THE
DREAM
CHASER

THE

DREAM

CHASER

If you don't build your dream,
someone will hire you
to help build theirs

TONY A. GASKINS JR.

WILEY

Published by John Wiley & Sons, Inc., Hoboken, New Jersey.
Published simultaneously in Canada.

For general information about our other products and services, please contact our Customer
Care Department within the United States at (800) 762-2974, outside the United States
at (317) 572-3993, or fax (317) 572-4002.

Wiley publishes in a variety of print and electronic formats and by print-on-demand. Some
material included with standard print versions of this book may not be included in e-books or in
print-on-demand. If this book refers to media such as a CD or DVD that is not included in the
version you purchased, you may download this material at http://booksupport.wiley.com.
For more information about Wiley products, visit www.wiley.com.

Library of Congress Cataloging-in-Publication Data:

Names: Gaskins, Tony A., author.

Title: Dream chaser : if you don't build your dream, someone will hire
   you to help build theirs / Tony A. Gaskins.

Description: Hoboken : Wiley, 2016.

Identifiers: LCCN 2016035957 | ISBN 9781119318903 (cloth) | ISBN 9781119318941
(Adobe PDF) | ISBN 9781119319054 (epub)

Subjects: LCSH: Success in business. | Entrepreneurship.

Classification: LCC HF5386 .G2513 2016 | DDC 658.1/1–dc23 LC record available at https://
lccn.loc.gov/2016035957

Printed in the United States of America

10 9 8 7 6 5 4 3 2 1

I'm dedicating this book to anyone who has a dream,
but you're afraid that you lack the time, resources,
education, and finances to achieve it.
I was that person at one point in my life, and I found a way.
I hope this book will help you find your way.
If you have a dream that you want to build,
you also have the tools to build it.

Contents

        First, I became an author.
        Then, I became a speaker.
        Then, I became a screenwriter.
        Then, I became a ghostwriter.
        Then, I became an author consultant.
        Then, I became a relationship coach.
        Then, I became a life coach.
        Then, I became a business coach.
        Then, I formed online courses.
        Then, I created audio projects.
        Then, I created phone applications.
        Then I created workbooks.
        Then I created my own tours.
        Then I started a real estate investment company.
        Then I started a referral business.
        Then I started a T-shirt line.
        That's all, folks.

THE
DREAM
CHASER

Chapter 1   The Birth Path

From the moment we are born, there is a path set for us. Our parents were born with a path for them, and they set a path for us. Some parents want their children to go to an Ivy League school and go on to become a doctor or lawyer. Some parents want their children to go to a state university and go on to work a solid job. Some parents hope their child goes to community college. Some parents hope their child just graduates from high school. Some parents hope their child lives to see at least their eighteenth birthday.

We all have a path set in place for us from the moment we're born. The problem is, we don't usually question that path. We just hop on and follow it and allow it to lead us to misery. Sometimes we reach the destination and then finally get the guts to get off of the birth path and to go in a new direction. Right now, there are artists who can change the world with their art, but they've settled for being a lawyer in their small city, handling routine cases. Right now, there are philanthropists who can help relieve hunger in thousands of lives, but they've settled for being an accountant because they were told that was a great major in college. There are so many people living beneath their dreams, walking the path set for them and never questioning it.

You have to question the path. We all need to write our own road map that will lead us to where we want to be, not where we were told we should be. Are you extremely happy doing what you're doing for a living? If not, you're on the wrong path. Are you at peace with your current lifestyle? If not, you're on the wrong path. Can you help others in the position you're currently in? If not, you're on the wrong path. If you were fired today, could you start your own company? If not, you're on the wrong path. As I was transitioning into entrepreneur life, I tweeted a quote: *If you don't build your dream, someone will hire you to help build theirs.* The quote went viral around the world. Others were quoted saying it, but I knew I wrote it. It came from my heart. It came from my spirit. It was deep inside of me, and I was feeling the pain of the truth in it. I feel that even if we work for someone else, that job should be our dream job. If it's not our dream job, then we should build our dream job, which will eventually replace our day job. Let a computer or robots do the meaningless, pencil-pushing jobs. A human shouldn't be doing meaningless work in the world. We all have a purpose to fulfill and filing papers just isn't enough. I used to file papers, so I know what it feels like; I used to stock groceries, so I know what it feels like. I used to work in a warehouse stacking heavy items on a pallet and driving it around on a forklift, so I know what that feels like too. I've done mindless work and it's a waste of time and energy. But yet that's the path that was set for many of us.

I remember my mother saying to me once, "Baby, I'll be happy if you just graduate from high school." I know you may think that's sad, but I didn't because I knew that's where her bar was.

All she did was graduate from high school, and her parents were happy about that. Where I'm from, dropping out of high school wasn't shocking. A lot of my cousins never graduated. Some family and friends died before realizing their potential. To graduate from high school was a real accomplishment in my family, and it was the most that most people did. On my mother's side, I knew only one family member who graduated from college. So the likelihood of graduating from college wasn't very high. That was the path.

Later in life, while in college, I said to my mom that I might become a schoolteacher and a high school sports coach. She told me she would be so very proud of me if I did that. She was always supportive of my dreams, but she didn't set the bar too high for me. She didn't want to see me reach and fail. She didn't want me to get hurt. She saw a certain level of reality around her and that was as far as she could see. My dad was the same way. He loved and supported me and gave me anything I needed to succeed, but he never set the bar high for me. He always told me to get good grades, but he never told me to try to become a doctor or a lawyer. I'm not sure that was possible in his mind. Often, we can only see as far as we've gone. It takes faith to see beyond that, and faith isn't as easy to come by as we think it is. My dad tells me often now that where I am is beyond his wildest imagination. I believe him. To be honest, I've actually surprised myself a time or two. It's because we weren't shown these possibilities growing up. Of course, we can't fault our parents for not seeing in us what we should see in ourselves. They may not be able to see more than what they are. They may want better for us, but they may not know how to help us get better. No matter what your age or where you are in life, you have to realize the path that has been set and start questioning why.

Ultimately, if you want to go where no one you know has gone before, you have to start leading yourself. You have to take control of your life and be willing to walk by faith. There's more in you than your parents know about. You have abilities and gifts that no one around you knows the full extent of. You can shock them, and you just may shock yourself.

The path that our society has given us is to get an education. You get out of college with more debt than our job affords us to pay. Then, you get a job in a major company or be the major in a minor company. Then, you try to climb the ladder in that company, so you can earn more and pay more taxes to keep the system going. Essentially, we are told to follow the set path to misery and debt; in turn, we compromise our happiness, peace, and prosperity.

The most ironic thing about the path set for us is that we are often told to get a formal education to work for someone who started a company without a formal education. The formally educated people start working to help build the dreams of the entrepreneur. You'd think that after paying tens of thousands of dollars for an education, you would have been educated in a way that allows you to buy your peace and happiness. Instead you're miserable while getting the education, and then still miserable after the education because along the way you never questioned the path.

I love formal education and I think it's necessary, but what's also necessary is that you get to know yourself along the way. What's necessary is that you question the path that was set before you, and that you start to tweak the road map so it leads you to a more desirable destination. Don't follow a path to misery. I was on that path because it was set for me and it cost me a lot. The wrong path was handed down from generation to generation. The American Dream became a nightmare for many because they didn't realize that the dream they were pursuing wasn't their dream. It was a dream someone else had created for them.

While studying in school, you should spend just as much time studying yourself. Get to know yourself. Fall in love with yourself. Write your dreams from the bottom of your heart. Question the path that you were put on. Don't be afraid of a detour. Don't be afraid to map to a new destination.

When I came to an age of understanding, I looked around me and I saw three options: I could be overworked and underpaid like my parents. I could be a pro athlete like Tracy McGrady. Or I could be a drug dealer, thief, or criminal like some of my friends and family. What would I choose? What could I choose? Published author wasn't a choice. International speaker wasn't a choice. Celebrity life coach wasn't a choice. Business consultant wasn't a choice. Business owner wasn't a choice. Everything I am today was not an option presented to me as a child, not at home, not in school, not in church. There was a path set in place, and until I questioned the path, I was lost.

It's interesting to see what happens when you question the path. When one person gets the courage to venture out, others do too. You can break a generational curse. You can start a ripple effect. I was on the phone earlier today with one of my cousins. He didn't finish high school. He dropped out at about 14 years old. He spent 20 years living the street life before he went down a new path. Today, he was on the phone with me asking how to publish an e-book, become a speaker, and turn his mess into his message the way I did. He's questioning the path. He sees that there are other options than what we were shown growing up.

My father is highly gifted. He writes, thinks outside of the box, and has a profound amount of wisdom. Even though he's never been where I've been or where I'm going, he was able to give me wisdom along the way. He's been writing all his life, but never questioned the path. He wanted to be an author, a filmmaker, and a speaker. He didn't know it was possible for him to do those things. He saw the path that was set before him and he followed it. Like my mother, he also was the baby in a family of 12 children. His mother was murdered when he was 8 years old. His father was a very wise man, but being one of 12 kids, my dad didn't get as close to his father as he would have liked. My father dropped out of high school, got his GED, and then went into the Army. Some of his older brothers had gone to the Army and fought in wars, so he was following the path. He left the Army after three years because it wasn't what he wanted for his life. He then went on to work several different jobs: a police officer, a mail carrier, a lineman fixing power lines. He worked in the hot sun 8 hours a day. He saw friends fall to their death from the power lines. His life flashed before his eyes many times. He didn't know that what I'm doing was possible for people like us.

I believe each generation should go a little further than the one before. I went as far as he had gone and then tested the possibilities. I laid new road. I found a new path. My parents were happy for me and they supported me, but they didn't hedge their bets and put up their life savings to assist me in my dream. They didn't know anything about the world I ventured into. But once I questioned the path it led my father to question his as well. A few years after I became an author, he became one too. Now he's written and published two books.

My mother, being the baby of 12 children, saw a lot growing up. I looked into my mother's side of the family, and I saw way more dysfunction than on my dad's side of the family. There was a lot of pain, and I didn't know where it stemmed from. There was abandonment, abuse of every form, crime, pain, and death. There was so much to get past. Relationships were a pain point on my mother's side. My mother followed her path. She told me that her teachers didn't teach her much in school. She said it wasn't long after integration when she started school, and teachers were still reluctant to teach black children. She said she didn't do any work really, but she always received a C from the teacher, just to pass her to the next grade. By the time I was in the fifth grade I could read and spell better than my mother. She wasn't illiterate by a long shot, but there was a lot she didn't know when it came to academics. That birth path limited her greatly because it told her what she could and couldn't do, and she didn't question it. She's said to me more times than I can count that she never applied for a promotion at work because she's insecure about her reading and spelling. She worked at a major insurance company for 15 years, so she was fortunate to be there, she felt. She watched those around her go higher in the company and make more money but she never tried. Even after her ceiling was made a little higher, she didn't try to reach it. I couldn't blame her because that's how she was conditioned.

As I was growing up my mother would always say to me, "Baby, you're so smart." She was so captivated by my writing, reading, and spelling. I was just a little above average in our school system but nowhere near the smartest. I was always touched that she was so impressed with me. She would tell me, "Baby, you need to be writing for Hallmark cards." That would make my day. All my life she kept saying, "You need to be getting paid for your writing." She wasn't talking about this type of writing; she was referring to my poetry. It wasn't that good, but it was off the beaten path for us. It wasn't common in our family, neighborhood, or city. Those words of encouragement my mother would give me ultimately played a large role in me becoming the entrepreneur I am today. Although she didn't venture off her path, her words gave me some courage to get off of mine.

It's deeper than just having parents who knew themselves and what they could become. I look around and I see some people who were given everything. Their parents graduated from college and became successful in life. They received the best education and attended the best college. Their parents supported them every step of the way financially, but still failed to advise them to get to know themselves. Now, though they are well off, they are lost. They have money, trust funds, business connections, and the world at their feet, but they don't know where to go from here. They have bachelors, masters, and some even doctorates, but they're still lost. Yes, their path led them further but it still didn't lead to peace and happiness. I've seen some of those individuals still end up in prison, on drugs, and as failures. It's mind-boggling to think that a person whose path seemed to have so many advantages could be led to the same destination as a person who was perceived to have no real options. It all comes down to if you question the path and get to know yourself.

Think about your path. List 10 people you know and analyze their paths. What path was set for them? Did they stay on it? Did they get off of it? What became of them? Now what are you going to do? Are you on a path that leads to nowhere? If you're not on the path that was set for you, how is the one you're on? Is it where you want to be? If it is, are you going to show others how to get on it?

To be honest with you, I still struggle today with the path that was set for me. It's always there. It's in my mind. It's all around me. I'm not on that path in my professional life, but what I realize is that our birth path is made up of many roads, and we all struggle with different aspects. One person may reach their goals professionally but suffer socially. Another person may reach their goals financially but suffer spiritually. Some suffer emotionally, financially, or physically. You have to recognize your weaknesses and pick your vices wisely. Question every path you're going down and make sure the destination is desirable.

Think of your path as a road to success. Each lane on the road has to lead to success. It will do you no good to make a million dollars and then die early from liver problems because of your drinking habits. It will do you no good to make a million dollars and then have a short miserable life filled with toxic relationships. Think about your paths. You don't have to be just what your mother or father were. You don't just have to be what your grandparents were. You can be more. Even if they are all great people, you can still be more. You can be better. You can grow and further the possibilities for generations to come.

Take some time to really think about what it is you want to become. Think about who you have already become. Confront the issues in your life. Look at the things you picked up without even realizing that you were taught how to settle or how to hurt yourself. Be willing to start fresh and new. Be willing to go alone and make a new path that your children can follow. Don't be mad at your situation. Don't blame your parents for what they didn't teach you because they could only teach what they knew.

Be thankful for what your parents could give you, and learn from their lessons, as well as their mistakes. It's time to make adjustments and get on the path you'd like to be on.

Anything is possible if we want it to be. We can start way behind the rest of the pack and still finish first. There is a lot of power in the human will. There will be distractions, setups, and setbacks, but you have to keep going despite everything else. There are those who will doubt you and count you out, but if you have a real desire to succeed, then failure is not an option.

We've heard so many stories of people who overcame obstacles that seemed unbearable and still made it. You can be one of those stories.

Chapter 2 We're Born Successful

No one is born a failure. You have seeds of success within you no matter where you're born, who your parents are, what race you are, or what religion you are. We accept limitations and we stunt our growth by believing the lies that were told to us about who we are and what we can become. No matter the level you were born at you can always go higher. You don't have to accept the limits the world tries to place on you. Any gift can make you a living. There is a business for everything imaginable and if there isn't, you can create it. Just because it hasn't been done or there hasn't been real success at it doesn't mean that you can't be successful. We see what others have done and we believe we can't go any further than they did. We tell ourselves what's realistic and what's not and we call it being a realist. I've found that everyone has something special about them, but it can be so unique that no one is ready to embrace it. Your gift can be so rare that it scares you and confuses others.

I look at my gifts, and I don't know where they come from. I write 100-page books usually, but I'm hoping this one finishes longer than that. I go away to a beach house and I write my books in two to three days. When I tell someone that, they are blown away, even some authors. I could write my book a thousand times over, and it wouldn't get any better because I write from my heart, not from my mind. What's on my heart won't change today or tomorrow because it's my true thoughts, feelings, and beliefs. So I sit down and I pour my heart out on the paper. I only took one computer class in school, but that class taught me how to type. I type as fast as I think, so my fingers can keep up with my thoughts and I don't have to suffer through writer's block. I'm not a prolific writer, but I can convey my thoughts and get a point across without it taking me weeks or months to do so. I came to realize that it's a small gift that has benefited me greatly. I don't know anyone else in my family who can do it, so I stand alone with my gift. We all have something like that. There is something in you that only you can do really well. There may be other people who can do it, but in your immediate circle you may be the only person who can do it that well. It could literally be anything. No gift is too small to embrace. No gift is too small to build a business around. Anything you are gifted at can be monetized and used in a positive way.

Think back to when you were young. What did you do that came so natural that you didn't have to think about it? What did you do that others talked about or gravitated toward? What did you enjoy? I remember meeting a guy in high school who talked nonstop. That's a gift. If I talked as much as he did, my head would hurt, my jaws would hurt, and I would become physically exhausted. But this guy talked nonstop, and the topics just seemed to fly off the top of his head. He was a freestyle talker. He also liked to write as much as he liked to talk. He also started to rap. Today he has a podcast, and I believe one day his love for talking will make him a living if he harnesses the gift and pursues a career in it. Some people are neat freaks. Well, that can be a cleaning service, an organizing service, a closet-cleaning service, or anything along that line. There are neat freaks that would be organizing and loving every minute of it and earning a living from it, but instead they're on someone's job slaving away and hating it. Don't sleep on your dreams. Don't curse your gifts. There are natural gifts inside of you that could change your life. Maybe you can't see them, but someone else can. Your gift may be tied to your passion, or it may be tied to your purpose. Whichever it's tied to, it can bring you peace and joy. You have to realize your gifts if you want to take control of your life. Your gifts shouldn't have to be your hobby. Your gift can be your job. It may have to be your hobby for a little while to build a business around it, but it can become your full-time job. I love what I do, and it doesn't feel like work. It's not fair either. I hate to see someone miserable while I'm happy. I hate to see someone asking a boss for time off while I'm creating my own schedule. It upsets me. It bothers me. I'm thinking to myself, *there are people whose ancestors were slaves, and they started life with every disadvantage. Why are they living the dream and you're living the nightmare?* There are people using their gifts and making millions of dollars. If anyone can do it, then I believe everyone can do it. I'm just that optimistic. You'll have what you believe you can have. There are no excuses.

When I was in the fourth grade, we had to write an essay in class. I wrote the essay from my heart. It was based on my life experiences, all nine years of them. I got an A on the essay, and my teacher asked me if she could read the essay to the class. I was shocked that she wanted to read my paper to the entire class. It confused me because there were kids in the class who were way smarter than me. Their parents were smarter and more successful than my parents, so those smarts were passed down to them. They read faster. They worked faster. They got better grades.

I was confused, but I let her read the paper to the class. All I remember from the essay was one line, in which I said: "I got a weapon so bad that I could not sit down." It should have said "whippin'" instead of weapon but the teacher thought I spelled it that way on purpose. She said, "I've never seen whippin' spelled like that, but that's a clever way to spell it." She thought I did that on purpose, and I took the credit for it. Sometimes your mistakes will look like you did it on purpose when you're operating in your gift. She read the paper, and after that day she wanted to talk to my parents. She told my parents that I was gifted, and she wanted to put me in the gifted class. I felt very special, and I accepted the offer. I went to the gifted class. My parents were surprised and elated. They didn't do anything special with me growing up when it came to academics. My elementary school started to get too hard for them to help me. I would ask for help, but they would teach me their way and that way wasn't the teacher's way; so when I realized that, I stopped asking them for help. They were trying, and they were happy that their son was a gifted student.

I didn't just write essays. I wrote poems later. That gift intrigued my teachers, and I kept hearing the same thing from English teachers all my life. The young girls I wrote poems for told me how much they loved them. My mother started praising my writing and telling me I could write Hallmark cards. I was really embracing this writing thing, and the more I did it the easier it became. I've always had bad grammar though. I never knew the grammar rules. I just knew how to put words together and paint a picture with them. Once, one of my teachers told me that my grammar could use a lot of work but that he couldn't give me less than a B just because of my writing style. Honestly, the only book I read was the Holy Bible growing up. There is a certain writing style in the Bible, and I believe growing up I emulated that style.

Not only was I writing a lot, but also I was teaching and advising. I remember in middle school I would walk to my friends' homes, and I would be teaching them about the Bible on the way home. I would teach them about life, sins, and forgiveness. I was a child. I was a baby. I didn't really know nearly as much as I pretended to know. Then in high school I started doing relationship coaching. I didn't call it that back then, but that's what it's called today, and it's become a substantial stream of income for me. I remember being on three-way calls with these two girls, and they would ask me questions about their boyfriends. I'd tell them why he was behaving the way he was and what they should do in response. Then they would call back with the results, and they would always say, "I did exactly what you said I should do and you were so right!" I never got tired of hearing that. I was operating in my gifts. One of the two girls ended up leaving her boyfriend, and she became my girlfriend. So I'd used my life-coaching gift to get her out of that relationship, then I used my writing gift to win her heart. I say all that because the gifts were evident even as a child, but I had no idea that one day I would earn a living using them.

You see writing and life coaching were gifts, but they were not options on my birth path. So I operated in them, but I didn't know that they could become a career. Had I known those were gifts that I could make a living from, I would have taken them much more seriously and honed them better. While those gifts were there, I was following my birth path and following one of the three options I had. The option I chose first was to be a professional athlete like Tracy McGrady. At that time Tracy McGrady was the only pro athlete I knew personally. I'm from Auburndale, Florida, and we had a population of 5,000 then. Tracy was the one guy who made it out and was making millions in the NBA. I wanted to be the next Tracy McGrady. That was one of the options on my birth path, but it wasn't the one for me. Tracy is 6′8″; I'm 5′10″. I make a much better writer, speaker, and life coach than I do a basketball player. I didn't think about that at the time though. I also played football. I excelled in basketball and football, so they seemed like natural gifts. I could have gone to the pros in either one of them had I put in the work, but again those goals were beyond what we could see in my household. I just wanted to graduate from high school, hopefully get into college, and stay out of prison or the grave. Becoming a pro athlete wasn't really taken seriously by anyone around me. I talked about it, but I didn't really work for it. I was good, so people thought that's what I would become if luck struck at the right time. But no one invested in me. No one took me to five-star camps or put me in a travel league or a real AAU program. I played one year of AAU, and that was with the Boys and Girls Club team. We weren't serious about it nor did anyone take us seriously. We were just going with the flow and hoping that we would get lucky. No one expected to make it out unless they were unusually gifted or uniquely built.

Then my senior year rolled around and that was a big year for me. I had to earn a college scholarship in basketball or football. I didn't know much about academic scholarships, and I didn't think I was smart enough for one of those anyway. I knew my parents couldn't afford to pay for college. They were struggling to pay the high school tuition, and it wasn't very much because I qualified for financial aid; and I had some supporters at the school who really liked me and helped me a lot.

Football came around first, and in the second game I popped something in my leg. I didn't know what exactly happened, but I heard a pop in my leg. It was treated as a high ankle sprain. The next week I tried to play but ended up with two carries and −3 yards due to my ankle. The next week I got a little better but still couldn't play. Then I had to sit out one more week. I missed three games that season, and we only played nine. I played the first game and the last five. I finished with over 1,300 yards in those six games, so I still averaged over 200 yards a game. I think a miscount happened though, because by my count, I had about 1,100 yards—but I went with what the newspaper said I had. Because of that ankle sprain I didn't have the showing I wanted to have, but I still received a lot of letters. The really big schools offered to let me join the team as a preferred walk-on. They just couldn't believe the numbers I put up, so they wanted to see it for themselves. I couldn't blame them. There were running backs that I was better than who went to big schools, so I knew I could cut it if it came down to it. But I was getting ready for basketball, and I wanted to make one last campaign just to see if I could get a scholarship in basketball. However, my dad and my coach got into a disagreement, because my dad wanted me to take two weeks off from sports and my basketball coach wanted me to come right into basketball. My dad told the coach that if he didn't give me two weeks off, then he wouldn't let me play at all. The coach said, "OK, then I guess he won't be playing then." My dad told me what happened, and I sided with my dad. My coach came and told me that it wasn't personal and that he had no problem with me and that he just wanted me at practice. For some reason I wasn't as excited about basketball anymore when I realized my coach wouldn't let me take a two-week break. I decided not to play, and I was banking on football 100% then.

The end of the year came, and schools started to come around. My football coach was telling schools that they needed a full scholarship to get me. He was asking for a bit much considering that we played at a small 1A school against virtual nobodies. But, I took the vote of confidence in stride. I realized that the full scholarships weren't coming in, so I started to market myself. I didn't notice then what was another gift of mine—to be a go-getter. I'll talk later about how I got myself on TV. But I looked up all the Florida colleges and I went to their websites and submitted my info on their football pages. Florida Atlantic University called me back first. They invited me to come down and look at the campus. I went down with my parents, and it looked nice. I wanted to play there. The coach asked me if I would come play, and I told him yes. Then when I got back home about a week later, I got a call from a smaller school, West Virginia Wesleyan College. It was a D2 school and somehow the coach had come up with a way to pay my full $28,000/year tuition. Florida Atlantic was only going to be $11,000/year. So I felt flattered that a school was offering me almost triple. We spoke to my AAU basketball coach because he was the only person we knew who went to college on a scholarship. He told us to follow the money, not the opportunity. He said that I could get hurt in training camp and then I would be stuck paying for college at Florida Atlantic, but at the other school even if I got hurt, my school was paid for. So we took that advice, and my mom's friend who coached at Florida State University told her the same thing. He said if you were good enough, the NFL would find you even if you were playing pick-up ball in the middle of the woods. So I packed my bags and I moved to West Virginia. It was one thousand miles away from home.

I was going away and taking all of my gifts with me. My gifts opened doors for me, and they made a way for me to get into college. I believe we all have gifts that can open doors for us, but we have to be willing to use our gifts and then walk through the doors that they open. We don't take ourselves seriously enough most of the time. We sleep on our dreams and we curse our gifts. I was stepping out on faith and taking a chance.

You see, someone else confirmed all of my gifts. We can feel good at something, but if a single soul doesn't believe in us, we won't have a chance. Sometimes we pursue passions instead of gifts. A passion can be different from a gift. My passion was basketball, but I wasn't good enough to get a scholarship in basketball. My gift was football, and I got a scholarship in that. I had to use my gift as a means to a better end. My passion for basketball could have become more of a gift if I had more resources and support in that area, but I didn't, so I had to take what I could get. Every school had a hundred spots on a football team, but a basketball team had only 15. So it was easier for me to make it to college in football. Sometimes we have to walk in our gifts until we can pursue our passions. There are a lot of people pursuing passions but getting nowhere while letting their natural gifts rot.

You may be good in graphic design and website building but not passionate about it, but yet you're passionate about music but not as good in it. Well, if you use graphic design to make money, then you can fund your passion for music. But if you ignore graphic design and just chase your passion for music, you may never get ahead in music because you don't have the resources you need to get really good at it. So take what you're naturally good at and use it to get to a point where you can dive into some of your passions for fun. We have to use what we have, not what we want. Gifts are natural, and they're free. Use them to get ahead in life. Look back over your life or at your life currently and identify whether there are any gifts you're overlooking. Are there any gifts you're ignoring or running from just because it comes so easy that it bores you at times? It bores you because you haven't given it a purpose. I can write without getting writer's block naturally, but if I'm writing about stuff that doesn't matter, then I'd be bored with the gift. I can coach people in their lives, but if I'm coaching them about things that don't matter, then I'd be bored with it. But because I gave my gifts purpose, I'm excited about them and they've come alive in me. Identify your natural gifts and build on them.

Chapter 3 Don't Take Your Gifts for Granted

There are gifts we have that we take for granted every day. We have an opportunity, and we don't seize it. We see this opportunity, and we know it's ours for the taking, but we let it slip away. I'm not sure why we do this, but for me I think I feared success. I feared greatness. I was afraid to be amazing. They say that everything that goes up must come down. I didn't want to go up to my highest heights because I didn't want to be knocked down. What I didn't realize at the time is that you don't have to be knocked down. You can do your time, run your course, and then choose to come down and retire when it's time. I didn't want to feel any pain of gain. I didn't want to do the hard work that comes with greatness. I was comfortable coasting and doing just enough to get by. But we don't get results when we're comfortable. Comfort is for the sleeping. If you want to sleep through life, then get comfortable; but if you want to be great in this life, then you'll have to stretch yourself.

Sometimes when your gift is your means to a better end, you have to become passionate about your gift even if you aren't. Your gift comes freely, but at times it may be a burden until you've found your purpose. It may even be a little painful until you've found your purpose. You'll have to sacrifice a lot before you get some time to relax and enjoy the fruits of your labor. When I was in college, my dad would often call me and always say, "Son, if you sacrifice the next four years of your life, it will never be the same." I had no clue what he meant by sacrifice. At this point his advice was too little too late. Sacrifice has to be instilled at a young age, and you have to know the pain of sacrifice in order to appreciate it. You have to be accustomed to sacrifice. It has to be engrained in you and become second nature. If you're not comfortable being uncomfortable, then sacrifice will scare you. I was scared to understand what he meant by sacrifice, so I told myself that I was already sacrificing. I told myself that going to practice every day was a sacrifice. I told myself that going in the weight room was a sacrifice. I told myself that getting up at 6 a.m. everyday to eat breakfast was a sacrifice, but I was lying to myself. I was lying to myself because I was only giving 50 to 70 percent at practice. I was only giving 50 to 70 percent in the gym. I was going to breakfast because it was mandatory. If I wasn't made to do it, I wasn't doing it. I was staying up late every night. I was eating badly every day. I was chasing the ladies every day. I was partying on the weekends. I wasn't focused. I was coasting by.

Have you ever coasted? Have you ever gotten off track? Have you ever done just enough to get by? That's what I was doing. I was doing just enough to get by. I think my dad understood that I was close to realizing the dream. I think he knew that I was good enough to make it if I would dedicate myself. He had heard about the chances of success from some reliable sources, I'm guessing. I knew guys in the NFL who played D2 and D3 football. I realized that you truly could make it from anywhere. I thought success would come easy for me though. I thought that it would be easy like it had always been. I was taking success for granted. I had to do more, but I wasn't willing to do more. Now I realize what my father meant by sacrifice is that I should abstain from sex and women. He meant that I should go to bed at a decent hour. He meant that I should put in extra work in the weight room and extra work on the practice field. I didn't want to think about that at the time. I wanted it to be easy, and I wanted to make it look easy. I wanted to look cool. I wanted to make it look effortless the way I had always done—but I couldn't get by with so little effort at that level. If I was skimping at a D2 school, I don't know how I would have made it at a D1 school. In a way, I feel like I could have done better at a D1 school, because I would have been challenged. It was still easy for me on the field at the smaller school. In every scrimmage I was averaging 8 yards a carry. That was a lot, and it felt easy. I was averaging that without using my offensive line properly. I would beat the pulling blocker to the hole, so I was facing defenders one on one much of the time and blowing past them. But I also didn't stretch well. I was making the defense look silly with almost-cold muscles. I was taking shortcuts, and I was soon to get cut short.

In my freshman season I was red-shirted. That meant I would have a free year that year and would still be able to play four more years. So my hope was that I could graduate with a master's degree instead of just a bachelor's degree, and it would be fully paid for. But I was cutting corners and not taking it seriously enough. One day in practice I pulled my hamstring. That was a result of never stretching properly. I came back from that hamstring injury, and then I pulled my other hamstring.

I remember that when I came back from the first injury, I was put on the scout team. That's where the red-shirt and academically ineligible players played. One day I was on the scout team kickoff-return unit. They kicked the ball off to me, and I darted up the field, saw a seam and hit it, and took off for a touchdown. It was a full field return. The coach screamed and yelled at the kickoff team. He was cursing and enraged. Then they kicked off again, and I caught the ball, saw a seam, hit it, and took off for another touchdown. I returned two kicks in a row on what was seen as the best defense in the conference. Then the coach screamed and yelled again. I know it was bittersweet for him because I was torching his kickoff team, but he also had to have some joy knowing that I would be eligible the next season. So they kicked off a third time, and this time I caught the ball and saw my seam again, but when I took off, my hamstring popped. This was a trickle-down effect—I tore my first hamstring because I didn't stretch properly, then I came back and tore my other hamstring because I didn't stretch properly. When I got to the field that day, I was late to practice. I think I was late because I overslept on my afternoon nap, but I really can't remember. The scout team were doing kickoff drills, and the coach told me to get out there immediately. I hadn't stretched yet. So it was somewhat remarkable because I hadn't stretched and I ran back two kicks, but then it was sad that I still hadn't learned my lesson from the first hamstring tear.

Things kept going downhill from there. I wanted the instant gratification. I didn't want to wait my turn or to trust the process the way we are supposed to. I got lazy, and I started taking dives on the field. If I saw a puddle of mud during a rainy practice, I'd slip in it and pretend that I pulled my hamstring. I wanted the easy route. I didn't love the grind. I tried to cheat the grind. But the interesting thing about the grind is that you can't cheat it. It knows exactly what you've put in, and you can only get out what you've put in. I didn't realize that back then. I tweeted that quote a couple years ago though, and it went viral; now I see my life lesson all over the web. It's funny how life works.

I kept cheating the grind, and I kept being penalized. I finally got through that first year of college and still had my scholarship intact. I put in a little work over the summer, and I came back the next year ready to play. I became eligible to play my second year in college, and I was ready. Our team had another running back from California, and he was pretty good. He wasn't better than me, I didn't think, but he was older and bigger than me. My coach respected seniority for the most part, and he loved big running backs. So he played him over me and made me the second-string back. I got to play in one game in the fourth quarter and got 62 yards. I think I had five carries. I remember many fans telling me after the game that they didn't know I was so fast and good. It was still kind of easy for me. I was physically healthy all that season, but I wasn't healthy mentally. I was more focused on the ladies. I was up late and still chasing the ladies and love.

When the starting running back went down in the second or third game of the season, it was my turn. I was ready for it physically, but my mind wasn't where it had been when I was really good. I went into the game, and everyone was excited to see me on a turf field. I was kind of excited, but I decided to not get nervous, so I blocked out all thoughts about the game. I was very mellow and nonchalant. I failed to realize that it was my nerves that had fueled me all my life. So I went into the game so mellow that I wasn't focused. My first two carries were fumbles. Fumbling the ball two times back to back was like suicide in the coach's eyes. I wasn't ready for my moment, and it was the next man's opportunity. I still ended up getting back in the game and finishing with 40 yards on eight carries, so 5 yards a carry wasn't too bad, but it would be my last opportunity as a starter. My coach moved on to the other athlete on the team because there were only two of us who ran at that level. The other guy was actually a really small receiver the coach turned into a running back. He was lightning fast and could hit open holes with a full head of steam and gain a lot of yards. That was good enough for the coach, so I was back to picking up garbage time in the fourth quarters.

I started to break down mentally, and I guess I got what I'd asked for by my actions. I started becoming a cancer on the team.

I started to do locker room politicking and carrying on. I was cutting corners and chasing the ladies. I was going downhill fast. On top of not being focused, more distractions started coming my way. One day as I was walking in the ice cold winter, I looked down and saw a little baggie. I picked it up; it was a $10 bag of weed. I didn't smoke at all and had no desire to. But I did know about weed because my cousins and some of my friends smoked it. I also had a lot of family and friends who sold weed. So I showed the baggie to one of my teammates who I knew smoked. He looked at it and asked me how much I wanted for it. Not having a clue what to sell it for, I told him he could just have it because it was my last one. I had now become a drug dealer. A very petty one, but still, I was a kingpin in my mind. Then I had to find a way to keep up this image because this cool guy on the team was impressed that I had been selling drugs under his nose even though he knew nothing about it. The word started to spread, and now I was back into the shine. I couldn't shine on the field, so at least I was shining off the field. It's crazy to me when I look back and see all the time I wasted running from greatness.

I remember going home over Christmas break, I believe it was, and talking to my cousin. This is my cousin I mentioned earlier in the book who had called me for advice about publishing his own book. Well, back then he was still in the street life. I called him and told him that I needed to talk to him. He came over in this old-school car with some candy paint and like 26-inch rims. I was thinking to myself like, *wow this is the life*. He has a mouth full of gold teeth, wearing gold chains, bracelets, and rings, and at that time a fleet of amazing cars. He was making option number three on my birth path look very attractive. I was in college getting an education, so I was on my way to being overworked and underpaid like my parents. I was playing football in college, so I was also attempting to become the next Tracy McGrady. So now all I needed to do was to try my hand at option number three, which was to be a drug dealer, like my some of my cousins.

When I talked to my cousin, he told me that he wouldn't advise me to sell drugs, but he also knew he couldn't stop me from doing what I wanted to do. I gave him a sob story about not having any money and how I wanted to put a little money in my pockets while in college. He told me that he wished he had the opportunity that I had, and he didn't understand why I'd want to sell drugs when I was in college playing football and good enough to make it to the NFL. He was blown away, and he thought I was lost and crazy. Here I had an opportunity that he would kill a man for, and I was choosing to take a major risk in my life. He said I was being stupid. But what I didn't realize then is that I had the heart of an entrepreneur. I was going about it the wrong way, but the fact that I was willing to take such a big risk was a sign that I had something in me that could pay dividends if I channeled that in a different direction.

My cousin told me to think about it a couple days and then let him know if I was sure. I called him back after a day or two and told him I was sure. He told me to come over, and he gave me half an ounce. I'm not even sure that was enough for me to go to jail if I had been caught with it. I drove from Florida to West Virginia, and I broke it down and sold the weed. This made me a little bit of money and gave me a little more street cred. I don't know why I wanted street cred on a Christian college campus. I was a product of my environment, and I was settling right into the stereotype. The football coach took the boy out of the hood but not the hood out of the boy. I was choosing to be like guys I saw while growing up, but I wasn't raised like that. My parents didn't sell drugs or use them. My dad raised me by reading the Bible and praying every day. I was in church every time the doors were open. My dad pastored his own church for seven years of my life from the age of 14 to 21. I was searching for myself. I was lost and didn't want any help being found. I was living beneath my gifts and taking my gifts for granted. It makes me mad typing this just to know that I squandered an opportunity trying to be cool.

I went back home for the summer and wasn't really selling drugs because everyone knew me at home. They knew I wasn't cut out for that life. I had a little weed here and there, and I showed my friends. They were shocked that I had it. I think I actually ended up letting my friends smoke it. I never smoked and I never tried it, not even one puff. I never even rolled anything, lit anything, or anything of the sort. I'd seen the effects of drugs and alcohol growing up, so I wasn't going to use those things. But I'd never seen anyone go to prison for drugs, so I was crazy enough to try to sell them. I had uncles who were drug addicts and aunts who were alcoholics. That kept me sober. My cousins, on the other hand, were living the high life with their drug money. They sold everything, but they only gave me the weed to sell. I couldn't touch anything white, and frankly I didn't want to. At that time, I was playing around in the streets. I wasn't serious. I didn't count the cost. I wasn't thinking about the fact that you could get hurt or go to jail. I never had enough on me to go to jail, but it was still a dumb idea.

I got caught up looking like I was successful, but really I wasn't. I think we sometimes do that in everyday legal lifestyles too. People can get caught up trying to look successful, but actually are empty on the inside. We spend money trying to impress others instead of saving money to impress ourselves. We dress a certain way, drive a certain car, with the hope that it will get us better treatment from others. It's a miserable and painful life to live if you ever get caught up in it.

I was there and I was lost. All this talent and it was going to waste. My athletic talent could have opened doors for me and provided a totally different platform. I could have been like Tim Tebow at least. He hasn't become a star in the NFL, but just because of his hard work and dedication he at least got the opportunity to impact lives. I look at Steph Curry, and I see the hard work he's put in and the platform he's gained and how he's touching millions from his platform. I honestly have to say that in my respective sport and position, I was more naturally gifted than those guys are, but they sacrificed and put in the work. Every year when the NFL Scouting Combine happens, I look at the numbers that the guys put up, and I compare them to mine from college—mine were better than a lot of running backs going in the draft. I didn't just have numbers, but also I had the talent. I knew a guy who played D2 and went on to play 7 years in the NFL. He sacrificed. I could have done the same thing had I wanted it bad enough. I was taking it for granted because I was afraid to be amazing.

I went back to college for my third year, and I had put in some work over the summer. My body was nicer, and I was ready to play. Once I got there and realized that I was in the same position and that coach didn't like me anymore than he did the year before, I got back into the same rut. I started to sell drugs to the smokers again. It wasn't anything major, but it was just something to get me a little street cred and keep my name relevant on the campus, because I was embarrassed that I wasn't getting any playing time. I was the best all-around athlete on the team, but I was on the bench. The other athlete was a step faster than me, but I benched 200 percent of my body weight and had nearly a 40-inch vertical. I was one of five players on a full scholarship out of 95 players, but yet I was riding the bench. The coach called me into his office to tell me he needed to take some of my money away. I told him he couldn't do that because I only came to the school because he offered a full scholarship. He told me that he didn't care how good I was, he wanted to see 100 percent every practice, and he didn't see that from me. He didn't like the fact that I wasn't fully committed and didn't go as hard as I should have. I couldn't blame him, but I just didn't think he could do anything about it. Little did I know, I was sadly mistaken. One day I was walking out to practice with a bruised hip. When I stepped onto the field, he yelled and told me to get off the field and that I would never wear the Bobcat jersey again. I was floored. I didn't know how to take it. My stomach sank to my feet, but I tried to keep a straight face. Eleven years later, it still hurts me to think about it. I ruined my opportunity. I took my gifts for granted. I took my opportunity for granted. So many people wanted the chance that I was given, and I let it slip away. I had worked all my life and had my parents sacrificing for me only to get to that point and fumble the ball. I tried to appeal the coach's decision with the school, but they decided in the coach's favor. I wrote an eight-letter appeal, and they still decided in his favor. They offered me $14,000 to come back the next year, but I wasn't going to go to a school 1,000 miles from home just for an education. I was only that far from home for football.

I was crushed. I was embarrassed. I hated my coach back then. I wished that he would have talked to me more and told me exactly what he wanted from me. I wished I had another warning. If I had known that would be the penalty, I think I would have gotten my act together. I say that now, but I'm not sure what could have reached me back then. I hated him then, but I thank him now. Had he not kicked me off the team I probably would have gone to prison in West Virginia just for being young and stupid. I was on a road leading to destruction. I had all the gifts and talents that one person could need, but I didn't use them properly. I was trying to coast. I was trying to be cool and fit in, not realizing that I was born to stand out. I realize now that we can't be afraid to be great.

We can't be afraid to be amazing. We have to be willing to give it our all. We have to be willing to sacrifice and accept the rewards of sacrifice. We have to prepare to succeed and be willing to accept all that comes with success. We can't shrink in the face of adversity or in the face of opportunity. We have to seize every moment and be glad for it. I didn't do my part. I let my team down. I let my coach down. I let my parents down. I let myself down. I could cry, but I don't think I ever did. Or maybe I did and I've forgotten it by now. I know some people were laughing at me when I was kicked off of the team. My false confidence became cockiness, and I rubbed some people the wrong way. I was fronting and pretending to be something that

I wasn't. I didn't know what mattered most. It's the grind that matters most, not the shine. I didn't know that. I wanted the rewards without the work. I wanted the prize without the process. I messed up a great opportunity, and it sent me on a detour that cost me years of my life.

Maybe it was necessary. Maybe I wouldn't be the man I am today without those experiences. Maybe, but I'm not sure that I'd do it the same way if I had the opportunity to do it over again. I wouldn't recommend it to anyone. I wouldn't say, "Make those mistakes because look where I am today." I'd say, "Be grateful for your opportunity and don't let the moment pass you by. Give your all and max out your gifts. Do everything you can to be the best you can and don't settle for mediocrity. Don't try to fit in when you can stand out by just being yourself. Don't pretend to be someone you're not and miss out on who you can become. We only live once, and we have to live life to the fullest of our potential."

I not only watched myself but I also watched others squander opportunities. There are people who have natural gifts and resources but are choosing to coast. I know some people who have the resources to get all the training and mentorship and start any company their heart desires, but they're sitting on their hands and letting life pass them by. They're partying and drinking the days away. There are others who don't have the resources, but they have the gifts; but instead of utilizing the gifts, they're chasing vanity just like I was. They are chasing a fantasy instead of a dream. A fantasy is rooted in pleasure. A dream is rooted in purpose. There are people who have natural gifts that can make them hundreds of thousands of dollars and some even millions, but instead of jumping on the opportunities, they're letting it slip away. They think it'll be there for as long as they want it to be. They think they've arrived and that they don't have to continue to sacrifice. They don't see that their end is near. They can't see that the window of opportunity is closing, and it'll be closed before they expect it to be. They think they will have the liberty of walking away from it when they are ready. They don't realize that it will be taken from them right before their very eyes. I saw it happen to me. I've seen it happen to others. If you have a gift, you better use it or you will lose it. You better buckle down and lock in. Treat it like you're running out of time and get everything out of your gift while you can. Today I wish I had 48 hours in a day. I wish I had three brains, four more arms, two more ears, one more mouth, and a lot more money to build more business. But I had to realize that I have enough right here and right now, and I have to use it to the best of my abilities. I realize now that I have to maximize my gifts and maximize my efforts. I can't shrink, and I can't live small.

I'm creating daily now, and I'm making up for lost time. If you're still breathing, then you still have time to get on track and to get your gifts out of you. You still have time to change your life. You still have time to turn things around and to start building like never before. Sure, you've made some mistakes. Sure, you've cut some corners. Sure, you've taken some of your sunrises and sunsets for granted, but you still have time to get it right. You can't sit idle. You can't settle for good enough. You can't get complacent with what you've done and where you are. You have more life left in you. You have more that you can produce. You have more time that you can utilize. Don't take your gifts for granted!

Chapter 4   The Valley Experience

There are times in which we are at our lowest. I believe it's those moments that can make us or break us. We can stay down, or we can decide to get up. We can lose hope and wallow in the valley of failure, or we can create a plan to get back on the climb to the top. I believe that it's in the valley where you gain the wisdom and clarity for the climb, then you grow as you climb.

What was your lowest moment in life? Did it break you, or did it make you? Did you fold, or did you get stronger? How long were you down? Are you still down? Did you get back up yet, or is it time to get up? Identify that time and make sure you didn't miss any lessons in the valley. It's at your lowest that you can evaluate your life and be honest with yourself about the things that have happened and devise a plan for the way forward. Anything can get us to our lowest point. It could be losing a family member. It could be losing a job. It could be being kicked off of a team or out of school. It could be an injury. It could be a divorce or a bad breakup. It could be a freak accident. It could be just a transition into a new period of life. There are many things that can knock us down, but can you get up? Absolutely, you can get up. As long as there is breath in your body, there's a fighting chance. You have to be willing to stay down long enough to get a lesson and then bold enough to get back up and get back in the fight stronger and wiser than before.

If you're in the valley right now, you have to appreciate it and see it as the training ground. You can't resent it. Life is a weird teacher, and the lessons it gives us are not labeled as such. We have to discern between the lessons and the tests. We have to allow our character to be built. You can't quit and give up. When you're knocked down, you can't wallow on the ground. You can't throw in the towel. If you're breathing, then it wasn't intended to kill you, so don't kill yourself. It was intended to teach you. So get the lessons and get back up. A lot of times we take the "woe is me" approach, and we miss the point of the valley. We think that the world or God is against us. We think God has turned His back on us and no longer loves us. That's not true. My mother would always say to me, "The greater the test, the greater the testimony." We have to know that hitting rock bottom is to build character, not to destroy it. We make a choice to make mistakes, but those mistakes can make us better if we allow them to.

I've seen people turn their backs on God because they lost something or someone in their life. They didn't realize that life was testing them to see if they could handle the blessings that were on the way. When they checked out of the fight, cursed God, and turned their backs, they showed that they couldn't handle the next level. If you can't handle the valley, you won't be fit for the top. The valley may be hard, but the top will be much harder. The top may come with some money, some peace, and some happiness, but it will also come with its share of tests. The air is thinner at the top. Rocks are thrown at you while you're at the top. People will try to convince you to jump from the top. Others will try to push you off the top. Don't ever stop learning. Don't ever wish you were in a different phase of life. Don't wish, just work. Your work, your growth, your plan, your efforts are what will transition you from season to season of your life. You can't wish your way out of hard times. You have to work your way out of hard times. There is growth in the climb, so don't stay down for long. I have a spoken word album on iTunes called *GREATNESS* that talks about this. You have to get up and get going. Everything that we go through in life is to grow us: the good, the bad, and the ugly. Everything is a test. You have to know that your answer to the test is your key to unlocking the next door of your life. You'll be tested emotionally, physically, spiritually, mentally, financially, and relationally. Nothing is off limits in life. You will have to sharpen every knife in the drawer, from the smallest to the largest. Life is about growth. Those who constantly grow live the fullest life. If you stop growing, then you start dying. You can't avoid growth. You will get stronger through it, or the weight of it will kill you. We all have to go one day, but be a fighter until that day. Don't lie down and quit, and don't take yourself out of the game. Don't disqualify yourself by making stupid choices on purpose. Don't be afraid of greatness. Don't be afraid to be amazing. I know because I've been there.

I had a valley experience, and it could have killed me or sent me to prison for a long time. I was lost, and I was confused. I was hurt, so I felt like giving up. I got knocked down, and I was afraid to get back up because I thought life would move in for the kill and hit me harder the next time. I stayed down as long as I could; I kept making bad decisions trying to run from my calling. I was trying to run from greatness. I was afraid of responsibility. I was afraid of change. I was afraid to grow. I tried a little bit, but trying was too hard. Trying stripped my ego and forced me to be humble. I didn't want to be humble. I wanted to be the man. I tried my hand at so much, but nothing seemed to work out right.

When I got back home for the summer break, I decided to apply to the University of South Florida in Tampa. There was the University of Central Florida, but I didn't like the idea of living in Orlando, which was basically Disney World and tourist capital. So I chose Tampa. I was accepted into the school, and I applied for financial aid. My classes were paid for, and I was given a couple of loans. I signed up for 15 credits that fall semester. I was trying. I was trying to get back up, but it was hard.

I started school and got my refund check. I think I went to the mall and shopped some and maybe paid my rent and my car note. I was a grown man now. I was 21 years old, and I had a car and an apartment. I had my mom's car for a while, but she needed it back. My parents tried to help me the best they could, but they couldn't carry me and I didn't want to be a burden. I tried to grow up and be a man. I got a couple bills, and I was moving forward. In that first semester I folded. I dropped all my classes after I'd spent all my money from the refund check. I wasn't focused on school. It was boring me, and my mind just wasn't in it. I had gotten a job as a grocery stock boy at Publix. I was making $7.50 an hour and working about 32 hours a week. It was hard for me to work that much and study, especially without any study skills. I started to feel the pinch of the school system I'd grown up in. I was a junior in college, and things were getting real in the classroom. Just listening in class and then passing the test wasn't cutting it anymore. You actually have to study, and I didn't really know how to study. I missed that lesson growing up. I dropped my classes, and I just worked.

I was getting ready to switch jobs because stocking groceries was embarrassing for me. Even though no one knew me, I felt like they did. Girls would come in the store who I'd want to talk to, but I felt like a lame stocking groceries. I didn't realize while working that job I was next to some of the strongest and smartest young guys around. They were doing it the right way, the hard way, and they had a plan. I didn't see that at the time. I just wanted out of there. I was able to talk to one of the young ladies who came in there, and she liked me. I don't know why I couldn't see that she appreciated that I had a job, a car, and a cell phone and was going to school. She probably admired that but I couldn't see that.

I quit the grocery store after a few months, and I applied at the Publix warehouse. I thought I'd give that a try because it was still an honest living, but it was behind closed doors so no one would see me but the guys I was working with. I wanted to make money without anyone seeing me sweat. I'm still kind of that way today. I don't like for anyone to see me sweat, stress, or worry. I've always wanted to make everything look easy. Life just doesn't work like that all the time. Sometimes we've got to grit our teeth and grunt while we lift. I was looking for an easy way.

At the warehouse I found out fast that there wasn't the easy way out. I was in there with guys who were star football players in high school just like I was. Some guys had done time in prison. Some guys had brief stints in the NFL. We were stocking groceries on pallets that were on forklifts that we drove up and down the aisles. A lot of the guys in there didn't seem educated, but the system they were working with was mind-boggling to me. First, you had to learn the Greek alphabet, I think it was. It was hard because I knew my ABCs but now learning Alpha, Beta, etc., was kicking my butt. We had a headset on and the lady would say a Greek letter and a number. Then you'd have to drive your little pallet lift to that aisle and get however many units she told you to. While I was trying to learn, I thought I'd never get it. I was looking at these guys around me who I thought I was smarter than and wondering how in the world did they learn how to do this? Once you learn the alphabet system and how to drive the forklift thingy, then you have to learn how to stack all the stuff you're picking up. You're stacking it on a pallet and then driving. So if you stack it the wrong way, it falls off when you start driving. I was in awe at the speed with which these guys operated. It blew my mind. You have an order to pull and the lady in your ear may say it's a

60-minute order. That means that if you're working at 100 percent, you should be done in 60 minutes. Some of these guys were pulling these orders at 120 percent, while I was pulling them at 60 percent. I got lucky a few times and pulled 100 percent or better, but that was very rare for me. The worst were the times when I would pull my order and have it stacked up and wrapped with the Saran Wrap, and then I'd turn a corner on my forklift and my order would come crashing down. I remember one time very distinctly. I was the new guy, and I was pulling orders; and I got this big order and was just about done. It was like a 64-minute order, and I was almost done. It probably had taken me about two hours. I was coasting just like I used to do in college. I was tired. It was backbreaking work because you're bending and lifting heavy boxes hundreds of times over. It was insane. They really need robots for that stuff. Everyone in there should be paid six figures, but that's not realistic. I was feeling the pain as I turned one of my last corners, and it was like a Jenga game when the blocks come tumbling down. Everything fell off and I had jelly on my order, so the jelly hit the ground and busted open; it was bad. I remember this one guy who was an all-star in the warehouse. He stopped and helped me clean up my mess. That touched my heart because here this guy was making a living for his family, and I was in his way slowing him down because I was in there coasting and being lazy. A few guys hopped on their lift and helped me throw the stuff back on the pallet. It was crazy to see the brotherhood. We were all black, and maybe a few were white. It looked the way a professional football or basketball team looks. This work was professional athlete work in my mind. It was hard.

At three months you have to be pulling at 85 percent. So that means if you have an hour order, you have to pull it in an hour and fifteen minutes. I think my math is right. Well, I was pulling at about 75 percent. I told the boss man that I didn't think I was going to keep doing the work. I couldn't remember what exactly I told him, but I knew I couldn't consistently pull at 85 percent, and I didn't see how anyone could. I honestly tried one day to average 85 percent, and I was drenched in sweat, my back was killing me, and it felt harder than any football practice I'd ever attended. Then I said to myself, *these guys do this every day?* I was blown away. There was one guy in there who averaged 120 percent. The faster you pull, the more you get paid. We started at $10/hour. This guy was taking home $21/hour. He was a beast. What upset me about him is that he was short with a potbelly. Here I was taller with an 8-pack, looking like a Greek sculpture, but only pulling at 75 percent. I learned a few things about the makeup of a man in that warehouse, and I had to come to realize that I wasn't a man yet. I wasn't ready for man's work like my father did all his life to raise me. I wasn't ready for man's work like what you have to do when you accept the birth path given to you. I wasn't ready for the man's work that you have to do when your consequences come home to nest.

I quit that job, and I tried something "fun." There were guys into club promoting, and they were my age. That club scene seemed fun. One of my friends told me I had a way with the ladies and that I needed to use that gift. Who would have thought that someone would see that as a gift? Well, he did. I took his advice, and I used my finesse to talk some ladies into being a part of a modeling/dance troupe called "Dazzlyn Dymes." My friend who gave me the idea was good at graphic design, so he designed our logo and our website. I got some shirts made for the eight ladies, and I got a couple Dickie's shirts made with the name on the back. Their outfits were black tank tops with "Dazzlyn Dymes" on the front in gold glitter and a number on the back of the shirt, with boy shorts, skirts, or leggings as their bottoms. These young ladies were in school to be doctors, nurses, lawyers, and so on. I guess they just wanted to feel pretty and do something out of the box. We did photo shoots. We hosted club nights. We were VIP eye candy at clubs. We were in music videos. We did all kinds of stuff. We weren't into prostitution, although some people thought it was. Our ladies were young ladies who were pretty, and they were eye candy. Our business only lasted a couple months, I think. I might have made $130 total from the business. It was a waste of my time and theirs. One thing that stuck out to me during that time was that one of my friends invested $900 into the business. He wanted to support me. I never forgot that, and I didn't realize how instrumental he would be in my life later on down the line.

My mother gave me a hard time about the "Dazzlyn Dymes." She wasn't happy about it. She didn't put the bar too high for me, but that was sure beneath the bar for her. She told me I needed a respectable job and that she was embarrassed to say what I did when her friends asked how her son was doing. My mother was always kind and sweet to me, but she always spoke her mind too. She could bite her tongue for all of one day, and then the next day you were going to hear exactly what she was thinking. I went back and forth with her, but it bothered me that she wasn't proud of me. I wanted her to be proud of me.

Another deciding factor in me letting the modeling troupe go was the fact that I'd gotten back with the girl of my dreams. I had met this young lady who swept me off my feet in October 2005, but I ran her off a couple months later. Then we bumped back into one another about six months later when I was working with the modeling troupe and was almost back into the street life.

One day my little sister came to me with some drugs that she found from her boyfriend at the time. Something happened; they had a fight and she left him, and he had left a bag of weed in her car. He was a drug dealer, and he was making decent money. He had mid-level weed that could sell for a little more than the regular kind. I can't remember how much it was worth, but it was probably around $300 to $600. It's crazy how life works, isn't it? You can be doing the right things, and then the wrong things will fall in your lap and give you a choice to make. The first time I got into drug dealing, it was free to me. Now the second time I got into it, it was free again. Things like that make me believe that there is a God and a devil. God sends the blessings and the way to escape; the devil sends the traps. I was so down and out, so I fell for the trap. My sister didn't know what she was giving me, and she probably thought I'd just give it away or just sell the bag to one of my cousins and be done with it. But silly ole me, I used it as a startup kit. There were some scissors, a scale, and some little baggies in the bag. So I went back to my apartment and bagged them up. Then I took this little backpack and got out in the streets of the apartment complex and flagged down cars of college students. Out of everyone I asked if they smoked, I think 100 percent said yes. Everyone became repeat customers too. It was easy. It went from little $5 and $10 bags to selling QPs, which is a quarter of a pound. Then it went to me buying a pound and breaking the weed up and selling it. By the time that pound was done my run was about up. Weed seemed like it was legal, so it didn't feel very dangerous. I was having fun because I was a full-time drug dealer, and I was living the thug life. I saw this all around me growing up and now I was in it. I didn't know how to act. I was playing a role, and it was like I was an undercover agent out there. I felt undercover because I knew I was faking. I wasn't forced into that lifestyle because I had lost my parents and had to find a way to make money as a kid. I chose that lifestyle as an adult. I didn't know what was worse: smoking it or selling it. My friends smoked it, and I sold it. I didn't know which of us was more stupid. I was living backward. I was all the way into option three on my birth path. I tried the athlete route. I tried the school route. Now I was trying the drug-dealing route for a living. It was harder than I thought. It wasn't all glitz and glam like I saw. Even in drug dealing there was sacrifice that had to be made. There was budgeting that had to be in place. You still had to prioritize and live an adult life. You just were making an illegal living. There were a lot of lessons there that I wasn't getting. I didn't realize that if I could work around the clock except for a few hours of sleep to make an illegal living, then I could do the same thing legally. I didn't realize that if I was crazy enough to be an illegal entrepreneur, then I could be an amazing legal entrepreneur. I was a product of my environment. I was living what I'd seen over and over. There were so many talented individuals from where I was from who could have done so much in the world, but they came back to be a drug addict or a drug dealer. You were one or the other. There weren't many of us who were neither. There were a few guys I knew who chose to be overworked and underpaid like my parents, and although back then I thought they looked like lames, I realize now that they were the smart ones of the bunch.

I was playing into every stereotype known to young black men. I had the long goatee that was in style back then. I had six gold teeth in my mouth. I had the fake necklaces, hoping someone would believe they were real. I had two cell phones, and I don't think one of them worked, but I wore them like they did. I had my Impala that I eventually put the biggest rims that could fit on, 22 inches. I was living the thug life and embracing it. I was a failure. I was in the valley and wallowing in my despair. I would be selling drugs around the clock. I slept from about 3 a. m. to 6 a.m. If I got a call for a $10 bag at 2 a.m., I was going to make that measly $10. I remember one night I went to sell a $10 bag to a group of guys who had chosen a different criminal route. They were jack boys or robbers. They would kick in doors of the apartments and go in and steal laptops and TVs and then keep some and sell some. I assumed they would rob people in person too. I sure thought they were going to rob me that night because about 10 of them were standing in a circle at 2 a.m. for a $10 bag of weed. I was blown away. I wasn't really scared because I was kind of numb to the danger at the time. I was young and dumb. I used to do something stupid and keep all of my money in the bag with the weed I was selling. So to flaunt I would show the money when I grabbed the weed. Dumb, I know. Well, I think one of the guys saw the money and told his friends about it. His friends would drive up from down South and rob for the weekend and then go back home. The guy who called me for the weed wasn't with the group. I think he was trying to set me up to be robbed. I'm guessing he was moving out and wanted to hit one last job before he left. Well, when I went to grab the weed out of my bag, I also pulled out my gun. Then one of the guys said, "Oh, you pulling guns? Are you gonna use that? You know you're not supposed to pull a gun if you're not gonna use it." Then I said, "Who said I wasn't going to use it?" He then said, "Oh, you're gonna shoot somebody? I thought we were cool with you." I said, "Oh we're cool, but I just gotta be ready. You never know these days—y'all boys brought 10 guys to buy $10 worth of weed; that seems a lil' strange." Then they got the weed, and we went our separate ways. Had they not seen the gun, things could have gone wrong that night. I'm not sure if they were going to rob me or not, but I made it out the best way I knew how.

You see, I was lost without a road map. I was losing myself. I was in a dirty game. I was bottom feeding. I didn't know if it was my rightful place in America or how I'd even gotten to that point in my life. I wasn't a killer or a kingpin. I was a lost and confused kid. I was doing what a lot of entrepreneurs have done in their past but are afraid to admit because they don't want to be judged. But I don't care about being judged because I'm not here for the people who judge me. I'm here for the people who are down and don't see a way out. I was there. Now I'm here. If I can get a lesson and get up, then so can you!

After that incident that night I was on my way out of the street life. I started looking for jobs. The woman of my dreams had come back into my life, and I wanted to straighten up. I knew she didn't want a drug dealer to be her husband and father of her kids. She was being patient because she knew she left me and my life went down after she left. She knew that I was searching for myself and pretending to be something I wasn't. She knew it, and she was patient. I think God gave her clearance to come down to the valley and help me up. I think God knew that neither my parents nor my friends could help. He had to send my woman.

She spoke life into me, and she told me I was better than the man I'd become. She told me I was gifted and that I had a bigger purpose in life. She told me I was smart and that I could become anything I wanted to become. Deep down I knew she was right. I knew I could be more. I had shown myself some things while I was in the streets. I got a product for free. I got knowledge for free. Then I made money from it. I packaged it. I marketed it. Then I sold it. I intensified the demand, and then I supplied it. I had shown myself that I knew how to be an entrepreneur and a businessman. I just needed to go about it the right way. I needed a purpose. I needed a meaning for life. I needed my Wife.

I applied for a job and I got hired. I was a counselor in a group home. I was working with men who had mental issues. They suffered from a range of issues. Most of them couldn't read and write well, but some could. They didn't understand much about adult life, but they pretended to know it all. They were like me in some ways. There were ups and downs with those guys, and I had to manage their mood swings. It was very interesting work, to say the least. I liked it, but it didn't pay well. I was making $8.50/hour. I would work 40 to 55 hours a week. I had gotten back in school, but I was in school to collect the refund checks basically. I was barely getting by in school. My wife was with me, but not my wife yet. She was helping me with school and would take my online tests. She was so smart that she didn't need to study for my tests; she could take them and get a B or C rather easily. She was in school as a biomedical science major, and her dream was to be a doctor. I helped mess that up because she became so distracted by me, and I became more of her focus than her schoolwork.

I was in the valley, and God sent an angel to whisper life into me. I started to get some strength to climb again. I started looking at my life and getting lessons from it. I knew I had to clean up my act. The mistakes I made took a total of about six to eight months, I'd say. During that time, I was evicted from my apartment because I didn't pay my rent for three months.

I almost lost my car because I didn't pay my car note for three months. I was spending my money on clothes, shoes, "Dazzlyn Dymes," and buying more drugs to sell. I had my priorities out of order, and it almost ruined me. I got a refund check from school and moved into a different apartment before the eviction hit my credit report. My mom bailed me out and paid up my car note, which was $900 past due. I was faking it and trying to make it. I learned some valuable lessons, but now it was time to get up, brush myself off, and get serious about life.

I want you to spend some time thinking about your valley experience. What did it show you? What lessons did you overlook? Did it make you stronger? Did it make you wiser? Are you ashamed of your low points in your life? Don't be ashamed of anything that you've done or that has happened to you. Don't think you have to tell every detail like I've done, but turn your mess into your message. Use that pain to propel you into a season of greatness. Let those lessons make you wiser. Don't stop learning from them. If you've made it out, don't go back on purpose. If you happen to be knocked down again, don't stay down. Get up and keep fighting. We all have valley experiences, but it's how you use them that will determine your success.

Chapter 5   Use Your Gifts

We have gifts lying dormant, and we are afraid to use them because we can't see how these gifts can make us a living. No matter what the gift is, there is a certain level of fear associated with using it. We look at the people who make millions from their gifts, and then we see others just as gifted who are poor or barely getting by. Beyoncé is amazing, but she's not the only person who can sing and dance. She's the one who daringly and boldly uses her gifts without letting fear hinder her. Michael Jordan couldn't jump the highest. He wasn't the tallest. He wasn't the biggest. He wasn't the strongest. But he used his gifts without fear. He outworked his competition, and he didn't hinder his greatness. We all have gifts, but we have to be bold enough to use them. It's scary I know. We will hear our parents questioning if we really want to do it. Our friends may ask us if we're sure this is the route we want to take. There will be books and videos from know-it-alls who advise against it. We will read all the statistics that say how many people fail at what we're thinking about doing. There will be those who flat out tell us that we're crazy and it's impossible. Some people who have no idea what they're talking about will lend their opinion. The people who are so programmed by the system will try to convince you to use your college degree or to go get one if you don't have one yet. They will tell you that's the only way to have a good life and that's the smartest thing you can do. They'll give you that advice with a straight face and smile to top it off. They'll advise you as if they are happy and content with their life. They are speaking from their birth path that they never questioned or the path that society told them they should take and they never questioned it. They weren't bold enough to take a chance on their natural gifts, so they'll try to convince you to play it safe and not take the risk of failing. They'll fail to mention that you can work all your life and then be laid off by the "safe job" your degree earned you. They'll fail to tell you that social security may fail us one day, and you'll only have what's in your bank account and your safe at home to live off of. They won't mention the risk of mediocrity or the risk of not taking any risk. They'll just advise you to play it safe and never think outside of the box. That's the life we've been conditioned to live, and that's what so many of us play into. We never question it. We never dare to be different. We never dare to take a chance. You can play it safe if you want. You can work on someone else's job and be miserable until you retire. That's a personal choice. You wouldn't be the first person to do that. Maybe your parents or your grandparents did it. Maybe it was the only way they knew. We live in a different world today. We live in a world of opportunity, a world that favors the risk takers, a world that gives chances to be great. There is so much you can do today. Failure is becoming nonexistent for those who believe. It's a world built for faith-walkers.

What are your gifts and how long have they been dormant? Have they been dormant for so long that you've forgotten what they are? Has your job made you feel untalented? Do you scratch your head when it's time to dream and plan? Are you so programmed by the system that you can't see beyond it? Well, it's time to wake up. It's time to wake your gifts up. You have to stir up something inside of you that will bring your gifts back to life. You have to live like you did as a child when you weren't afraid to dream. The dreams you had when your mind wasn't clouded by the dreams your parents put in your mind. Yes, those dreams. Those wild and crazy dreams that made the world seem like your playground, those dreams that had you at the top of the world. The dreams that made you feel like you couldn't fail. Those are the dreams that you have to ignite, and only your gifts can make those dreams a reality. I'm a fan of dreaming big. Dream so big that it scares you. Have a vision so big that certain parts of it are blurry and it only clears up as you walk by faith toward it. Those are the dreams and gifts that have to come back to life. Don't continue to let the doubters tell you what you can't do. Prove it to yourself that it can't be done if it can't be done. Don't let someone who has never tried to do it tell you that it can't be done. Take a chance and you just might surprise yourself. Walk, run, jump, or leap—do whatever you have to do, but do it in faith. It doesn't mean you have to drop everything today and dive in head first, but it means you have to start the process. I'll tell you in the next chapter how I balanced my dream and my job, but first let me share this story with you of when I rediscovered my gifts. It can happen at any time for you, but you have to want it to happen and you have to will it to happen. It has to be your every waking thought. It has to come from your heart and be your deepest desire. You have to know that you want something different for yourself and that you're willing to put in the work to make it happen. If you're not there yet, get there. There is power in that space. There is hope in that space. Your destiny starts with a decision.

I was transitioning in my life, but I wasn't operating in my gifts. I remember looking at my life and wondering what happened to my dreams. I was wondering how I would become the success that I'd dreamed of all my life. I couldn't believe where I was in the world. I was shocked and hurt. I made all the choices on my own that got me to that place. I couldn't blame my parents, my cousins, my friends, or anyone. I couldn't blame my teachers, the police, the government, or anyone. I had to look at myself in the mirror and realize that I made bad choices over the course of my life. I knew right from wrong, and I chose to do wrong. I had to admit that fact. I wanted more out of life. I was 22 years old, and I wasn't getting any younger. How was I going to make it? I didn't enjoy school. I had changed majors from business management to criminology. It was ironic that I was majoring in criminology while I was selling drugs. I looked at my job options with my major, and I wasn't impressed. I saw that the pay maxed out at $65,000 in most cases, and I'd have to risk my life as a cop or prison guard. I wanted to work for the FBI or CIA, but I knew I was too honest of a person to beat a lie detector test. I proved myself right later in life when I applied to be a detention deputy. I was going through the motions at the time but hoping and waiting for a sign. I needed a sign that would push me in the right direction. The job that I had as counselor would max out at $12–$13/hour, if I became the manager of a group home. I saw how hard they worked and how they worked around the clock, and I knew I didn't want that job. The other jobs in the company that paid more required degrees in behavioral science or something similar and I knew I wasn't interested in that.

My gifts were tugging on me. I could feel them tugging, but I didn't know what to do. Then one day I saw a picture online of one of my younger friends I used to mentor when I was in high school. He was playing college ball and on his birth path doing well. He wanted to be a pro basketball player. So I wrote his sister and told her to give him some advice from me. She asked me why, since I used to do what he was doing at the time, and I told her. She then told me that I should write a book about relationships because I was the biggest player she knew. Well, at that time I wasn't a player anymore. I loved to give advice because I was a life coach before I knew what a life coach was. I also loved to write, so it made perfect sense for me to write a book giving advice. I was able to marry my two passions. My passions also happened to be my gifts, so my gifts worked perfectly. I told her to gather some questions that her friends had about guys. She did that, and then I added a couple other questions that I wanted to touch on, and I had 10 questions. I sat down on my work breaks and on my days off, and I wrote the answers to the questions. I wrote from the heart, and I didn't pull any punches. I didn't know how to pull punches back then. I've gotten better over the years though. You can't say everything you think, feel, or know because the world just may not be ready for it. You have to time your message perfectly. I've gotten better but still nowhere near perfect. Back then I had no filter. I was very blunt and real with my advice. I wrote the book in what felt like five to ten days. It didn't take me long at all because I was writing from my heart. It was strange, but I had a very deep understanding about why I did what I did as a man. I realized that my truth was also the truth about most men. My observations of several other men proved my assumptions to be correct. I wrote this matter-of-fact book, and I was pleased with it. I let my wife and a couple of female associates read it. My wife wasn't my wife yet, so the book could have ruined me with her, but it actually just made it a lot tougher for me because it was the blueprint for a woman to understand a man. She was very smart, so she read it and took every word of advice and used it perfectly on me. I was beat at my own game. What she did to me with my advice showed me that I was good at giving advice on things I know something about. Here I was with my gift in action.

My first book came about in a weird way, but that's how life works. We will find our way to doing what we are meant to do.

You have to pay attention to the signs because they will be all around you. That wasn't the first book I tried to write, but it was the first book I was really passionate about, so it flowed much easier. The crazy thing about me writing the book is that I wasn't a reader. My wife is a reader, but she couldn't write the way I did. I started to notice that most readers aren't writers, and a lot of writers aren't readers. You either have the gift or you admire the gift, although you can have the gift and still admire it. At the time that I wrote the book I don't think I'd ever read a book cover to cover. I read the Bible almost daily growing up because my dad required it. I believe I read a short version of Martin Luther King, Jr.'s story and also one on Malcolm X. Other than that I hadn't read any books. I knew what a book looked like, so I formatted it the way I'd seen books done. I made my table of contents, my dedication page, my title pages, and my note from the author in the back. It looked just like any other book. I was 22 years old, and I'd written my first full book. It was 130 pages in book form. I was ecstatic. I'd done it. Writing the book wasn't enough. I had to publish it. I think my friend who gave me the idea was surprised that I actually wrote the book. I don't think she realized that she just spoke it into existence. She nudged me on the path. She was a vessel God used to push me into purpose. Then my wife supported me, and my mother and sister inspired me. All women—that's funny how that worked out. I wrote the book for women who were being played by men or just didn't understand men. My mother and sister were in that boat, so I wrote the book with them in mind.

Then it was time for me to publish the book. I didn't know any published authors, so I was on my own on this stage. So I turned to my adviser, Google. Google was always there for me when I needed it. I searched "how to publish a book" and all the Internet publishers came up. All the sharks in these muddy waters of publishing. The world was changing, and it was set up so that people like me could become a published author and essentially have our books for sale in the same places as traditional authors. The companies were charging for their services, of course, and getting a piece of your sales earnings, but it was publishing. I saw that there were a couple former celebrities who self-published their books through these Internet publishers, so I chose the top one. They beat me across the head with their inflated prices, but it was a learning experience. I became a published author, and I couldn't have been happier! It cost me $1,300 to publish my book, and my wife gave me that money from her refund check from school. She gave me another $300, so I could print some business cards to promote the book and get a little website made for it. She was supporting me because she wanted me to walk in my gifts instead of selling drugs. She not only pushed me into purpose, but she supported me along the way. After my book was published, the publisher would sell you copies of your book for about $8 a book. My mother gave me the money to order my first 100 copies. I was getting support from the women in my life, and it motivated me to keep going.

A couple weeks after my book was published, I landed my first speaking engagement. I wasn't a speaker, but I knew I had to get out and promote the book somehow. I was a very shy person, so speaking was far beyond anything anyone ever saw for me. Honestly, I didn't see it for myself, but I had to do it because I had to change my life somehow. I didn't know any professional speakers, so once again I was on my own in that department. I thought outside the box, and I found a way. I met a guy who played basketball for Bethune Cookman University. I wrote to him on Facebook and asked him if he knew the person who organized the campus events at his school. He told me her name, so I looked her up on Facebook and wrote to her. I told her I was the author of *What Daddy Never Told His Little Girl* and that I'd love to come speak at her school because my book was written for that demographic—African American women ages 18 to 25. I just thought that group would get the most out of my book. To my surprise, women of all races and ages read my book and got something from it. I went to speak at the university, and I was so nervous. This is where my dad came in with his support because I was stepping out and doing something that he had wanted to do, but he didn't know where to start. He also knew that speaking was unchartered waters for me. He traveled to the school with me where I would be speaking for $65 and some chicken wings and pineapple slices. Yes, that's what I charged them for my services. Remember I had no mentors about this, so I had no idea what to charge when she asked me for my fee. Sure enough, when we arrived, they handed me a check for $65 and also had my chicken wings and pineapple slices in the dressing room. My dad sat in the back with me and looked over my notes for my speech. He changed everything around for me and told me what to say. I rewrote my notes and went out there and read from that sheet of paper like a pro. Then I opened up for Q&A and answered a few questions. All I can remember is my wife and my sister sitting in the audience. My sister raised her hand and asked me to step from behind the podium to show off my outfit. I had on a brand-new Miskeen outfit and some fresh white Air Forces that my wife had bought for me. She still wasn't my wife yet, but we were about to get married because she was five months pregnant with our son. She was in the audience claiming me and making sure all the college girls knew I was taken.

After the speech, I did a book signing. I sold the books for $15 and I sold 15 copies of the book. I was so happy. I was too happy. The young lady who arranged the event had never met me before, but she came up to me afterward and said that "you and your dad looked so happy in there tonight." She could tell that we were off of our birth path and excited to be there!

So here I was, a 22-year-old black man who came from very humble beginnings, and I was on a different path. I was now an author and a professional speaker. Yes, it was on a very small scale, but it still could be scaled. Everyone who knew me was shocked. I had done something that no one we knew of had ventured to do. I had a cousin who had written a small book and had it printed and stapled it together to hand out, but this was at a different level. You could get my book online from Amazon and all of the websites of the major book retailers. We were blown away. We were a little country, a little ghetto, and very simple people. Our families worked hard and minded our business. We didn't know that there were any other options outside of what we'd seen. I was in a whole different league now. My friend who told me to start the "Dazzlyn Dymes" had designed my book cover. My other friend who invested $900 into "Dazzlyn Dymes" bought 15 copies of my book the day it was released. It was cool to see that those same friends were still along for the journey and supporting me along the way.

It wasn't all roses though. The book brought some heat. My mother-in-law was looking at me sideways because of some of the truth I'd put in the book. My mom called me, yelling and almost crying because of some of the truth I'd put in the book. My dad talked with my mom and was very upset with me for some of the truth I'd put in the book. He later told me that they weren't comfortable with me being so transparent. They were private about their business. They were divorced and my book stated that, but my dad said some of his friends didn't know about their divorce yet. I was like, oh well, sorry about your luck folks, but I have to come up out of this ghetto living. Now, of course, we didn't live in the ghetto, but to me the ghetto is a mindset, and I felt that we still had that mindset. I felt like we had a poverty mindset, a mindset full of limitations and lines that we couldn't cross. We were free from slavery, but we still acted like slaves in a lot of ways. I wanted to be free in every way. I wanted to break the shackles of my past. I wanted to be free in mind, body, and spirit. I wanted to live a fulfilling life and reach my full potential. I was no longer willing to be average. I had tried everything I knew, except for using my natural gifts, and now was my time to try it. It was almost like I chose to wear colors when everyone else was comfortable wearing black and white. I got some strange looks. My guy friends I grew up with distanced themselves from me. I had given away the game and broken the guy code. I was a sellout. But I didn't care at all because I wanted to change my life. I didn't need a friend as long as I had my woman, my child, and my immediate family. To be honest, living my dream felt so good I was willing to lose anyone who couldn't be happy for me. When my mom and dad were upset about the book, I didn't lose any sleep over it. I knew they loved me and that they would have to face their truth and get over it. They came around after a month or so.

I was operating in my gifts, and there was no turning back. About a month after my book was released I turned 23 years old. I got married 22 days after my 23rd birthday. Our son was born a month after we got married. There I was, 23 years old as a husband, father, author, speaker, and still working 40 hours a week. I was growing up fast. We were still broke, but we had dreams. My wife was 20 years old and still in school full-time and working full-time. We both worked for the group home, but for some reason they gave my wife a promotion right away. So she was making $4 more than me per hour. I wasn't too happy about that, but we thought it was funnier than anything. I was blown by how she came in and got promoted just like that. But her birth path was very different from mine. She was raised to become a doctor or something of the sort. She was very book smart. She was well spoken, very pretty, and put together. She ran track in college and maintained almost a 4.0 grade point average. I married up if you can't tell. I don't know why she was attracted to me, but I thank God for her because she helped to change my life. I didn't make her life easy nor did I change without a fight. It was tough, but we were working toward being better.

I was operating in my gifts and it felt good, but I still had a long way to go. I knew nothing about what I was doing, so I was setting myself up for some major disappointments. I didn't really understand how Amazon.com worked, because I'd never shopped there. I just assumed that people would be looking for books on Amazon and see mine and just buy it because it had a nice cover. I told my wife that I would probably sell 1,000 books a month. I was that naïve to the world of publishing. I knew that I was making $4.20 per book so I told her that if I sold 1,000 books a month, then every royalty check would be $12,000, and if I got four checks a year, we would be making $48,000/year from my book alone. Then I would start speaking and so on. I was so excited, and my wife knew nothing about the publishing industry, so she was quietly excited too. I was spending the money before it came. I had made a list in my mind of all the stuff I was going to buy. We were talking about the house we would live in and the cars we would drive. We were excited about how life was about to change.

However, there were some lessons from this process that I needed to learn. One lesson is that your gift never leaves you; it's just waiting for you to use it. You may be 16 or you may be 60; your gift can be used. Don't get caught up in the system so much that you fail to do what you were born to do. Tap into your gifts and use them to help make your life better.

Another lesson is that there will be some learning curves on the journey. You have to be okay going forward even if you don't know everything. If you wait for everything to be perfect or to know everything about the industry you're in, you'll never make anything happen. You have to be willing to make a move. I went and spoke at the university for $65 when they probably would have paid me $1,500, but I didn't know any better. It was a lesson learned. I was paying a publisher $8 per book, when I could have gotten them for $3 per book. That was a lesson learned. I didn't even know I could become an author, but Google taught me otherwise. There is always a way—you just have to find it. Don't ever feel like your gifts can't be used or your dream is too big. Start somewhere and do something. It may not be perfect and it may not be easy, but be willing to make something happen.

Also know that not everyone will agree with your choices, but if you know you're doing what your heart desires, then they will just have to get over it. Don't let anyone talk you out of your greatness. People doubted me and people questioned me, but now those same people see the fruits of my labor. Some of those same people who doubted me are now benefiting from me. That's just how it works. You have to know what you were called to do, and you have to do it. If you listen to opinions of everyone else, you won't get anything done.

Don't be afraid to dream big. The vision I saw when I started on this journey is what I'm living now. I didn't know it would take this long, and for some reason I thought the rewards would come right away. I was wrong, but I didn't stop dreaming, and I didn't stop believing. Things got desperate at times, and my faith wavered from time to time, but I kept pushing forward. You can't be afraid to dream big dreams. If you dream unrealistic dreams, then your reality will eventually become unrealistic. You'll have what you see in your mind if you believe it in your heart and work toward it with your actions. I'm still dreaming. I'm still tapping into my gifts. I'm still digging deeper. I'm nowhere near my peak. I've done a lot and I've seen a lot, but I know my gifts can take me further. If I told you my dreams, you may become one of those people who think I'm crazy, but I know one day you'll see that I was the sane one and you were crazy for not dreaming big dreams for yourself.

Operate in your gifts! Don't let them die inside of you. You were born with them, so you might as well use them. If you don't use your gifts to benefit you, then someone else will see your gifts and use them to benefit them.

Chapter 6 Balancing the Dream and the Job

This stage of your career may be one of the most important stages you'll ever go through. So much hangs in the balance when you're dreaming, but you're also on someone else's job. It's hard to stay focused on your job when your dream is calling your name. Your boss may be a horrible person. Your coworkers may be petty or too nosy. The paint on the wall starts to look ugly to you. The smell of the building turns your stomach when you walk in. The food you eat there or the food you bring to eat there just turns to gravel in your mouth. It feels like your air supply is being cut short while trying to breathe in there. It's bad. It's beyond bad. If you could go to prison for your thoughts, you'd be serving a life sentence for the things you've thought about doing to your boss. Maybe you've thought about setting a part of the building on fire, so they'd have to close down for a while and you'd get some time off. I know it's rough, but you have to stay the course. There's a balancing act that has to be put in place. You can't just up and quit your job. You can't just jump into the next thing without a plan, especially if you have a family to feed. You have to be smart about it. You have to take your time. Change the way you look at the job. Instead of looking at your job as though you're an unappreciated slave hand, start looking at it like a training ground. Pretend that your dream job sent you there for paid training. This training ground is to prepare you for everything you'll face on your dream job. If you can learn how to deal with these people on your job, then you can deal with anything or anyone on your dream job. If you can learn to smile at your boss when he or she gives you another task to do, then you'll be able to smile at anyone when you leave. If you can be happy in this pit, then you'll be able to choose happiness anywhere you go in life. That's how you have to look at it. You can't let your job suck the life out of you. You have to realize that it's a part of the path. Yes, we should build our dreams, but there is a part of the world that has to be sustained until we find a better way. These jobs need us as we are passing through life on the way to our dream job. For those companies that require humans to run it, there should always be a revolving door because the job should be for people passing through, not for people to sit and rot on the job. A company should be happy to see you leave because they know you were motivated by what's ahead for you, and now they get to hire someone fresh to fill your spot. A smart company would help you balance your dream and the job, and they should make that balance easier for you. A smart company would realize that there will always be someone on that part of their journey where they need to work for someone else. With that in mind they should provide tools and opportunities for you to build your dream—then they would get more out of you. I know not many companies think like that and maybe yours doesn't either. But that's why it's up to you to change the way you look at your job.

Your smile should be confusing to your boss and your coworkers. They should literally ask you why you're always smiling, laughing, and upbeat. They should wonder if you're on some type of drug. And when they ask, you should tell them, yes, I'm on a dream drug. Let them know you're happy in the moment because you can see what's coming in the future and that if you're sad in the moment, it will drain your energy for what's to come. They'll be confused and think you're crazy at first, but after a week or so they'll want some dream drug too. Give them a copy of this book, and then they'll understand. You'll have to confuse the people around you with your peace and joy. Don't stoop to their level. Don't let them suck you dry. Don't become a doubter when dealing with doubters. Don't become a settler when dealing with settlers. Operate on a higher level and force them to elevate to your level instead of you stooping to theirs. If you refuse to be pulled down, they'll eventually climb up. You can be a workplace rejuvenator right where you are. You can train yourself on how to change the energy in a company from the inside out, and then one day be paid to change companies' cultures. That's what I did at my company with anyone I came in contact with.

It's all up to you. You can't depend on anyone else to make your experience better. If you want it to be better, then you have to change it. If you don't change it, then it will only get worse. When it gets worse, it will start to slowly kill you. Don't let your job be the death of you. Don't let your job break you down and make you sick. You have to lift the job up and change the environment to one that will serve you instead of defeat you. Be a workplace shifter, not a workplace drifter. Impact the culture, and don't let the culture impact you. Inspire your boss with your attitude and work ethic. Make them want to give you a raise to keep you, but at the same time don't get complacent in your pursuit of your dreams.

The balance is very important. You have to work to help build a solid foundation. I was on my job for nearly five years. I worked every week, 40 hours a week. I didn't take a vacation. When I started working at the group home, I was working from 3 p.m. to 11 p.m. On this job there were no lunch breaks or any breaks because the clients were on 24-hour supervision, so I had to do everything they did. There was always an opportunity for overtime, but because I had a dream, I couldn't afford to work overtime. Their overtime couldn't afford me either. I knew they couldn't pay me what my dream would pay me, and I had to work toward my dream. The clients would go to bed at 10:30 p.m., so while they were sleeping, I would use that last hour to work on my dream. I wrote books during that hour. I would write every day I had to go to work. While I was at work, if I didn't have to be fully engaged at certain times, I would put one earphone in and have a motivational podcast playing in my ear. I would be growing while I was working. I would listen to podcasts for the whole eight hours. Sometimes I had to talk to people or pay attention elsewhere, but I would keep the podcast playing so it at least would enter my subconscious mind. I was deprogramming myself from the birth path the world gave me, and then feeding my mind with the knowledge I knew I needed for the journey ahead. I wasn't listening to people who thought like me. I was listening to people who thought differently. Everything that went in my ears had to move my life forward. I was rewriting the script of my life, and if a scene didn't move the story forward, I cut it. I could not settle for mediocrity. My job thought they had me, but I had my job. I was being paid to learn and to grow. I was on the job, but I was not in the job. I knew what was ahead for me.

I had to grow into the space I mentioned earlier, and I learned the hard way. Before I adopted that mindset, my job was draining me. My job was killing me slowly. It was changing me, and I was becoming a different person. My job stole some of my drive. I would look around and see people who had been there for 20 years, and it discouraged me. I thought to myself, *who would do this for 20 years?* There was nothing wrong with the job, but there are phases to life and that job was a phase to me. If that job had been my ideal line of work, then I would phase out of that job and start my own center with my own rules and regulations. I wouldn't forever do that job in someone else's way. I would want to make it better and make it my own. I didn't want to do that work for my entire life though, so I despised it. I was growing impatient for a while, and I was starting to snap. I would snap at the clients, and I would snap at my bosses. I was becoming fed up. No one saw the dream but me. I sounded crazy to anyone who'd listen because I wasn't speaking my dreams from a place of hope and happiness. I was speaking my dreams from a place of pain and resentment, so my dream didn't resonate with my coworkers or my bosses. I was tired of my job. I was breaking down and losing myself very quickly. My resentment would affect my attitude at home as well. I started cringing when it was time to go to work. When I got to work, I did not want to get out of the car. It was getting harder by the day. I was losing the battle between the day job and the dream job.

Then the shift happened—I was working so hard on my dream that I started to see the light at the end of the tunnel. My dream started to look real for me. I was making progress, and then I knew I had to keep the progress going and my energy needed to be right for that to happen. I would be at work preaching to my coworkers about entrepreneurship. I would share my dreams, hopes, and goals, then I'd listen to theirs. I was life coaching on the job. I would listen to their relationship problems and give advice. I'd also listen to their business dreams and give advice. They could tell that I was thinking outside the box, but I'm not sure they believed it. I think they saw me making moves, but they probably thought I was just doing it to appear different or special. I don't think they knew I was serious and that I wouldn't be on that job forever.

I remember one of my coworkers saying, "You can't be doing too good if you're still coming here." I believe they were referring to someone else in the company who claimed to have outside business going on. There were a few of us who claimed to have a life outside of the company. I don't think any of us believed anyone else. We started telling everyone that we were just there for the insurance and that we made way more money in our side business. They were lies for the most part but we were trying to dream. I saw some people move on, but they didn't move up. I didn't see the point of moving on unless I was moving up. I had a good job, and I figured I would stay there until I could go full-time into my dream job instead of just starting over in another dead-end job. I stayed put. But I wanted to leave so bad. Had I been single, without kids, then I may have left sooner, but I had a wife and a son so I had to stay put. I had faith, but because I had responsibilities, my faith wasn't enough. Even the good book told me that being married meant that I had to tend to the things of the world, because only singles can tend fully to the things of God. What that meant to me is that I had to consider my wife and son in all of my decisions, and because of that I had to build a stronger foundation.

While I was on my job I saw people around me taking the jump. I could tell that most people would take the jump out of ego, pride, frustration, or resentment. They wanted to prove their job wrong, and they wanted to succeed so much that they left without a solid foundation or a building plan. I couldn't do that. I saw an associate leave his job and go full-time into his dream job. The sad part was that he had no work coming in on his dream job and had to live off of his savings. Then after a few months this person had to move to another city and crawl back to another job just like the one he left. This example proved my point about balancing the dream and the job until your dream becomes your job. The associate would talk about the dream and what all he wanted to do and how he wanted to do it. The other sad part was that this person wasn't all that gifted at his dream job. It was his passion, but not his gift. If you're going to jump, you have to jump into your gift, not your passion, unless your dream job and your gift are one and the same. So this person was walking by ego, not by faith. He kept saying that God told him to leave his job, but I knew God wouldn't tell him a lie like that. I knew God would not tell him to leave his job and then leave him stranded with no money and no opportunities. After saying that God told him to leave his job, he would go right into how much he hated his job and how he was frustrated with his job. But I knew that God gives peace in the midst of the storm. When you leave your job, you should be at peace, not in turmoil. God is not the author of confusion, so He's not going to confuse you. There will be a peace to walk by faith even if you can't see the bridge through the fog. You'll be at peace because you know it's there. Don't leave out of pride, or you'll be coming back out of humiliation.

I didn't have any money, but I had wisdom. I had enough wisdom to hear God and to know God. My associate who left his job was much older than me, but he didn't have a lot of wisdom. Ignorance is bliss until the consequences hit. I started learning from the mistakes of others. I had already made my fair share of stupid decisions, and I had to be smart. This was not easy to do because I was so anxious to find a better way to feed my family. I had to stay on my job because my book wasn't paying well. Remember the $48,000/year I thought I would be making from my book? Well, that wasn't happening. I was making more like $1,200/year from it. I remember getting that first royalty check and being afraid to open it. When I got the check, it sat on the table for probably an hour. I started daydreaming about the new apartment we were getting ready to move into. I was ready to move on up like the Jeffersons and the Joneses. I had a big grin on my face just knowing I'd made a smart investment. I had my wife all happy with me, and she thought she was going to get the chance to prove her mom and dad wrong because she was looking like a failure somewhat by getting pregnant and married before graduating from college. Well, we opened the royalty for the big reveal. I think my eyes multiplied the zeros just because of what I was expecting to see. The report said I sold a whopping total of 70 books and made a life-changing $320. This had to be a printing error. The publisher had to have my check confused with someone else's. You mean to tell me that a sales rank of 1,141,300 on Amazon meant that I was ranked there and not that I had sold that many books? I was shocked and appalled. Something in me made me believe that the Amazon sales rank could have meant that I sold over 1 million books. Yes, I was a dreamer. That pitiful royalty check knocked the wind out of my sails. I think I may have cried. I felt so bad that I let my wife down. But she took it in stride. I think she even started laughing about it sometime later. I couldn't do anything but laugh with her. I was so down at first that I went back to the street life long enough to sell half an ounce of weed.

My wife left me when I did that. She told me that she didn't care if we were flat broke, but she refused to be with a man who was going to live an illegal lifestyle. She left me, and I had to call and beg her for three days to come back. She finally decided to give me a second chance. She came back with some stipulations in place this time. She made me promise to never go back to the streets again no matter how poor we were. She made me start doing coaching sessions with my dad to learn more about manhood. She made me cut off my friends who supported my decision to go back to the streets. She also made me go back to church with her. This little incident happened right after my first royalty check disaster and right before I realized the importance of balancing the dream and the job. I couldn't leave my job with a hope strategy. I needed a solid plan and then a dose of faith.

I stayed the course. There were some ups and some downs, and staying the course was hard to do, but I had to balance. When my son was born in April of 2007, he had to spend three months in the Neonatal Intensive Care Unit because he was born 10 weeks early and was only 2 pounds and 10 ounces. My wife had to stop working, and I was the only source of income, making $9.50 an hour at the time. So after my son came, and then my royalty check didn't bail us out, I again thought the streets were my only option for some extra income to provide for my family. But because my wife showed me that she would rather be broke than for me to go backward in life, I knew then that she believed in me and that she would stick by me through thick and thin. That's when my balance started to kick in. I had to find some patience in the process. It was one of the hardest things I've ever done.

We were living in the apartment complex my wife had lived in while growing up. She had a rough life growing up because her single mom's finances weren't always plentiful. Knowing that, I wanted even more to give my wife a better life. The apartment we were in was built out of wood that looked like termites were going to take it down any day. We couldn't afford any living room furniture. We had a $99 bed; a 19-inch box TV that was about five years old; a cheap dresser set; and that was it. When my son came home, we had a dirt-cheap crib for him. We lived off the dollar menu at Wendy's. I would get paid and then after paying the bills, we would have about $25 left to our name. My wife had a way of staggering the bills so that we could afford to live. We would pay for things right before they got turned off. We actually made a mistake a time or two in the bill-staggering technique and got our lights turned off. I had a Wachovia account back then that would let me go $400 into the negative, so we lived out of that for a while. I think Wachovia is out of business now, so that may be why. They carried people like me. My wife thought I had money put away, but what she didn't know was that Wachovia would let me withdraw $100 out of the bank even if it wasn't in my account. I don't know if they actually did that on purpose or if it was God who rigged my account. I'll have to ask someone who used to work there one day. I remember one time our power was turned off, but we had a newborn so we couldn't stay at the apartment. So I booked a hotel on my Wachovia card and it cost $99/night, and we stayed for three nights. My wife was scratching her head wondering where I got this money. But I was spending the bank's money that I would have to pay back later. I was doing a balancing act and trying not to let her see me sweat.

God gave us a peace eventually, but at first things were tight, so we argued sometimes just out of frustration. I was focused on how I would make it and provide for my family, so I wasn't always present-minded for my wife and my son. I didn't understand her needs, and she didn't understand my pressure, so we both were struggling. It was a painful process, and it hurts to look back on it. We would eat ramen noodles like they were gourmet. If I had a few dollars, then I knew I could eat a few days on the 99-cent menu at Wendy's. Because I worked at the group home, I could eat at work. I could also bring my wife a plate of food home so she could eat too. In the group home system, there is a lot of corruption, so sometimes the managers would buy the staff groceries out of the money that was allotted for the clients. The staff would gladly take these groceries because we were all struggling and we knew the group home's refrigerator would always be full no matter what.

My wife and I were both still in school pursuing our degrees. I was working full-time, and she was a full-time student, mother, and wife. She was only 21, so she was in deep to be so young. I've seen men leave their job to be an entrepreneur and put their family in a bind, but I couldn't do that. I've seen men quit their job and make their wife work, but I couldn't do that either. My wife just wanted me to be happy. She was supporting me and pushing me and encouraging me. I made some stupid mistakes as a young man, but as long as I was willing to get back up and get back on the right path, she was going to be by my side.

I saw some of my coworkers quit the job out of frustration, and then a few months later they would be back. I never wanted that to be me, and the fear of having to come crawling back kept a lot of people stagnant. I told myself that when I leave, I'm leaving for good. I set a goal to be on the job for five years. I was working my butt off to reach my goal. I was working 70 to 80 hours a week. I would work 40 hours on their job and 30 to 40 hours on my job. They always had overtime and they would offer it to me, and I would tell them, "No, thank you. I have my company I have to work for." They didn't understand why I had such pride in my dreams. It didn't make sense to them. My coworkers couldn't understand how I could turn down money in the present with the hope that I would make money in the future. I was working my job for free so it seemed. But I was laying the foundation and planting the seeds. I knew the harvest would come later. I was growing patient in the process. The vision started to become more clear, and I was comforted by the fact that I knew my life wouldn't always be the same.

On my two days off, I would still work eight hours on my dream. My wife was very understanding and supportive. She saw me putting in work, and she wanted to make it out of the struggle too. She brought in $10,000 a year in refund checks, and my son brought in $8,400 a year in social security checks. These were loans that we would have to pay back, of course, but it helped us during the times we needed it the most. Things were tight because life is expensive. I know my wife wanted more of my time, but she understood the bind we were in. My son's checks stopped coming after a couple years, and we had grown dependent on those checks because those checks almost paid the rent. Of course, my son's medicine could cost us $1,400 a month. He had creams that we paid $500 for. His illnesses were very costly—another reason I had to balance the dream and the job. I had insurance from my job that also covered my wife. My son had Medicaid, so he was covered. Even when I felt like I could leave my job because my company was starting to bring in some money, I realized how helpful that insurance was, and I had to be still and keep the patience.

I was building my brand online while I was balancing. I was marketing myself online and spreading the word about my book, which was still barely selling. I was making connections and pitching myself to Hollywood. I wrote a movie script and started attaching Hollywood talent to it without any money. I was still dreaming and believing. It was this balancing act that prepared me for entrepreneurship. I learned how to be patient. I learned how to be hungry but yet be content. I learned how to have an honest grind. I learned the value of sacrifice and hard work. I learned how to dream bigger and more often. I learned who and who not to share my dreams with. I learned how to inspire others and how to shift the culture in a workplace. It was very humbling because I started building my brand online and I'd become a Twitter celebrity, but I was still working a full-time job. My coworkers started to see my tweets and my following online, so they were wondering why I was still on the job. The reason was because my season of balance wasn't over. My company started earning twice as much as my job was paying me, but my season still wasn't up. I had to stay put because my foundation needed some more firming. I needed the insurance until I could make enough to pay for outside insurance. I needed more consistent business. I needed more security because I have a family. I wanted to make sure my heart was in the right place when I walked away. I didn't want to leave because I was tired. I wanted to push through the tiredness. I didn't want to leave because I was frustrated. I wanted to push through the frustration. I didn't want to leave hating my boss. I wanted to leave in a way that my boss could celebrate the success I was stepping into. The job was paid training. I started going to work listening to gospel music the whole way. I would listen to a gospel song for the first hour or so at work. I had a song on my heart all day. I would go back and forth between the gospel music and the motivational podcasts. I took control of my spirit-man and my energy. I stopped letting the job dictate my feelings, and I chose peace and happiness. I appreciated the balance; it was necessary to my growth.

I want to encourage you if you're in that space of balance. Don't get weary. Don't give up on yourself. Regain your focus and your clarity. Utilize this time to grow. Let your job make you better, not bitter. Take it for what it's worth and change the way you look at it. Don't let your job break you; let it make you. Walk away on your terms, not on theirs. When you know you're ready to leave and you've built enough of a strong foundation to leave, stay just a little longer. Stay to that point where you can feel the peace because you know you have something better waiting for you. There is so much bliss in that space. It feels so good to go to work knowing that you don't have to be there and that the job doesn't own you or control you. Walk out and close the door gently behind you because you go in peace, not turmoil. Let them be confused by your composure. Have a goal but don't be afraid to rework the plan. Be realistic in your approach and count the cost before you jump. You can work toward your dream job without immediately walking away from your day job. Trust the process, embrace the tough times, and get every lesson you can along the way.

Chapter 7 The One-Man Show

I'm not against having a team. But I have heard so much about how we need a team to succeed. Well, what is success? If success is to be a Fortune 500 company, then yes, you may need a team to do that. But if success is to make $100,000, $200,000, $300,000, $400,000, or $500,000 a year, then no, you don't need a team to do that. If success means to live your dream, you don't need a team to do that. If success means to be your own boss, you don't need a team to do that. If success means to travel the world or become a celebrity at what you do, you don't need a team to do that. The question is: How do you define "team"? I define "team" as a group of people you hire to help you reach your goals. A team is a very tricky thing because there are different levels of help. First, you have the professionals who will only help if they're paid. Then you have the interns who will help for free, but because they're learning about the business, their help may not be very helpful. Then you have the friends and family members who will help you, but they may also feel like they own you or a part of you. Then you have the partner who believes in you and what you're doing and will help you from the ground up for a payday down the road. Any of those team members could become your worst nightmare or become your sweetest dream.

I've coached clients who had a partner in business who they just couldn't see eye-to-eye with. It drove them crazy. Each had a vision for their baby, and because they were afraid to embark upon the journey alone, they brought on a friend, and this friend hindered their progress with their lane-cluttering ideas. The creator loses creative control and starts to have the creator's vision watered down or distorted with the opinions of others. You can't expect someone to understand your grind if God didn't give them your vision.

I haven't found a team to be necessary yet. I'm sure the day may come, but I've been able to make a lot of progress and change my life without a team. I utilize independent contractors. Those people realize they do not work for me alone. They have to get several clients if they want to make a living. Those people realize that they don't have any say-so over my companies or my brand. They do what I ask them to do, and they only give their opinion if it's asked of them. There's only one person who can see your vision and that's you. That doesn't mean you have to be a tyrant or a dictator, but it does mean you have to be very careful about who you add to your team or whether you need a team at all. I've had people who were paid by me weekly, but I considered them seasonal employees, not team members. A team implies that everyone is an equal contributor and everyone has equal say-so. Even if that's not how you have your team set up, it could easily end up that way. There is a reason we see so many teams split up and groups break up and certain individuals go solo and restructure their brand from the ground up. We saw Beyoncé do it. We saw Justin Timberlake do it. We saw Michael

Jackson do it. You have to be careful when building a team. If you were meant to stand alone or build a personal brand, then a team has to take on a new meaning.

Beyond needing a team, there are times when you can't afford a team. Don't hinder your progress or implode your business by paying boatloads of money to people who are only collecting a paycheck. Make sure you don't hire a full team just to look successful or to appear to be doing big things. Some people hire a team for their ego. They feel like a one-man show makes them look cheap and unprofessional. But it all depends on where you are in your brand building. I've seen people bragging about their team and taking pictures and flaunting their team because a team makes us look more successful. A team can also make us more broke. We could be splitting profits when we don't have to. If you're the brains behind your brand and if you are your brand, then you may not need a team right away. I'm not against having teams, so don't get me wrong. I'm against having a team when you don't need one or having a team for the wrong reasons.

Hearing people say you need a team has always been a thorn in my side because, for some people, it means they've failed before they've started. Not everyone can have a team. I was one of those people. I came from a place where no one thought outside of that small town of five thousand. Big dreams meant moving to the next small town within the same county. People stayed in the same area all their lives. There are people where I'm from who will never leave the state, never get on an airplane, or never move. So to be told that I needed a team I was like, a team from where? I'm a country boy, so that means anyone I spoke to thought I was dumb. They thought that country meant uneducated and slow. So I would be on the phone with big-city people listening to them fast-talk and lie. I had to show these people over and over that just because I'm country doesn't mean I'm dumb. That was another thing that made building a team hard. The next thing is, everyone wanted money because no one believed in me. How can this country boy make it? How can a young black man without a degree go where he says he wants to go? The result of that was them saying, "yes, I'll help you, but you're going to have to pay me up front and pay me ridiculous amounts."

Another hard part about building a team is that people will claim they made you. I've never had a team, but I had help along the way. It may be an idea here, a tip there, and a contact here. I remember one lady wrote me after it appeared to her that I had made it, and she accused me of using her and not giving back. I barely knew the lady. I never met her in person, and we only spoke on MySpace in the message inbox. I honestly couldn't remember how she helped me or what she did. I still don't remember to this day. I think she said she used to talk to me and give me tips. *Well, if you got all the tips, how am I doing better than you? Why didn't those tips work for you? Why don't I remember the tips you're speaking of?* Those were some of the questions I was asking myself. It also reminded me why I have to be very careful about building a team. I realize that as humans we all want credit. We all want to be recognized. We all want to be thanked and appreciated. We all want to be compensated in some way. I'm fine with compensation; it just has to be in proportion to the job being done. I was writing public relations people who wanted $1,500 to $10,000 a month and had no real contacts. I met graphic designers who wanted $700 to design a book cover but had no real portfolio of work. I met people who said they didn't want anything up front, but they wanted a 50/50 split. I realized quickly that if you don't protect yourself, no one will.

So I took a different approach to building my brand. I decided to do it alone until I was forced to hire team members. I wanted to build my brand to a point so that people couldn't say they made me. I only wanted God to get credit for my success, not man. I was very careful what I accepted from people. If someone did something for me, I paid them or I returned the favor. If I didn't pay them or return the favor, then they are still on my blessing list, and they won't make it out of here without being blessed by me. I made everything a business transaction. I don't accept favors because they've always come with a snare. People will say they don't want anything in return, then remind you a year later what they did for you. As humans we want to be appreciated in some way. Nothing is for free. You'll pay now, or you'll pay later. If they say it's for free, then make sure they believe that God is the one who will pay them back. When I give freely, it's because I'm giving to that person as if I'm giving to God. I know God will meet my needs when I'm in need, so that's why I met the needs of others. Nothing is free though. Everything we put into the world comes back in some form. Every seed will reap a harvest of some sort, somewhere. I don't accept free. I have to pay you, or I don't want it because I don't ever want you to say I owe you.

I started getting knowledge and implementing what I learned. The people who would give knowledge weren't doing it for free. It was a part of their marketing plan. They would give knowledge and then hit you with the big sticker price at the end. I learned early on that they give their best stuff for free, and then when you pay them at the end, what they give you is basically the same stuff over again with a little extra added onto it. There's always a price to pay somewhere by someone. I would get on free teleseminars and listen to the free advice. Then I would get off the call and go implement what I'd learned. I remember one time I wrote a PR lady and told her that I was on a call she hosted and from that call I used the information to pitch myself to Oprah and Tyra Banks. She wrote back that she was blown away. Although I had spoken to her in the past, now she wanted money and I didn't have any to give her. I couldn't blame her for not working for free. I don't like to work for free either. I was writing her to let her know that I made it anyway. I did it because I initially wrote her and poured my heart out for help. If a person couldn't hear my heart and see beyond the quick money and help me, then I was determined to prove them wrong. I didn't have to pay her because she gave away the information for free trying to get people to pay, so I know somebody paid her enough money for the both of us. Like I said, every seed sown will reap a harvest somewhere. She took my email and used it on her website as promotion for her business. She used it without my permission. She gained clients from that testimonial I'm sure. Who wouldn't hire a PR person if they saw on the site that she helped a client get on *Oprah*? I remember getting emails from people asking me if the lady was my publicist and if she got me on *Oprah*. Then another PR lady I met talked to me about the appearance, and she made an info product and put it online. She did an SEO for the website, which would come up at the very top when you searched "Tony Gaskins on Oprah" on Google. She was selling my information. The first PR lady asked me to be on a call to teach my tips about getting into the media to her students who were paying her for PR insight. I was being used left and right, but that's the nature of the beast. It's another reason I stayed away from teams early on. Everyone I ran into had an angle. Everyone was a scavenger. It was hard to meet honest people who didn't have motives. The biggest crooks will tell you to trust people more and not be skeptical of everyone who tries to help you. They tell you that in order to get you to drop your guard so they can take advantage of you, and I've watched it happen over and over again.

I started learning the game early on. I had a family to feed, and I couldn't feed my family if I was paying everyone else. I invested in myself, not in others. If a person had a product that was reasonable, I would get it if I felt it could help me, but I wasn't going to pay anyone $1,500 a month for marketing me when I could send an email myself. I learned how to pitch myself, and I pitched myself daily to the media. I had a routine every day. I would pitch myself to Oprah, Tyra, then CNN. I would write a different pitch every day. I used the free advice I got from teleseminars, and I used my gift of writing to craft it. It was short and sweet, with a punch in it. I called it the perfect pitch.

I learned a concept on the free teleseminar called "a timely pitch," and I used it. What "a timely pitch" meant was that you should pitch yourself when something relevant to your story happens in the media. I'll go into details about this later in the book. I pitched my butt off.

I wrote my own pitches, and I sent my own pitches. Then they had social media managers. One young lady told me she charges $3,000 a month. To me she's out of her mind, but I know there are many people who would pay it. I didn't let anyone touch my social media. I post every message myself, or I let my wife post it if I can't. I saved myself between $400 and $3,000 a month. I was actually investing in myself. I invested in myself with my time. It takes time to build a brand. Those free teleseminars I was on cost me because that was time I could have spent with my wife and kids, but instead I was on a call. That's an investment. I googled my fingers off, and I read up on a lot of stuff. For anything I needed to know I would talk to my adviser, Google. I would read several articles and then compare and contrast. I would chew the meat and spit out the bones. No matter what I read I made sure that it sat well with me. I consider myself to be smart, so if it doesn't make sense to me, I don't listen to it. I never took anyone's advice unless I agreed with the advice, expert or not. I'm an expert too. We all are experts, so you have to value your own opinion just as much as the next person's. They could be right, but if you don't agree with them, then you have to live with the consequences. I'm fine living with the consequences of my choices. I'd rather live with my consequences than someone else's. There are so many experts who have never accomplished anything other than building a site and writing articles that they've never implemented. I learned early on that you could make more money teaching someone how than actually doing it. For that reason, there are more teachers than doers. If you look online, you'll see so many info products, but if you look into what the teacher has actually produced, you won't find much. That's why I only teach what I've been very successful at. I started to realize that I knew more than a lot of the experts. I think we all know a great bit, but we talk ourselves out of our genius and believe in someone else's genius. You have to believe in you first. The PR lady who had me on her call had been doing it for 20 years, but she wanted me to teach her class and I'd only been doing it for two years; that blew me away. What I learned from this is that we know more than we think we know.

I was my own manager too. I handled all my own negotiations—yes, even the $65 speaking fee I garnered when I was 22. Maybe a manager could have gotten me $2,000, but maybe I would have never known about it because the manager would have had the school pay their company instead of me. I saw things like that happen firsthand, so it made me very skeptical. Not only did I see on TV how so many athletes and entertainers were going broke because their manager or agent took all their money, but I saw it with my own eyes. I remember a guy coming to me and asking me if I knew a certain celebrity. I told him yes, I'd met her through Twitter, and I could reach her. I actually went to her manager and emailed him over and over. The guy's offer was $30,000 for a cruise ship performance. This artist was on a downtime in her career, so I knew she would have jumped on that $30,000 offer very quickly. But her manager never responded to my emails after the first one. I was blown away. Later I spoke to the artist directly about what had happened, and she was very upset. She called and ripped her manager a new one; then he finally called me back and tried to rip me a new one. I told him that he knew he was wrong and that he had dropped the ball and needed to do his job better.

Another one of my celebrity clients had a manager who was smarter than my client. Her manager structured a deal so that my client didn't know that the company was supposed to pay the manager's company directly instead of my client. So when the very large payout was made, the money went to my client's manager instead of my client. My client had a family to feed and could have really used that money.

I've seen that happen over and over again, and it taught me a valuable lesson. Do your own work until you can't do it alone anymore. I've structured my business very differently, and I'm not sure I'll ever do it any other way. I'm not interested in someone else handling all my work. I need the money to come to my bank account, and then I'll pay who needs to be paid. I need to see every contract, and I'll sign it, not have someone else sign for me. I need to be on the calls so I can hear exactly what's being said and what's being agreed to. If I need an agent or an attorney's input, I'll send them the document, have them send it back to me, then I send it to the company I'm dealing with. All final documents must go through my hands. I don't believe in the middleman. I am the middleman. Guess what? I've never lost any money to someone working with me.

If the work becomes too much for me to be involved, then I have to question the territory. If I can't be a part of the process, then why even process it? If it's my brand that's being represented, but I'm not representing, then why do it? My dad recently went to a publishing seminar under the name of a great American speaker who many know and love. Well, at this seminar the speakers he had there representing his brand were charging innocent people $40,000 to $50,000 to publish their books. Those people probably won't sell 500 books nor will they ever see their investment again. The seminar was a complete scam from everything I heard about it, and it's this speaker's name that will take the ultimate hit. That's why I do my own work. I don't want to send anyone out on a speaking circuit in my name because no one can represent me but me. I don't even want my two sons to represent me; they can build their own brand and represent themselves.

Do your own work. Life is about living it. Don't turn over all your hard work to someone who doesn't care about you or the work you've been called to do. Be active in your brand. Do the servant's workload. If you can't get your hands dirty, then it's not meant for you to be doing this. Get out of the way and let someone else have that space.

I still do all my own work. Yes, I've spoken around the world. I've earned millions of dollars. My messages reach tens of millions of people every week, but I still do my own work. I have attorneys. I have publicists. I have managers. None of them are on salary. None of them can sign on my behalf. None of them are on calls on my behalf. None of them can make a call on my behalf. None of them have access to any of my accounts. None of them can receive a check or send a check on my behalf. I do my own work. I call my own shots. God gave me the vision, so I have to see it through to the end. No one else can see it, not even my wife. Why? Because God didn't give it to anyone else other than me. If I get too busy, then I need to go back to the drawing board. If it starts to outgrow me, then I need to pause and make sure I can still have a servant's touch to my work. I don't want to be worshipped or treated like a king. I don't want fans. I want real people who are real supporters. I want to be able to be reached, to be touched, and to be felt. I want to remain a human and let God be God. There are so many leaders who want to be god-like. They want to build something so large that they become the king, and the fans become the peasants begging for food. I don't want that. I understand that some things will grow beyond the proportions I've seen in my mind, but I always want to be accessible. If I have to charge for my time, then I'll charge for my time as a professional, but I want to be reached.

I cannot entrust the work that God has entrusted to me to someone else. One of the main reasons we scale things is to make more money. Is money your God? How much money is enough money? What are you doing with the money? Are you changing the world? Are you clothing and feeding the needy? Or is the money to fund your greed versus your dream? Has your dream become a fantasy? Are you living and appreciating the grace and favor over your life? Or are you lusting after the material things that money can buy?

We have to question our motives and make sure they are pure. You're reading a book from my publisher, and I negotiated the deal. It's not the world's greatest deal, but I'm fine with it. I'm comfortable with the deal. They told me I needed an agent to get a deal with a major publisher, but I don't have an agent. I spoke to authors and agents, and I found out what percentages authors get in publishing deals and guess what? I got that deal. If I had an agent who had to feel special and to feel successful, then I'd be losing money in the deal. But my publisher will be paying my company, not an agent. Maybe an agent could have gotten me a little more, but what would a little more do for me if the agent were getting 15 percent? I did my own work, and I learned for myself what needed to be done on a deal. I made contact with the publisher before I had an agent, so the hard part was already done. The contract negotiations were going to be pretty standard with or without an agent because the publisher isn't hurting for my business. We are both taking a chance, so why give up another 15 percent on my end? A company is going to give you what they want to give you, and you have to know what you want from the deal. Ask for what you want, and if you don't get it, walk away. Another opportunity will come.

Because I work alone, I just ask my heart what I want for the deal, and that's what I ask for. If I don't know what the deal pays, then I ask a professional, and I pay them as a consultant for their information. If I lose some of it, I know it'll come back around. If I get less than what I was supposed to get, then I know they can afford to pay me a few more times. Either way it works; I'll be taken care of because I'm doing the work my heart desires to do, and there's more to life than money. The money will come.

Be humble but be firm. That's the motto I've built my business on. I'm hands-on with my brand, so it's built the way I want it to be built. I get out what I put in, and I owe no man. I've fared just fine working with companies with them being able to talk directly to me. I honestly feel like it gets me better deals because it's harder to talk to me directly and try to get a deal over on me. It's much easier to try to get a deal over on a manager. I just signed a big deal, and I let them know how I run my company and that they would be speaking with me directly and not with anyone else on my behalf. Because of that they told me they want to do more work with me because they've never worked with a personality as humble as I am. I asked around to some agents who have worked with this company, and they told me that their clients have bigger brands than mine, but I was paid double what their clients were paid. I don't know how it happened, but I know it happened and I'm glad about it.

We live in a do-it-yourself world. So don't be afraid to get your hands dirty and do your own work, especially at the ground level. Although I've done a lot, I still consider this my ground level. I'm still building, and I want to build something different and unique. I want to rewrite some of the rules because this way has worked for me. I want you to know if you'd prefer to be involved and be hands-on in your brand, then it can work for you too. I'm tired of seeing people learn the hard way. Although I'm looking for a manager now, I have some stipulations in place, and I'll keep looking until I find a manager who is okay with my stipulations. Even with what I'm asking, there will still be some ways the manager can get a deal over on me or at least try to, but it'll be harder to do. I think people talk to me on the phone, and I sound easygoing and naïve. I may even look naïve, but I'm far from it. If they send me an agreement and the deal never goes through, then I know they are sitting and wondering why the country boy didn't fall for it. I didn't fall for it because I knew it wasn't a fair deal. I've worked too hard and built too much to be taken advantage of. I know my worth and what I bring to the table. I know what I need in order to feel comfortable, and I won't settle for less. I'll work alone until I find what I'm looking for. I know it's out there, but good things take time.

You also have to consider the possibility that God may want you to do something so unique that people look at what you've done and say there must be a God because there is no way one man can do that alone. I'm open to the possibilities of being one of those people who reach certain heights without being owned by others. Don't get me wrong. If you're blessed enough to start your career with an amazing team, with an amazing structure, and you know there is no way you can do it alone, then by all means take that deal. But if you can't find anyone to help you on your budget, then don't be afraid to go it alone. I still do the work of an assistant, a manager, a publicist, an agent, and much more. It's fun and I love it. It helps me sleep at night. So trust me when I tell you, it's possible to work alone until the right people come along. If they don't come as fast as you'd like, keep going, don't give up, and don't quit just because you can't find good people to work with. Anything is possible.

Chapter 8   The Ram in the Bush

I believe that if you're doing what you are called to do, there will always be a way made for you. I was building my brand alone. I couldn't afford to hire anyone. I was balancing the dream and the job, and I was working nonstop. I spoke about my dreams to others. I didn't talk to people who were doing what I was doing because I didn't want to give away any of my ideas. I learned my lesson about that because I've had quotes, ideas, and plans stolen by others who were doing what I was doing. I would only tell people who weren't competing with me.

I published my first book in 2007. I promoted myself all of 2007, 2008, 2009, and 2010. I was building my brand organically, which I'll go into detail about in another chapter. I was investing in myself. I built something that was unique at the time, and it still is kind of unique today. I built a personal brand; I built it from scratch and against the odds. Considering my background, I was an anomaly so to speak. I think what I was building shocked and surprised a lot of people. There were a lot of spectators, but no real supporters. It's funny how that works. I think some people may hate you so much that they can't allow themselves to support you. People let jealousy get in the way. But you can rest assured that whatever you're building, people are watching.

I wrote the book, then I became a speaker in 2007. I don't remember anything special from 2008, so it must have been a year of groundwork. Then in 2009 I landed myself on *Oprah*, *The Tyra Banks Show*, and *The 700 Club*. You can't find any recordings of the shows because no one knew who I was, so no one cared to record them. I didn't record them either because I didn't want to see them again. I went on those shows talking about toxic relationships and how I once was a horrible boyfriend in college. I told that story because it related to my first book. The story was five years old when I finally got to tell it on live television and my book was a little more than two years old. I was making moves and making things happen. The story I told was shocking to people because no one knew that side of me. I was quiet and shy in public, so for me to tell a story of being a toxic and controlling boyfriend was news to a lot of people.

Right after my TV appearances in 2009, I started a Twitter account on the advice of a friend. I started building my brand, and I did so for two more years before I became attractive enough to an investor. I was building and building. I was balancing the dream and the job and I was coming up on my five-year mark. Remember, I set a goal to be off of my job in five years. It's important to have goals. I didn't write it down, but I didn't have to because I reminded myself of it every day. It was etched in my mind. I spoke it into existence, and I let people know that was my goal. If you see when you want something and you believe it, you will attract it. You'll attract it because it will be in your thoughts, on your heart, and it will come out of your mouth. You'll speak it to anyone willing to listen. That's the point I'd gotten to. I was telling my dreams. I had my weary times on my job, and then I found a peace about the job and changed the way I looked at it. I knew my time was almost up. But stuff really hit the fan when I asked for two days off because I had an event to attend, and my bosses denied my time off. I went above their heads, and I talked to their bosses. Even they denied my time off. I told them it wasn't fair what they were doing because I'd seen other people take time off when they needed to. I let them know that I'd even found coverage for my shifts. They were trying to railroad me. I wasn't going for it. I filed a claim against the company for discrimination, and we settled out of court with a mediator. The company had to pay me a certain amount that I agreed not to mention. They paid me over the course of three months. They also asked me to leave in the mediation, but I turned that down and let them know that I'd leave when I was ready to. I was outgrowing the job and even they knew it. I had gone on national television like a celebrity and then came back to this for another two years. If I were being led by ego, I would have quit the job two years earlier after those appearances. I was getting all I could out of the company, and it was paid training. Then as I was nearing the end of my payments from the settlement, which wasn't much at all, I was getting ready to leave the company. I told them in the mediation that I would be resigning soon anyway. I didn't know when or how I would be resigning, but that's what I told them. I was walking and talking by faith, but I didn't know how a way would be made.

My brand was getting bigger and bigger and gaining more exposure. Just the year before in 2010, I became a speaker for the NBA. First I spoke for the National Basketball Players Association. Then they called me back a couple months later to speak to the NBA. I spoke on choices, decisions, and consequences to the top one hundred high school basketball players in the country. Then I spoke about embracing manhood to the sixty NBA draft picks. That was huge for me. It was huge for anyone who did this. It was just a great stamp. I was one of only two speakers under the age of 30, so it meant a lot. My investor saw that too. He was watching everything. Someone is always watching, and you never know who is watching.

Then one day a friend reached out to talk to me. He was the same friend who invested $900 into the "Dazzlyn Dymes." I call him a friend, but he wasn't really a friend. We went to school together, were cool in high school, and knew one another, but we were very different, so we didn't really run in the same circle. He had been there all along. He was watching, and I'm sure he was shocked at the things I was doing in my life. We had a conversation, and he asked me what I needed in order to go to the next level. I was just talking to him, but I didn't expect anything to come of the conversation. I guess God had other plans. He was my ram in the bush. I had walked by faith for four years in the making, and I was speaking things into existence with no idea how they would come about. Then in talking to him I told him that I needed to be able to take a year off from working for someone else, and I'd never have to go back to a job again. He asked me how much I made a year and I told him $20,000. I did not know he had $20,000 just lying around. He came from a good family, and they'd made smart investments and put some of them in his name, so as a young man he came into some wealth and was investing it wisely. He had money invested in many different areas, but I guess not as a driven individual. He told me to give him 20 percent of my company for $20,000. I said of course. I saw that as 20 percent of nothing at the time so I felt like it was a win for me. Then my broke-minded ways kicked in, and I knew I would need to splurge a little. I'd want to upgrade from an apartment and rent a house. My wife and son had struggled for the last four years; I wanted to take us up a notch. At the time my company was making $40,000 a year, and my job was paying me $20,000 a year. So I was earning $60k gross. Even though my company had outgrown my job, I still couldn't walk away from my job to be a full-time entrepreneur because that entrepreneur money was funny. I didn't know how or when I would make money. And because it came in funny, I spent it funny. So I needed some security. My plan was to get the money from an investor and then pay myself biweekly the same way the job had paid me. I would be grinding all week for myself then; I would be able to travel and network and build my brand. I asked my investor to up the amount to $35,000 for 35 percent. Yes, it was a horrible deal to give away 35 percent of my brand, but this was just one company, and I felt like if I made a million he deserved $350,000 for doing this for me. He accepted the deal very easily, which made me wonder just how much money he really had. I couldn't fathom giving someone $35,000 for the life of me. And this wasn't drug money or any funny business. This was legit money and a legit deal. I was floored, but I knew then that God was real, for real. I started my second company on March 11, 2011, and my last day on my job was March 13, 2011. I had just turned 27 years old on March 8. I was a full-time entrepreneur and free man at 27 years old. That may be old for Mark Zuckerberg, but for me that was very young, considering my parents were still working their jobs and no one we knew was a full-time entrepreneur that young. Not the legal way anyway. I couldn't believe it. My five-year anniversary on my job would have been May 6, 2011. I beat my goal by two months. It was a surreal feeling. I just couldn't believe it.

It was a real grind. People who are in the grind understand that, but the people who are watching the grind don't understand. People watching the grind from online thought I was already rich and famous. The people online had no idea that I was still working a full-time job. They thought I was a full-time author, speaker, and life coach. I had to hurry up and make that a reality. My investor was heaven sent. I don't see him as a human. I see him as an Earth angel. A lot of days I don't think he's a real person, and I don't think he knows what he's doing. I think he's a vessel and doesn't really realize it. I always tell him that he sowed seed on good ground and that he's going to reap a harvest that will blow his mind. I believe it with everything in me. The beautiful thing about it is that he doesn't need my money. He has his own money. He helped me, but he doesn't hound me for money. I've paid him back for loans that he gave me after the initial investment, and he's stuck by my side. I've blown him away time and time again. He earns his money differently because he is part owner of several companies and doesn't actually go into work on a daily basis. He's an investor. He's worth more than me, but he tells me that I earn more than him in income. I don't really believe that but I'll take it. By leaving my job and focusing solely on my brand, my income started multiplying very quickly. My goal was to be a six-figure earner before the age of 30, and I did that. I started earning six figures right away, and I just kept building.

From what happened for me, I tell people all the time to keep the faith and to keep working hard. Someone is watching you every step of the way and waiting for the right time to invest in you. It may not be a person investing money. It may be a company signing you to a deal. People invest in those who invest in themselves. My partner knew me when I was kicked off of the football team in college, but he didn't invest in me then. He knew me when I wrote my first book, but he didn't invest in me then. He knew me when I showed my book to the world on *The Tyra Banks Show*, but he didn't invest in me then. He knew me when I became a speaker for the NBA and the NFL, but he didn't invest in me then. He watched me and paid close attention to my grind. He saw that I was making waves and making moves without any handouts. I knew him all those years too, and I'd never really asked him for anything. It happened when it was supposed to happen. It happened at the right time. He didn't just invest and then expect a return right away. He helped me build. He was the ram in the bush. People were watching and looking and wondering how I was doing the things I was doing, but they didn't understand how God sent provisions for the vision.

You have to work and work like you're the only person you can depend on. Stop asking for help from everyone you talk to. Just work. I didn't ask my partner for an investment; he asked me what I needed. When it's meant to be, it will be, but you have to put in work first. I meet people who just started yesterday, and they want a handout today. It doesn't work like that. I meet people who want me to put my brand on the line to stamp them, and they just started speaking a couple months ago. It doesn't work like that. People write me all the time, and they want to partner on a project because they want brand alignment and to benefit from what I've built because they are weary on the journey. It doesn't work like that. People invest in those who invest in themselves. The best investment you'll ever make is investment in yourself, not in the stock market. If you invest in yourself long enough, then eventually someone else will invest in you and help you get over the hump.

I didn't have to walk off of my job into uncertainty. God showed me how I would eat. I still had to walk by faith because anything could happen, but God sent provision. If He tells you to build it, He will give you the tools. He won't tell you to build it and then turn His back. That's how I knew when someone was listening to their ego instead of God, when they would leave their job and then have to go back to their job after a couple months. That's not how God operates. He doesn't give gifts and then take them back. Wait until it's your time to walk away from your job. You'll be elevated to the next level when you're ready, not when you want it. I wanted to quit my job in 2008, 2009, and 2010, but I had to wait until it was my time. My time was almost five years; yours may be three, or it may be 10. You have to wait until it's your time. It will be painful and you will get weary, but if you keep the faith, you'll see the ram in the bush.

I'm a firm believer that we get what we most often deserve. Yes, there are bad things that can happen to good people but a purpose often comes from it. On average, things happen the way they are supposed to happen. If things aren't happening for you, then you have to check your heart, check your motives, and look into your character. I meet people all the time who want more favor over their life and they want a big break, but their heart isn't right. They can't see the ram in the bush because they aren't being obedient to the calling to begin with. They don't know the giver of gifts to begin with. They are doing it on their own grit and for their own merit. They want the fame and the power. They want the money and the respect. They don't want to be a servant; they want to be worshipped. They want to be an idol. Their heart isn't in the right place. In order to see the ram in the bush, you first have to be willing to make a sacrifice. If you aren't obedient enough to sacrifice, then you'll never get relief from your burden. You have to be able to hear the voice, and then be obedient to the voice. You have to follow the calling, not the crowd.

I believe that everything has to be in order for you to receive your breakthrough. When I got my breakthrough, my character was on point. Everything in your life has to be in order. In 2007, when I wrote my book, my heart wasn't right. I wasn't a good man. I was tiptoeing the line. I was halfway in the streets and halfway out. In 2008, I still hadn't become a great husband. I was still coasting and just getting by. In 2009, doing the TV shows went to my head. I got the wandering eyes, and my spirit got weak. I was feeling the buzz around my name, and I wanted the attention from the ladies. By the end of 2009, I snapped out of it and realized that my wife was the only woman for me, and I might as well stop looking around because no other woman would do for me what she did for me. The year 2010 was my year of pruning. I was being prepared for the journey. I was being set apart. I had to be separated before I could be elevated. I was growing in my marriage, on my job, and in my walk with God. Come 2011, I was ready! I was a man. I was focused. I was a good husband, a good father, a good employee, and a good boss. I was operating with integrity and leading with character. I had tens of thousands of followers online and I was leading courageously. My heart had shifted. When I started, it was all about the money. I wanted money so I could live the good life. I didn't realize the good life has nothing to do with money. It's how you live your life that matters most. I shifted to a purpose mindset. I stopped focusing on the money, and I started focusing on the people. When I made that shift, I showed that I could be trusted with the call. I showed that I was ready for the call. It won't happen until you're ready.

You say you're waiting on God, but truth be told, God is waiting on you. He's waiting for you to get your ego out of the way. He's waiting for you to stop counting dollars and start counting people. He wants your goals to shift from how much money you want to earn to how many lives you want to touch. Money is a by-product, but it can't be the focus. If you're chasing money, you'll always be lacking. Chase purpose, and the money you need will chase you. You've never seen a righteous man forsaken. The righteous will always be redeemed.

Are you ready for your breakthrough? Are you ready to go full-time in your purpose? Are you tired of your job? If the answers are yes, then do a heart check. Sit down with yourself and really check your heart. Don't be fooled by what you can fix your mouth to say. Let your heart speak. Hear what your heart is saying. What are you really doing in your life? Are you treating people right? Are you arrogant? Are you condescending? Are you manipulative? Are you backbiting? Are you scandalous? Are you a liar? Are you a cheater? How do you treat the people who can do nothing for you? Do you steal ideas? Do you steal anything at all? Check your heart. You don't have to be perfect, but your intentions have to be pure.

That's one thing I always tell people when they ask me how it happened for me. I tell them that I got my life in order, and then everything else fell into place. I remember seeing a guy who had the gift. He was charismatic, energetic, and gifted with words. He was shown favor early on in his life. He got into a great school and got an education. He had some big breaks in his life that seemed like they would last forever. He was way ahead of the competition.

People were looking up to him and praising him. He had some big breaks on a level that put him ahead of his peers and his family members, but on a larger scale he still had a way to go. His résumé was building, and it looked good on paper. He had what seemed to be all the pieces to the puzzle, but what was on the inside wasn't right. He didn't know how to treat his wife. He was controlling. He was demanding. He was a cheater and a user. He had her bear his children, but he didn't know how to be a good father. He wanted to be famous. He wanted to be rich. He wanted to be world renowned, but he needed that touch. He needed that real touch of favor from the creator, but he just couldn't get it because he couldn't be trusted. He tried everything on his own will and might, and although it got him some places and it opened some doors, they were not the big ones that he wanted opened. Then here I came. I wasn't as gifted of a speaker. I didn't have the highlight reel and the résumé, but doors were being opened. When I looked at the difference between us, I felt like he should have been the one getting the blessings that I was getting, but his life wasn't in order. He went from marriage to marriage and continued to fail in them. I knew what his issue was, but I don't think he realized it. How can God trust you with the world when he can't trust you with your own home? Yes, you may go some places and you may do some cool things, but you'll never get the ram in the bush until you're humble enough to sacrifice completely. Until you put your heart on the line and you lay down your will for a greater calling, you'll always find yourself spinning your tires and being stuck.

You'll ask for help, and it won't come. You'll look for help, and won't be able to find it. You'll pray for a breakthrough, but you won't be heard. You'll have to get in line. You may look left or look right and see the next person appearing to prosper, but you don't know their behind-the-scenes footage. You see what they show you, but you don't know what's really going on behind closed doors. You don't know what demons they are battling or what fate awaits them. You can't get caught up in what it appears to be. You have to look in your mirror and come to terms with your truth if you want to see a change happen. I've watched people fail over and over again and have all the talent in the world, but none of that matters if your motives aren't right. You can try and try, but if you know right from wrong and you still won't get right, then everything will continue to go wrong. If you've never known the right path and you've never been on it, then you may be exempt from the laws, because you've lived all your life in ignorance to the way. Once you know the way and you choose to go astray, you'll struggle and you'll pay a much greater price than the ones who never knew.

Get ready for your ram in the bush. Be in expectation of your blessing, but work like never before. Train yourself to live the right life and trust that things will work out in your favor. I always say work twice as hard as you pray. You can pray and have faith, but you need to do your part and work. Once you've worked and done all that you can do, then you can expect your blessings to pick up where you left off, but if you don't do your part, it won't ever happen for you.

Don't rush the process. Don't be desperate. Don't depend on someone to make anything happen for you. You can't wait on someone to give you a handout or a hand up. You have to climb as if no one will ever look down to pull you up. You can't expect to be carried to the top. You may do enough to attract an investor or a partner one day, but you can't want just a deal. You have to have a plan on how you'll make good on the deal. I meet people all the time who want a deal, but they have no idea how they'll pay that person back. I know my plans will make my partner way more than he's ever given me. I know that one day he'll look back and say, "Wow, I was really fortunate to have met Tony and made an investment in him." I don't have a doubt about it. It would have to happen otherwise to prove me wrong. Get ready today; don't wait any longer to change your life and get aligned for your breakthrough. Don't beg for it; work for it and know that it will come when it's supposed to come!

Chapter 9 The Leap

I've heard a lot about people wanting to take the leap. We get tired of our job. We get tired of being unappreciated. We want to do our own thing, make our own money, and be in charge of our own schedule. It's fair to feel that way. I've been there. I want to share some insight with you just in case you're thinking of making the leap of faith. I know you've heard that if you're unhappy doing what you're doing, then stop doing it. You've heard that if you don't like your job, then quit your job. Those things are correct, but you can't take them so literally. You're where you are for a reason. Your life experiences and your knowledge got you to that place. Now, if you want to be somewhere else, you have to make sure you have the knowledge to get there. It's a process, and it doesn't just happen overnight. Don't just wake up tomorrow and quit your job without a solid plan. You may have a plan of action, and you may even have savings or an investor. Those things are great to have, but they don't guarantee success. You have to have more than just what's on paper. You have to have favor. You have to have a calling. Some people are called, and some people just came. You have to make sure that you're not one of the people who just came. Don't just do it because you want to be like the other entrepreneurs you see online. It's going to be a sad journey for you. Do it because there is something tugging on your spirit every day, and you can't shake it no matter how hard you try. Do it because the thought of your calling keeps you up at night. You can't stop thinking about it. You can't stop talking about it. You're drawn to it in every free moment you get. The calling has to be bigger than you. The calling has to scare you a little bit. The calling doesn't have to be religious. It could be something that will just solve a problem or boost self-esteem like the lady who created the Spanx line. That's not an earth-shattering idea or going to rid the world of disease, but it does solve a problem, boost self-esteem, and help millions of women get dressed with a little more ease. It changed her life, and it's touching the lives of many others. It could be something like that, but even with that you have to be strategic.

You have to make sure that you've worked out the kinks in your armor. You can't make this leap if you're not spiritually and mentally ready. You have to train yourself, teach yourself, test yourself, and trust yourself. I didn't do that. I've kind of purposely forgotten exactly what I did because what I did was very stupid of me. I made the leap, but I didn't leap very far. I had the wind knocked out of my parachute rather early. When I left my job, I believe I spent my $35,000 in about three months. I used like $10,000 of it to pay the first and last month's rent on a three-bedroom, two-bath house in a gated community on a lake. I bought new furniture for the house and all. I used $2,000 of the $35,000 to pay for a book proposal to be written up for me to submit to a publisher. The book never got picked up, because the agent I had didn't have many connections to the publishers

I needed, or maybe she didn't submit it at all because she didn't really like the book herself. I think she was the opposite of what I was writing about. There was $12,000 gone already. I can't really remember what I did with the rest of the money, but I know some shopping was done, probably upgrading my wardrobe a little so I'd look like a successful entrepreneur. It wasn't long before I was back at my investor's door needing a "hold me over." Fortunately, I was connected to the right people, so I was able to borrow when I needed to, but it built a mountain of debt for me. Now just imagine if I had made the leap without strong backing and did it on my $35,000 savings? I would have had to go crawling back to a job in only three to six months. That's what I watched so many people do.

You see my leap was favored. My leap was covered by grace and mercy. There were provisions in place even for my shortcomings. Not everyone is as fortunate, so you have to make sure your plan is solid. I'd hate to see you leave your job because the idea sounds good, and then you're right back where you started in a few months. The truth of the matter is that a lot of people who do what I do will lie to you. It's so easy to say "leave your job and take a leap of faith." It's so easy to say "if you don't like what you're doing, then quit." I've heard people say that they were sleeping on a couch with a few dollars in their account and now they're millionaires. Something in that story is being left out. You heard Donald Trump say his father gave him a small loan of a million dollars. Wouldn't you like to have that small loan as a starting point? You see there's always something that happens in a person's story that they leave out because they don't want their success to be discounted or taken for granted. They leave out the financial help they received along the way. You have to look deeper.

I watched a guy with a couch story who appears to be a millionaire now. I heard the couch part with a few dollars in the account, but then the story went from there to investing in some companies and making some money and becoming rich to now wanting to teach others. Umm, how did your money go from $100 in your account and you're on a couch to enough money to invest in some companies? I think maybe someone died and left him some money and then he invested it. Or did he spend it strategically to look like enough of a success to implement his plan and sell you on his strategies for sale? Something happened in the story that isn't being told, and that's what you have to take into account. Did someone die? Or did he meet a billionaire with a few hundred thousand to blow? Or was it dirty money? Don't just look at someone like myself or someone on YouTube or TV and not get the full story.

If you had an investor who could float you a million dollars, I'm sure you could make some things happen. If you had an investor who could even give you $100,000, I'm sure you could make some things happen. You may not get that and you may not need that, but you have to be smart before making a leap that you could regret. People are waking up and quitting their jobs today and will be begging for their job back next month. Don't make the same mistake. What I suggest is that you ask for a vacation instead. Use all of your vacation days and take that time to dream and plan. Map out your plan. Look at how you'll generate income as an entrepreneur. Look into who you could ask for an investment or a small loan like Donald. If you won't be asking anyone and you're going to do it on your own, then look into what bills you can cut back on. Map out how you'll pay yourself from your savings. Account for emergencies by looking at the emergencies you've had over the last five years. What were they, and how much did they cost? You can never predict everything, but you can come close. It's very important that you count the cost of your decision before you make it.

After you have the plan in place, now implement it while you're on your job. Let your dream job checks go to an account that you don't touch. Live without the things that you decided to cut back on. Create a mock emergency and put $2,000 away into an account like you had to give it away. Make money from your business the way you plan to. If you say you need to be off of your job to make money in your business, then use your days off from work as your workdays in your business. That may mean you only work two days a week, but that's good practice for the life you want to have anyway. You don't want to become an entrepreneur to work like a slave, do you? So work two days a week on your dream job and make something happen. Do that for three to six months and see how it works. At the end of the six months you'll have saved a lot more money, gotten some simulation of entrepreneurship, and had a better idea of what it will feel like. You have to build while you dream. You can't just dream and then jump. You have to plan. I worked my butt off for four years before I took the leap. Had it not been for my investor, I still may not have taken the leap. I could have left my job and probably could have done it on my own, but I would have been very afraid. I had mouths to feed, so I had to be smart. I was earning $40,000/year in my company, and some people can live off of that. We could have lived off of it, but I still wanted to make sure.

When I made the leap in 2011, I didn't count my income that year. I can't remember what my taxes said. The next year I made $147,000 as an entrepreneur. That was the launching pad. It started tripling from there. My guess was that if I could work on my dream every day all day, I could be a six-figure earner. That's what I told myself. That's what I told my wife. That's what I told my investor. I was right. My estimation was because I saw what I made while balancing the dream and the job, and then I figured in having 40 extra hours a week to build and to brand. I did simple math and that's what I came up with. I was hitting my stride after my leap, so my income was climbing fast. A couple years after my leap I had built a seven-figure brand. It looked like to some that I was shot out of a cannon and became an overnight success, but I had been working for half a decade behind the scenes. I had a couple flashes of greatness early on, but I still had to put in the work.

I urge you to count the cost. It felt so good giving my two weeks' notice. I worked with a smile those last two weeks. I was coaching my coworkers on their dreams. I was treating my clients extra special. I was so happy. I looked at my bosses with a look of satisfaction. They thought I would work a job like that all my life. They had said, "Oh, he must not be making any money if he's still here." They tried to block my progress by not approving my time off. They did whatever they could do. Some people don't want to see you do better for yourself because you doing better for yourself may mean that you'll be doing better than them. You have to understand that fact and use it as motivation. Don't let it make you angry or resentful. Let it make you hungry. Let it drive you to work harder and to get better at whatever it is you want to do.

Never forget the underlying stories that aren't told, and try to identify yours. Somewhere in your story there is a hidden blessing that is waiting to be activated. As a life coach, I've coached the wives of many successful men. Hearing the stories of some of these successful men, I realize that we have some similarities. Remember it was my wife who gave me $1,600 to publish my book, get some business cards, and a website. Had she not given me that money, who knows when the book would have seen the light of day? In hearing the stories of some other successful entrepreneurs, it was their other half who supported them when they had nothing. I've heard stories of men chasing their dream to be a comedian, a film producer, or an athlete. These men were working regular jobs and then got to a point where the job wouldn't support their time off, so they had to quit. They quit the job, and then the gigs and opportunities weren't flowing in and they were flat broke. In those times it was their women who worked 40-plus hours a week to pay all their bills, pay for their flights or rental cars, take care of the kids, and be the backbone for them. A lot of those men make it and then try to inspire you and let you know you can make it, but they never put their women on a pedestal and say, "If it wasn't for her, I wouldn't be here today."

I see men today who get married and then quit their job to pursue their dreams while their wives are working to pay the bills. If you're a single mom and you're looking at a male entrepreneur without any kids, you can't listen to everything he says. If you're a single parent and you don't have a spouse who can help pay your bills, then you can't just take a plan from anyone. You have mouths to feed, and who is going to help you when your kids are about to miss a meal? Count the cost!

There is another side to the leap that we often don't take into consideration. There are many female entrepreneurs. We see them living this dream life and building their company. It may seem as if they are entrepreneurs, but many of them still work full-time jobs. Some of them don't work full-time jobs, but they may have a rich father who pays all their bills because she's daddy's little girl. Then some of them may have a rich husband who pays all the bills, funds her company completely, and lets her spend whatever she makes on new purses and clothes. I know this because I'm in the playing field with them while you may be in the stands watching. My wife doesn't have to work, so she could blog every day and post products on her blog and have ads on the blog and look like she's making great money on her blog. But I could be taking full care of her, and she may not be making anything from the blog. There are always pieces to the story that you don't know. You may not need a team, but most likely you will need some form of help from somewhere; and if that help is going to be your savings account, then you need to be extra careful.

Never forget the part of the story that isn't told. What part of your story are you trying to gloss over? What missing piece to the puzzle do you need to find before you make the leap? You see the finished product, but you need to understand the process.

After you've done all of that, then you're ready. When it's time to leap, know that it's a beautiful thing. Don't get stuck pondering on the leap for too many years. No matter how much information you get or how much planning you do, there will always be an element of faith that's needed to make the leap. When I finally took the leap and left my job, I didn't know what to do with myself for the first month. It felt so weird to wake up every day and not have to go in to work. I was smiling all day. I was pinching myself. Fear also set in because I thought to myself, *this can't be life*. I found a way to make a living from home and only fly out a few days a month. So I was home every day with my wife. I could go to all the school functions for my son. I could go to breakfast every day with my wife. Then I got to vacation whenever I had to work because I would be flying to a new city to speak. It didn't feel like work at all. It's still not work. Don't go from a job to a job. Go from a job to a dream job. If you're going to do it, then do it right. Moving from one plantation to another to do a different type of slave work isn't freedom. I knew I had to create a new life. It's still in the making, but it feels a whole lot better than what I was doing before. I can make my schedule, and I can break my schedule. That's what the leap is all about. Don't go from stress to stress. Go from stress to bliss. I remember just lounging around some days. Work felt like a vacation. After being on vacation for about a month, then I said it was time to get back to work. Then I realized my work was fun. I could sit down and work for eight hours straight and not remember to eat or drink. That was fun work. I was blown away that you could make the leap of faith and then not have to work anymore. I believe in taking that next step because I believe this is how life is supposed to be. We go through phases, and working for someone else is necessary. There is a lot of growth in the climb, just as there is growth in the valley. It all works hand in hand, but life is meant to be lived through, not suffered through.

Get excited for your leap. Don't overthink it and don't stress about it. Make the transition as smooth as possible by patiently going through all the necessary steps. Listen to your heart, not me or anyone else. I said take three to six months, but your heart may say to take 12 months of planning. Follow your heart because it's your path. Don't believe everything you see online. Look at your reality because that's your truth and that's the truth you have to plan and prepare for. You can't plan for someone else's reality because you don't know their full truth. You only know what they show you, so look at your behind-the-scenes and work to make them look like a highlight reel. Today my behind-the-scenes look like a highlight reel. I've been able to create a dream. When I have a nightmare, it's because I brought it upon myself by the decisions I've made.

It's almost that time for you, so embrace your dream and get ready for what's to come. I wouldn't lie to you. Life can feel like a dream. You can go from favor to favor. You can wake up and do what you truly love. You don't have to be a scam artist to be an entrepreneur. You don't have to be a snake to make it on your own. You can live a purpose-driven, fulfilling lifestyle, and earn a great living while doing so. Get ready for the leap.

Chapter 10   The Organic Brand

There is something special about building an organic brand. You've heard of organic food, right? Well, I guess an organic brand is similar. There are so many brands online that it gets kind of confusing when you try to figure out who's the real deal or not. There are so many copycats. We all say kind of the same stuff, and there is nothing new under the sun. We're building the best we know how and doing it the way we know how. There are differences in brands based on race, age, demographics, and so on. I've seen some people who may not know the things I know, but they have an amazing website builder who makes their stuff look terrific. Then I see some people who know more than me but they have no website. There are people who know nothing for themselves and piece together everyone else's work and call it their own, and they build a very believable brand.

One day I was having a talk with an industry insider, who was telling me about a couple of brands that I've seen online. One guy on YouTube paid $200,000 in YouTube ads to expose his video to millions of people to sell them a course. Thousands of people have bought his course, and it made him millions of dollars and an overnight authority. The guy says he reads a book a day, so that implies he's teaching you stuff he's learned from other people and making a great living from it. Then there was a guy on Facebook with millions of likes on his page. Well, that guy boasts about Facebook ads and promotion. He spent hundreds of thousands of dollars in Facebook ads to get millions of likes. If you have the money to spend, you can spend like that, have the gift, and then get the attention of Oprah and anyone else you'd like to reach. Money talks. Are they gifted? Yes! It's a gift to be able to see an opportunity and then capitalize on it. It's a gift to know how to market yourself and convert leads into sales. That's clearly a gift. But is it the only way? No.

I know you may be like me. Maybe you don't have a rich father. Maybe you don't know any rich people who will give you hundreds of thousands of dollars to market yourself. Maybe you don't have a great corporate job paying you hundreds of thousands of dollars that you plan to leave and spend that money on yourself. Maybe you don't know how to market. Maybe you don't want to become an overnight celebrity. Maybe you want to grind it out because you realize that the process is everything. Okay, maybe that's too many maybes, but you get the point.

I took a different approach because I had to. I also wanted to learn. I can afford to buy ads now, but I still don't spend more than $100 on an ad. I'm not in a rush. I'm not money hungry. I'm perfecting my craft. I'm perfecting my pitch. I'm taking my time. I started with 34 followers on Twitter. Those followers were the people in my contact list that Twitter automatically made follow me. Before Twitter, there were MySpace and Facebook. I want to share with you how I built an organic brand. I'll leave

MySpace out since it no longer exists really. On Facebook, when it was just about friends, I broke the code and I started friend-requesting strangers. I mean it is the World Wide Web, so why just interact with people you already know? I built my friend list up to 5,000 because it wasn't just about being friends with 5,000 people; it was about free marketing. I figured that I had something that people wanted to hear about, so I invited them. Then, once I wrote my book, I created a Facebook group for the book. I invited all of my friends, and I asked some of my friends to invite their friends. I got about 400 to 700 people in the Facebook group. I can't remember how many. Then I started creating discussions about the topics in the book. I was getting my feet wet with Facebook. I was learning on the go. I was thinking outside the box and doing some things that I hadn't seen anyone else do. Such groups are very common today, but in 2007 there weren't many groups for books in my demographic. In fact, there weren't many authors my age, so I was introducing a lot of people to something new. Facebook started to phase out for me after a while. Then I heard about Twitter. I was late to Twitter by a couple of years.

I joined Twitter in 2009—March 25 to be exact. It was right after I was on *Oprah* and had filmed *The Tyra Banks Show*. My friend who would later become my investor gave me the idea to join Twitter. He was into the tech stuff and probably bought some early stock in Twitter too. I joined Twitter, and I was still using Facebook. On Facebook, I started using my status updates to post quotes. I wanted to be deep. I felt deep, and I loved deep people. I downloaded a motivational quote app on my phone, and I would read the quotes daily. I didn't read books, so reading these quotes were like my books. I would then post the quotes on my Facebook, and I would even credit the author, unlike many people who use my quotes. I was quoting these great people from C. S. Lewis to Vince Lombardi. As I began to read the quotes more and more, I started to realize that I could write quotes too. I had always been a poet. If you notice, I start a lot of my sentences the same way in some paragraphs; I do that because for me writing is poetry. Poetry doesn't have to be grammatically correct or follow any rules because it's an art form. I loved poetry because I could be less educated but still feel smart. I took that gift, and I started to revise the quotes at first. I would add a line to it, or I would flip it around. If it was a quote that I didn't understand fully or I didn't agree with fully, then I would reverse it and say the opposite. That's how I taught myself to write quotes. Once I learned how to write my own quotes, I stopped reading the quote app and started reading my heart. I would sit and analyze my feelings and thoughts in the moment, and then I would articulate it poetically. The thing about wisdom and knowledge is that none of it is new; we just say it differently. That's how I know my quotes when I see them even if they don't have my name on it. A lot of my quotes I've only written once, but many of them have four or five different versions online. The reason why is that I may use different words at different times to describe the same feeling. When I write a quote, there is always four or five ways I could say it, and I just go with the one that feels best in the moment.

I started quoting because I wanted to be a great. I wanted to go down in history and never be forgotten. I wanted my wisdom to be written in books and shared around the world. I didn't want to live and die as just another social security number. I was quoting on Facebook daily, but it felt limiting because you only could have 5,000 friends. Then there was Twitter where you could get as many people as you could earn. Twitter stole my heart from Facebook, and I started learning more about it. I saw that people were tweeting their day-to-day activities, but that was kind of boring to me. I asked myself, *who cares what I'm eating for breakfast or what I'm about to do next?* I'm very confident and I know my gifts, but I'm not vain. I felt that it would be vain to just post my every move in life as if someone cares. I wanted to use it differently. I decided that I would use the space to motivate myself, remind myself of my goals, write out wisdom that life was teaching, and hope that it could reach others. I started with 34 followers, and it seemed like a daunting task to get followers because a person had to choose to follow you and then choose to put up with your thoughts on a daily basis. It's hard to do that with people we love, so imagine how hard it is to do that with strangers. Nonetheless I set out on this journey to build a following on Twitter. The first mistake I made was not following people back. I think you learn as you go. I noticed that celebrities didn't follow many people back, and I wanted to be a celebrity, so I was following their lead. It was a mistake because I wasn't a celebrity. So for a long time I only followed 25 people. Then it hit me one day, who are these 25 people? They are non-celebs just like me, so what makes them any different than anyone else on Twitter? By that time, I had amassed thousands of followers, so I just started following like 100 to 200 people a day; and I realized that it helped me grow my following even more because now those people felt appreciated, and they shared my message more. It also made me more accessible so people could present deals to me.

I started gaining followers by tweeting quotes at key times throughout the day. I did a little research and talked to a couple people about what were the best times to tweet. What I landed on was sending a quote out at 8 a.m. when people are just getting to work and sitting down to procrastinate before beginning to work. Then send a quote at noon when people are on their lunch break. Then send a quote at 4:30 right before people are getting off at 5 and on their phone wasting time. Then send a quote at 8 p.m. right after dinner. Then I did a tweet rant from 10 p.m. to 10:30 p.m., tweeting a punch line every five to ten minutes. My quotes throughout the day were poetic, so they were easy to retweet. I didn't tweet about me because people don't want to share bits about me on their timeline. Instead I tweeted quotes that anyone in the struggle of life could relate to. My 34 followers started retweeting me eventually, and after a month or two I was finally at 100 followers. Then I kept tweeting and I got to about 200 followers. I wouldn't tweet after 10:30 p.m. because I wanted to pretend to be asleep so it would look like my life had balance. It looked really bad to me when I would see people tweeting at 2 a.m. and stuff. I was like, wow, you're showing the world how miserable and unorganized your life is. I know we all are messes, but you don't have to show it to the world. That was just my thinking. I wasn't just tweeting away. I created a growth strategy for Twitter, and it was working slowly but surely. I had a couple other things going for me. I used my name @TonyGaskins. I wanted to be known for who I am. I wanted my name to go down in history. I didn't want to be @lilformerthug84. Forgive me if that's actually someone's Twitter name, but I hope it's not. I was branding myself. I was beginning with the end in mind before I ever knew Steven R. Covey taught that in his book on the habits of highly successful people. That lends to my point that we are born to be successful; we just have to trust ourselves. Another thing in my favor was my picture sitting talking to Oprah. I milked that picture greatly. I went on *Oprah* in 2009, and I talked about being a toxic and controlling boyfriend in college. Oprah didn't mention my book or stamp it. She did say that I'd dedicated my life to helping others to not make the mistakes I made. That was it. The show was a live taping, and it never re-aired. So no one could rewatch it or find it online. So when people saw the picture, they assumed that Oprah had interviewed Tony Gaskins the author and speaker, not Tony the former toxic lover. I used that picture as my background on Twitter and another picture of just me as my avatar. When you put all those things together, I had a recipe for success on Twitter.

Then one day it hit me that I needed to reach a celebrity. I needed to get the stamp of a celebrity to get me over the hump. I was tweeting some of my best stuff, and only a couple hundred people were seeing it; and some of them were stealing it and putting it on their timeline as if it was theirs. Then I developed a plan. There was another guy following me who I went to college with. He was "the man" in college, and he had an entrepreneurial spirit and wanted to be a famous celebrity. I was watching his climb, and he was reluctantly watching mine by default because Twitter made him follow me when I signed up and connected my contacts. He was a rapper who has a buzz in the city of Tampa. I sent out a tweet that said, "I'm thinking about doing a youth summit with @HisName and @AliciaKeys." Now, I was clearly lying because I didn't have youth summit money, connections, or anything else to do one. I had a good feeling that Alicia Keys would see the tweet though. After I sent the tweet, I sent the guy a direct message and said, "Did you see that tweet, watch what happens?" He wrote back, "Yeah I seen it but what do you plan to do with it if anything comes from it?" He had no idea who he was talking to. I had my plan mapped out. He realized that later. At the time he had like 10,000 followers to my 200. I knew without a shadow of a doubt that I was going to catch and pass him because I had a plan. I didn't know if his followers were real either because you could somehow buy Twitter followers, but I refused to do that. A little while after I sent the tweet, Alicia Keys followed me back. Why did I choose Alicia Keys? She had done some great things in her career, but she was kind of quiet at the time. She looked very humble and down to Earth. I felt like she had a good heart and would want to help the youth. I also could tell she was a deep soul and would appreciate my quotes. I also knew as a woman she looked up to Oprah, so her seeing me sitting next to Oprah would mean something to her. I had this all mapped out in my mind. It worked. It wasn't like she followed everyone who followed her. She had 350,000 followers at the time and was only following 99 select people. I became the hundredth person. She followed me for a while and that's what helped me get over the hump. It helped me because her fans would look to see who she follows and being that I was the last person, they would follow me too. The same things that made her follow me were the same things that would make anyone else follow me. We are all human, and we think alike for the most part. After about three weeks of her following, she retweeted me one morning. I woke up one morning feeling blessed for a reason I can't remember and I tweeted, "I woke up this morning only to realize that God had been working on my behalf while I was asleep." She retweeted it and she wrote, "LOVE THIS" in front of it. That tweet got a lot of retweets and people were blowing up my phone telling me that Alicia Keys retweeted me. That was a huge deal in 2009 or 2010. I went up to like 2,500 followers rather quickly because of Alicia Keys. I owe her a steak dinner or something. She was an angel in cyberspace and she didn't even know it. God used her in a special way for me. Getting her to follow me was my only deception in business, but I didn't see it in a bad way. The good book says to be wise as a serpent but harmless as a dove. I was being wise and I wasn't hurting anyone. A lot of people were begging for followers. I never once tweeted, follow me. I never once tweeted, tell your followers to follow me. People were begging to be followed but had no clue where they were leading people. I knew where I wanted to lead people. I wanted to lead people to the same place I was headed, to peace and prosperity.

When Alicia Keys retweeted me, it exposed me to every celebrity on Twitter. She's a legend, so she was one of the first people everyone followed when they joined Twitter. All the other music artists followed her, so then they all knew my name. The plan was working. I eventually ran Alicia Keys off after about a year or so. She probably woke up one day and wondered why she was following me to begin with. It could have been an intern or assistant who followed me, who knows? She helped me at first and then many other celebrities helped me. Some celebrities started using my quotes without quoting me, and that's when I learned how cruel cyberspace could be. I started seeing my quotes everywhere, and they were going viral left and right. Everything I tweeted was original material, so that's what made my page so ripe for the quoting celebs trying to build their following organically. They saw how it was working for me, but they had hundreds of thousands of followers to my tens of thousands. So they felt they could just repurpose my content to their following and eat heartily. I didn't know who was running their own account and who wasn't. Assistants could have been stealing my quotes because they probably thought I stole them too. As I started talking to people, most people said they couldn't believe the quotes were mine. This was kind of an insult and a compliment at the same time. On one hand, I heard this as if they were saying, *how can a young black man be this deep?* On the other hand, I heard this as, *your gift is so amazing; I can't believe you wrote it.* I'm not sure what they meant, but I kept hearing this. I called out a few people who stole my quotes, but they would tell me they saw it somewhere else without my name so that's why they used the quote and they had no idea the quote was mine. I was learning quickly how the Internet could help and hurt you at the same time. I was putting out life-changing content, and it was making it into movies, TV shows, books, radio shows, and so on. I would be watching TV and hear one of my quotes in the lines of a new show. I would be online and see a major company using one of my quotes in their marketing campaign. It was mind-boggling to me, but it also was a sign that I had a gift and that one day it would pay off for me.

As I said earlier in this book, one of my early quotes that went viral was, "If you don't build your dream, someone will hire you to build theirs." Some people thought it was Steve Jobs's quote but then found out it wasn't. People didn't know who said it first, but once they saw me, they definitely didn't believe it was mine. I didn't read books back then, so I definitely didn't read it anywhere, and I'm sure versions of it had been said before. Heck, it could have been said before exactly like that, but if that was the case I'd say, great minds think alike. Nothing is new. The quote went viral around the world. One lady who met me in person found out my name was Tony Gaskins and said, "Wow, those are your quotes I see all over the place, but I would have never thought you were black. Your name sounds like some French guy or something." She was black, so that's how she was able to say that to me just in case you thought it sounded racist. It made me laugh, and I knew that to be true because if my name were Tony Williams or Tony Johnson, then there would be a 50-50 chance that I could be black, but for Tony Gaskins, there's a small chance of me being black. I was blown by the power of Twitter one day when my partner went to a tech conference in Brazil, and the keynote speaker said my quote and quoted me. My partner went up to him after his speech and identified himself as my partner, and the speaker showed him my quote tattooed on his rib cage in code language because he's a web developer. This blew me away. I searched for the quote just to make sure it was mine, because it was getting so popular. We did a copyright for it, and I put it in one of my books just to seal the deal. When I searched the quote, I saw a couple other guys had been cited for the quote. One guy was an Indian guy who had passed away. I had a web developer who lives in India, so I asked him about this guy. He told me that he had been an entrepreneur, and now his young sons run his companies. He told me his sons probably saw my quote and used it as their dad's in his marketing and branding because his life embodied the quote. My partner bought the guy's book to see if it was in there, and he said he didn't find anything close to it. Another guy who my quote was attributed to is an African American guy who has used a lot of my quotes without permission, so I already knew what happened there. His life also embodied the quote, so it made sense that he would use it. But the overwhelming majority of the sites that used the quote attributed it to me, so that spoke for itself. I remembered when I wrote the quote because I was sitting in my car at work before I got out. I would always send a tweet right before I went in to work. I was in transition and getting ready to leave the job and that's when I tweeted it. At the time I had over 25,000 followers and several quote pages and sites followed me, and that's how it went viral around the world. There were a few pages with over a million followers who would share my tweets every day. Their pages were quote pages, so they needed great quotes to keep their pages alive. They utilized every single one of my tweets.

That's how my Twitter started growing organically. It was all from the power of retweets. I never spent a single dollar on fake followers. I never spent a single dollar on promotions or marketing on Twitter. I never sent a single tweet asking for people to follow me. That never made sense to me anyway, because the tweet only goes to the people who are already following you. The things that make you scratch your head on Twitter were crazy. I had a strategy and that was to empower people. I didn't want to make it about me and what I was doing. I wanted people to be able to read and tweet and say, "Hey I'm going through that," or "I agree with that, so let me share it."

I wanted to be a leader online, but I realized that in order to be a leader you have to be humble. That's why I started to follow people back, and I took it a step further. In my growth after the Alicia Keys tweet and the celebrity retweets, I started getting 150 new followers per day, and some days I would get between 300 and 400 new followers. It was crazy how fast Twitter was growing. I started seeing all kinds of people abandoning their Twitter practices and copying mine as close as they could. It wasn't working for them for some reason, but I felt that it was probably because they were not being authentic. People can read through fake stuff. I went a step further than just tweeting. I started sending a personal message to every new follower. I messaged literally hundreds of people a day. Some never responded because they thought my message was probably automated. Maybe some didn't want to connect; they just came to watch. But some responded in shock and asked me if that was a real message or from a robot. Some responded and thanked me and then took me up on my offer. My message read, "Hey, thanks so much for the follow. If I can help you in any way, please let me know." I really meant it. I wanted to connect and meet people. I wanted to build organically. I really wanted to network and build a net that actually works. I wanted a brand with a personal touch. I didn't want to be a celebrity or a god, or to be worshipped. I wanted to be able to be reached, touched, and talked to. It was cool when people saw me as a celebrity. That was flattering and funny because I was only a Twitter celebrity. I was still working a full-time job from 2009 to 2011, which was my first two years on Twitter and my heavy growth period. I was making $9.50/hour on someone's job, and that's why I tweeted so much about building your dream and taking control of your life.

Another strategy I used is only tweeting quotes that were 110 character or less. I did that so they would have 30 characters left to retweet me. Back then, there wasn't a retweet icon that just puts the tweet on your timeline. You had to hit retweet, then it would retweet it with the RT:@TonyGaskins: in front of it. Sometimes people wanted to add a little comment or a reply just like how Alicia Keys wrote "LOVE THIS" in front of my tweet. So giving them enough characters to do that wasn't an accident, it was a part of the strategy. I saw so many people that I knew personally trying to emulate the way I ran my Twitter by only posting quotes, but they used all 140 characters. I found that to be another problem with replicating versus creating.

In addition to just tweeting quotes I had other strict guidelines for my Twitter. I never responded to the same person on my timeline more than once each day. Some people would try to start a fake conversation to get on my timeline with the hope that others would see them and begin to follow them. Many people asked me why I direct messaged them instead of tweeting them back publicly. If you wanted to talk to me, you could talk to me privately in a direct message, not on my public timeline. If a person didn't want to talk privately, then I knew the tweet was a marketing ploy and not an attempt to interact authentically. My timeline was for motivation, not conversation.

I also would never retweet anyone unless it moved my life forward. I wouldn't retweet just to retweet. The retweet had to be something that added to my timeline in a different way. I also made a practice of not retweeting people I didn't know personally or who didn't have a track record. I didn't want to stamp or endorse anyone who could be a fraud. I was very careful with brand association. If everyone had that same practice, then it would have limited Twitter's growth greatly; but not many people did, so that let me know I was onto something that wasn't common practice. My picture with Oprah helped me though. Although people didn't see the show, they saw my content and they saw my bio, which stated that I was an author and speaker, so that was my track record.

Another practice I had was I didn't read tweets when I started following people back. Twitter is a very dangerous place if you don't use it correctly. Anytime I took a scroll through my timeline there would be so much junk and filth. I noticed that a lot of people on Twitter weren't progressing because they weren't using it properly. They got caught up in the celeb gossip, the commentary, and meaningless rhetoric—they got stuck in the mud. I guarded my eyes and my ears very closely because I was growing. I only read my mentions when I went into Twitter.

I maintained a block policy as well. If a person said something that was hurtful, they got blocked. I didn't play games about my space. I protected my space and my energy. I didn't argue with fools. I would respond to a fool once, but never twice. I'm a firm believer that if you argue with a fool, you'll become a fool too. I'm paraphrasing but while listening to my audio Bible, I heard the man say in the book of Proverbs, "Respond to a fool once because it may save his life, but respond to a fool twice and you become a fool too." Now I could be totally wrong, but that's how I made sense of it. It sounded like a plan to me.

Twitter was a very hard space for intellectuals. If you were ignorant on your Twitter like comedians, then you could do amazingly well, but if you were tweeting knowledge, it was a long way to the top. I wanted to make sure that I was consistent and that I continued to build with the people following me.

I never referred to them as followers or fans in public. If I mentioned them, I would say my supporters or my friends on Twitter. I was very cautious about that. I never started a Twitter team either. I wanted everyone to be their own boss and push their own brand. A lot of music artists gave their followers a name, but I never wanted to do that. I didn't want a tribe or followers. I wanted supporters who I could inspire to find their own identity and push their brand and their products, so we could support one another the best we knew how.

I took it a step further and paid close attention to my retweets. Now Twitter bunches the retweeters in groups of 10 or more, but back then they showed them one by one on the app I used. I got a lot of retweets, but I'm a visual person so I could easily remember a face. If I saw a person's face twice I would send them another message that said, "Hey, thank you very much for your support!" They would appreciate the fact that I took the time to recognize them. That turned followers into real supporters, and it opened a lot of doors. A lot of times I would thank a person, and they would have an opportunity waiting for me. I was shocked to see how many speaking engagements I received from just saying thanks. It was so interesting to see. I would think to myself like—*wow, you've followed me all this time. If you had an opportunity for me, why didn't you say something a long time ago or write in through my site?* I guess the difference was that I went that extra mile. When I showed up in their inbox to say thank you, that's when I separated myself from every other talking head on Twitter. That's when I became a real person with a real heart and a real mission.

I mentioned earlier in this book that I became a speaker for the National Basketball Players Association and also the National Basketball Association. Well, those opportunities came from my Twitter strategies. For example, there was a young lady in Atlanta who I saw in my mentions more than once. I sent her a direct message to thank her for her support. She wrote me back and said, "No problem, I've actually been meaning to contact you because my aunt works for the NBA and the NFL as a health consultant and I think they would love to have you speak to those guys." I was like, "Wow, I'd love to speak to her; let's set up the call." I was on my 40-hour-a-week job at the time, but we hopped on a call and I stepped outside and left my coworker and the clients in the house. I had to build this dream. I got on the phone with her aunt, as she called her, and the lady was so nice. Ms. Mac is her name. I thought she was going to be this very proper-talking, condescending doctor. But I found out she was an older, female version of myself. She was country, passionate, and self-taught. She knew what she knew, and she walked in her calling. She asked me if I was a speaker and I told her yes. At that time, I had only spoken a few times and only once for pay; that was the $65 I earned at Bethune Cookman University. Bethune, y'all owe me another gig! But anyway, it's amazing how perception works. I was seen as a bigwig online because I had a picture with Oprah, but I was just an average Joe. Well, Ms. Mac told the NBPA about me, and I was later on a call with her and one of the reps from the association. They offered me a chance to speak. I had nothing online that they could see, but they were taking a chance on me. It was a blessing from God. They probably don't want me to share this, but it shouldn't be a secret: They offered me $2,500 to speak for 20 minutes. The rep, Mrs. Lu, told me on the phone that she knew I was used to getting more than that, but that's all they could offer. It's crazy how perception works, isn't it? Little did she know, I was only making $1,200 to $1,800 a month! So that was for 160 to 200 hours' worth of work, and here she was offering me $2,500 for 20 minutes. I was 26 years old, so this was a huge break for me. To think that it came from Twitter. I called off work so fast I made heads spin. I had to accept this opportunity. I was broke, busted, and disgusted. I know the staff at the NBPA may laugh when they read this, but they helped raise me. They really gave me my start. They kept bringing me back every year too. They upped my responsibilities, and they upped my pay. They watched me grow into who I am today. Perception is key. I looked bigger than I was. I looked like I made more than I did. I looked more successful than I was. I carried myself like a success. When she told me that she knew I was used to getting more money for a speech, I didn't correct her. I didn't say, "Oh no, well actually I've only been paid $65 for a speech and that was three years ago." I walked in my calling because it was time to elevate. When I got on that stage, they couldn't tell I had never been on a stage like that because I'd been there before in my mind. I'd delivered that message a thousand times in my mind. I thought like a success. They called me back a couple months later to speak to the NBA rookies. The NBA paid me $1,000 less. I thought that was so strange that such a big organization that pays these guys millions was only paying speakers $1,500, but it was about more than the money for me. It was the opportunity I wanted. The opportunity was worth way more to me. They only paid me $1,500 for the 20-minute speech, but I delivered a million dollars' worth of advice to those young millionaires. They told me that the guys wouldn't remember what I said an hour later, but some of those same guys still call me today and can tell me exactly what I told them. I knew where I was supposed to be. I knew that I was in my calling. I wasn't counting money. I was counting the impact.

From then on Twitter started to bring in so many opportunities. I was building my brand, and my message was spreading very fast. I was able to earn more money because of the following I built and because of the way I built it. Because there was a personal touch, when I finally created a product it sold well. I was able to earn months' worth of income from a tweet.

Once you build one network it becomes easier to build the others. Each network has its own language. You can choose to do it right or choose to do it wrong and just hold your space on the network. Some networks I chose to use wrong, but just hold my space. The next thing I did after Twitter was create a public figure page on Facebook. This was my partner's idea. Keep in mind he told me to join Twitter, and he also told me to make a Facebook page. It's important to pay attention to the advice people give you and ask yourself whether it can hurt you. If it can't hurt you and you haven't done it yet, then it's worth a shot. I got on Facebook again. We closed my personal page by merging it with my public page. Facebook had a feature then that would turn the friends into likes on your business page. After 25 people were on your business page, then you could make a custom URL. Of course I wanted to make mine www .facebook.com/tonygaskins. I had to wait until they merged my pages though. It took a week or so until the pages were merged. Then I tweeted the Facebook link a few days in a row to get some people over to Facebook from Twitter. It wasn't long before I had 30,000 Facebook likes. It took maybe a couple weeks. I was blown away at how fast it was growing, considering how long it took me to build Twitter. I didn't care much about Facebook because I thought it was dead. Boy, was I in for a surprise! I was letting my partner post for me on Facebook, and boy, were those posts terrible—the pictures he used, the quotes he chose, and even the wording. One day he posted, "Hey fans," and I almost lost it. I realized then I had to take over. I got behind the wheel and started to drive this thing. I realized then that I had a gift and I had to use it. It's not easy to build an organic following, so when you learn how to do it, you have to do it yourself. But I was grateful to my partner for getting me on Facebook.

I remember it like it was yesterday; it was in December of 2013 on a Friday. Maybe it was Friday the 13th. I was trying something new with my quotes. My partner kept me up to date on what Facebook was doing with its algorithm. One day Facebook would say viewers were favoring text posts. The next day Facebook would say they were favoring picture posts. The next day they would say they were favoring videos. Then it was native videos instead of video links. Facebook had so many rules. I think they were trying to tick off Internet marketers and trying to find a way to make more money or set themselves up to make more money. I didn't want to post text posts because I felt it was too easy to just copy and paste them. At first I was posting quote memes. I didn't really see quote memes when I started posting them; everything was text. I saw that memes were becoming a big thing, but they were all based in comedy. I said to myself— *well what if I post memes since they are viral, but instead I'll put a quote on a picture card*. I started doing it, and it hit big. I started getting more likes than usual. Now people could decorate their Facebook wall with my quotes as pictures with colorful backgrounds. The ladies loved it. The quotes were catching, on and I started to notice that some people were taking my picture quotes and cropping them just high enough to cut my name off. This was the cruelest thing ever. My little sister showed me local guys who were posting literally every one of my quotes as their own. Then when people would thank them for the quote, they would write back stuff like, "You're welcome, it just hit me this morning." I wasn't big enough on Facebook yet, so their friends on Facebook weren't on my page. I had to change that. So I decided to use the quote app on the iPhone to put my picture as the background and then put my quote on top of my picture. You won't believe this, but when I started doing this, I had never seen it done online, but now it's everywhere. A lot of the major speakers weren't even using social media back then because they are so much older than me. I think they thought it wouldn't make a difference in a brand. They were snail mail, landline telephone, and cold-call guys. I was an email, text, and social media guy.

I started putting my picture behind my quotes, but I did something special to the picture. I would turn the brightness all the way up on the background so that it would fade my picture, so you could see the font of the quote better. So the background became almost white, and then I'd make my font black. I did it so that if people cropped my name out, my picture would still be in the background. I intended for this look to become as popular as the McDonald's golden arches. The first time I did it the quote with my picture on it went viral. Some people said it was vain, but then some people would defend me and say, "It's called branding and marketing. If you knew what that was, you'd think differently." I was like, yes, thank you Lord; we have some smart people in the world. I blended out my picture for the very reason of not appearing vain. I didn't want to showcase my face; I just wanted to watermark my quotes to make them harder to steal. I saw it the same as the special markers on checks that let you know it's a real check, or like on our money. I was tired of being ripped off. Even though I did that, some people still took the time to open the quote on the computer and then retype it into their own app, leave my name off, and then post it as their own. That really took the cake. I was shocked and appalled, but that's the world we live in. I had done all I could do, and I couldn't worry about the rest.

Back to that Friday in December of 2013. I posted a quote with my picture behind it, and I let it sit all weekend. I decided that I wouldn't post on Saturday and Sunday because I wanted to take a break from the phone and spend the weekend with my family and also appear to have a life outside of social media to my followers on Facebook. Well, people were visiting my page throughout the weekend to see what I'd posted and because I didn't post anything else besides that quote, it got a lot of views and interactions over the weekend. Facebook had started showing me how many people each post reached. I kept watching this post, and it kept climbing each time I would come back to look at it. By Monday it had reached over a million people, and I was blown away. I guess that meant the post was viral or something because then my page started to explode. I came back online on Monday with a new energy and started posting my relationship quotes twice a day, once in the morning and once at night. The posts kept going viral. Each post was reaching over a million people. My page started to grow by 20,000 people a week. It was insane. My page grew from 30,000 people to a million people in 11 and a half months. During that period of growth my income went up so much! My booking email was flooded. I was getting six booking invites a day. Before that I would get about two a month. My page exploded. All I could do was thank my partner for his suggestion. He gave the suggestions, and I did the work. My page became a trendsetter because I looked around and every speaker and author started posting quotes with their picture behind them. That was the funniest thing to me. Some of them had no clue how I did it, so they were posting theirs with a full-color picture as the background, and you couldn't see the quote because of it. Some thought that my posts were graphically designed, so they hired graphic designers and started paying hundreds of dollars to have quotes done professionally. They still didn't understand the point of the faded picture, so they would do a full-color picture and put the quote beside it. That defeated the purpose because no one wants to plaster a full-color picture of you on their wall. So they still weren't getting visibility or growth. I knew I was onto something when I saw everyone copying it. The bigwigs came on the scene and started doing the same thing. It was a beautiful thing to see. Graphic designers started approaching me and showing me the other authors and speakers they designed for and asking me if I wanted them to design for me. I'd politely tell them that I saw what they were doing, and they were doing it in a way that I wasn't interested in, so no thanks. I remember meeting with one designer who told me that he thought I was paying a designer to do my quote pictures. He said, "Who does those pictures for you?" I said, "I do them myself." He said, "Oh, you do graphic design?" I said, "No, I do it on my phone on an app." "What app?" he asked. "That's a branding secret," I said. It gave me a chuckle to know that people were paying money to do what I was doing for free. But it also confirmed in my spirit that you have to do what makes sense to you, not what you see someone else doing. If you create the trend, then you'll find the best and most cost-effective way to do it. If you see someone else doing it and try to copy them, you'll probably spend a lot of money trying to figure it out. You'd be better off reaching out to them and hiring them for a consulting session and just asking them directly how they did it and why they did it that way.

The next thing I did with the quote picture marketing was use my @ name instead of writing out my full name. I noticed that everyone was writing their full name under their quotes. It was cool and all, but when the quote goes viral it's too much work to find you, or people don't think to find you. I was writing Tony A. Gaskins Jr. under all of my quotes. Some people told me they saw the quotes, but never knew who Tony A. Gaskins Jr. was and thought it was some dead guy. It was flattering to know that my name sounded like a famous dead guy, but I had to change that. I started putting @TonyGaskins under all my quotes. As a result, I noticed that all my social media accounts started to grow faster. As a result of my quotes going viral every day, they would be all over the web. Well, if someone on Twitter saw it, they would search me to follow me on Twitter, Facebook, and Instagram. I saw it as cross-promotion, and it worked. Then it wasn't long after that I noticed that other speakers and authors who were writing their full name out changed theirs to @their name. Once again I knew I was on to something.

My Facebook page blew my Twitter page out of the water. Facebook had risen from the dead for me, and I was indebted to my partner and the team. In 2014, I finally gave in and joined Instagram. I was very reluctant at first because I hated following the crowd. I wanted to be a trendsetter, not a follower. But, some things you just can't get around. My wife was in my ear about Instagram because she joined and she loved it. She told me there were other speakers and authors on Instagram who were filling my void and would replace me if I didn't get with the times. I couldn't have that, so I decided to give it a try. I hopped on and started posting my picture quotes and then sharing them on Twitter. I used Twitter as my social media network jump-starter. People were excited to know I finally joined Instagram. I had to get my name on there, but a fashion page was using my name. I guess it was just a page by some entrepreneur who knew people were searching for me and since I wasn't on there, they just used my name. The page had like 100,000 followers or something crazy. It made perfect sense because most of my followers are women, so if they searched my name and found a fashion page, they would probably follow it anyway. One of my celebrity clients who I was coaching at the time asked me if I wanted my name on there, and I told her yes. The next day I had my name. I guess she had a connection at Instagram or something. I got my name Instagram.com/TonyGaskins and I was off to the races. With Facebook and Instagram, I had to tweak some things because they were different from Twitter. On these two sites I was posting picture quotes and to do that all day could get annoying, so I posted two to four times a day. I would let the work speak for itself, but the frequency of posts was my main strategy. Some speakers and authors would post 10 times a day, but that just showed they didn't have a life. Being that Instagram is a picture site, I didn't want to follow anyone other than my wife. I didn't want women to think I was watching them, and I didn't want to watch men either, so I only follow my wife on Instagram. I've been on there a couple years now, and there have been fewer than five people who have barked at me about only following my wife; and as soon as they do, some of my supporters jump down their throat to tell them to mind their business. I like Instagram because the people who follow you really ride with you for the most part. There's an occasional hater here and there, but much less than those on Facebook and Twitter. At least that's the case for me right now. On Instagram, I was upset at myself for joining so late because I saw other speakers with hundreds of thousands of followers when I started with zero. I felt like I would never catch up. I noticed it in the beginning, but I wasn't going to check again. I make it a habit not to watch others unless I see them just by happenstance. I never search anyone's name in the search bar though.

I stuck to my strategy on IG, and it paid off. I let the content speak for itself. I taught mostly. I showed my family on occasion just to let people know I'm a real person with a real life. I never followed anyone else just to let the women know that I'm only interested in my wife's pictures, and if they have a problem with that, keep it moving. My page was building at a decent rate. Of course, a few celebrities found my page and would post my quotes to their millions of followers and @ me, and it would send thousands of new followers at once. I just spoke from the heart, and the messages would hit the hearts of others; and they would share the posts. Guess what, my wife brought it to my attention that I passed all of the speakers she told me about when I joined IG. I don't know what to attribute it to other than the content, the consistency, the realness, and the favor of God.

I don't really utilize the message inbox on Facebook or Instagram. I had the message box open on Facebook at first, but my message is so blunt and real that I started to offend some people and they would send their hate mail to my inbox. It started to drain my spirit and make me change my messages. It was my style that made my page go viral, and now the critics were making me hesitant to be as real and transparent, so I shut down the feature. On IG, I just stayed away from the messages altogether. I was at a different point in my career, and as you grow you have to tweak some things. Always remain humble, but you have to change your accessibility guidelines to protect your brand and your image. There are a lot of traps out there.

Then there's YouTube and LinkedIn. I am just holding space in both of those networks. I don't use LinkedIn at all really because it seems to be more for job searchers, not entrepreneurs, although I'm sure some entrepreneurs have found it to be useful. YouTube isn't as much my style because I'm shy faced. I don't like people to look in my face up close and for long periods of time, so I only post videos on Facebook and YouTube when something is really pressing heavy on my heart. On YouTube I've taken the laid-back approach. I teach real messages with a low production value. It's definitely not the way to go on YouTube because the competition is very stiff. I've seen You-Tubers make millions and build massive brands. One of my former mentees built his brand on YouTube, and it got him TV and movie deals. I've seen speakers utilize YouTube, and it made them world-renowned speakers in the corporate and private sectors. Anything can work if you work it.

My approach has always been and will always be real. I'm real and I'm transparent, and that's just what I respect. Just how I shared all my tips in this chapter and even shared actual numbers that I was paid. I respect real. I could say I'm a speaker for the NBA, and you may assume that I was paid $10,000 and that may discourage you if you feel you'll never get that amount. Or it may disappoint you if you get the opportunity and you're expecting it to be $10,000 or more and they offer you $1,500. I just want to be real and be honest, so you know exactly what it is and what it isn't. That's not smiled upon by some people building a brand. They love the mystery of it all. I have some mystery to me, but I'd rather not live a lie. There is a time and a place for everything, and if you really want to help people, you have to be real. If it's just about you, then you can keep the mystery going. I just choose to do it differently.

I call this the organic brand because I never paid for anything other than knowledge. I never paid a PR person to market me. I never paid a manager to manage me. I never paid a speakers' bureau to get me speaking gigs. I never paid an agent to be my agent. I never paid Facebook to get me over a million people on my page. I never paid for fake likes, views, or retweets. I did it the hard way, and I took my time. I did it on my own terms and with my own gifts. I wouldn't recommend doing it any other way if you want to be an influencer and have lasting impact. Build organically, and if it takes 20 years to peak, oh well. You'll be taken care of on the journey, and you'll enjoy the journey. You can't buy your way into a position of lasting influence; time will prove that. You don't have to take my word for it now, but you'll see over time. If you're faking it to make it, eventually people will realize you're fake and it will be a long fall back to the bottom. But if you're real, it may be a long climb to the top, but you'll be learning and growing along the way, so when you get your platform, you'll be ready for it. Don't rush it or you'll ruin it. I started building my brand online in 2009 with 34 people, and today in 2016 it's over 2.5 million. It's not a lot in the grand scheme of things, but it proved to me that you can reach millions of people if you have the right heart behind your work and you take your time in the building process.

Chapter 11   The Hands-On Strategy

This strategy is similar to the one-man show but not the exact same thing. You can be a one-man show but have a lot of virtual assistants, interns, or other people who you delegate everything out to. I like to be involved in my work. If you're going to work, then why not work? There is time for vacation and your work may feel like a vacation at times, but you're still doing the work. Do you want to be rich and relaxed, or do you want to have an impact? If you just want to be rich and travel, then the hands-on strategy isn't for you. If you want to have an impact and you want to be active and enjoy your work, then you have to be hands-on.

While writing this book I'm away at a beach house, so I can be alone and in my zone, but today I had to coach a client for

30 minutes. He's a professional basketball player, but he also wants to be a fashion designer. I'm going to use our session as a real-life example as to why I feel the hands-on strategy is important. He's ready to build his business, and that's evident because he's paying me a nice little consulting fee to bounce ideas off of and be held accountable. In our conversation I asked him whether he has a manufacturer for his clothing line. He said that his assistants were working on finding the manufacturer, and they've sent him a few, but he hasn't had time to look at them just yet. I asked him whether he had looked into any manufacturers himself, because I believe in doing your own work when you're building from the ground up. There may come a day when he's a huge fashion brand and the groundwork has already been laid and he won't have to be at the ground level, but for now that's not the case. He then asked me, "Well, what about the creative process?" I told him that the creative process has to be factored into his daily work. Find the time period when he creates the best and block that time off as the creative process, and then in the other hours of the day block off time to do the groundwork. There is a lot of groundwork, and the owner of a company needs to know how everything works.

Then I said, "You know, what if I came to you and said, 'Hey, I have some manufacturers and they are really good and could produce your line without a problem. The only thing is that you need to have a manufacturer's code to work with them. I already have my code, and I've done a lot of business with them, so I get the work done cheaper. If you want to produce 1,000 pairs of jeans, I can get that done for $40,000. It'll be $40 per pair because of the top-quality materials they use. You sell your jeans for $200 a pair, so your profit margins would be amazing. The only thing is that if you go to them, they will charge you more, but if you go through my company, you'll get my friends and family discount because I've worked with them for years. So you can just wire me the funds, and I'll wire them the money under my account to save you. I'll just charge you 10 percent of the total for the finder's fee, so you only have to pay me $4,000, but I'm saving you about $36,000. How does that sound?'" He then said, "Yeah, that sounds good, and it sounds believable." He wasn't talking about the numbers but about the story. I mean we've all heard someone say "go through me and use my discount," so it's a believable story. I then told him that if he wired me the money and I was a crook, I may never wire the funds to the manufacturer and instead take a vacation. Or I may wire the funds to the manufacturer, but the true cost is $20,000 for 1,000 pairs of these high-fashion jeans, and I've pocketed $20,000 plus the $4,000 I charged him. He's trying to build a profitable business, but he would have just given away $24,000 if he has no knowledge of what the manufacturers charge.

I instructed him to make it a part of his daily work to search manufacturers and get quotes. Find the companies, get pictures, and even visit them if possible. Get an idea for himself what the cost would be to mass-produce his product. So then, even if he does go through someone else to have the work done, he will know if the numbers they are throwing at him make sense. His assistants could even make a connection with manufacturers and get a referral code and then send him to that manufacturer, and they'd be getting a kickback from the deal. If you're not hands-on with your work in the beginning, anything can happen. I've made those mistakes. It happens all the time when we aren't hands-on in our brands.

Let your company force you out of the groundwork. Learn every aspect of your business and then move up the ladder. When you start a company, you should be the intern, the assistant, the business manager, the CEO, the president, and so on. Even if you don't hold all of those titles, you have to know what every part does or else you can be taken advantage of. It's great to have smart and capable people around you, but you have to know what their work entails. You don't need to know every detail, but you should know the basics. There are so many people who get taken advantage of.

I'm a life coach to a lot of pro athletes. Yes, they make millions of dollars and during the season they are fairly busy, but yet they spend hours every day on social media. A lot of them have someone who has access to their money, and that person sends wires to their friends and family members. Well, if you have a lot of money going out and you have tens of millions in the account, you may just start feeling like a boss and a kingpin and stop checking your account to see where everything is going. Maybe you check for the first three to six months to see if everything is on the up and up, but then you stop checking because trust has been built. Well, it's when you get complacent that you get taken advantage of. I tell my clients to take an hour off of social media and learn how to send a wire. Then have a "wire day." Make a list of every wire that needs to be sent, add them to the online bill pay portion of your account, and log in and pay those bills. You can send all your friends and family the money you give them, and pay all your bills in that one hour. By doing it that way, now your finance person has been paid hourly to consult you on how to do those things instead of monthly, and this reduces their opportunity to take advantage of you. Learn how to be hands-on in your brand.

To be honest, we have more than enough time to run our brands if we use our time wisely. God doesn't make mistakes, so he made enough time in the day. You just have to utilize the time wisely. It's not the time that is short; it's your management skills. I've been hands-on in my brand since day one. Yes, I've delegated authority but only on certain tasks that I can't be taken advantage on. I love what I do, and I want to be a part of it. If you're so caught up thinking of ways how to get out of work, then you're in the wrong line of work. People say you need more time to create, and they are right. You can have a creative day or days if you need to, but you also need time to pay attention to the work being done in your brand or company. I'm taking a week off from work to write this book. Next week I'll be back to answering emails, negotiating deals, and running my social media accounts. How much work can there be? Can you scale it and still be involved? I believe you can. If you receive a thousand emails a day asking for advice, having an assistant answer those emails won't solve the problem because that assistant doesn't have your advice to give. But you can do a mail sweep and add all of those people to a list, then offer them online courses answering their questions or do free Q&As for an hour a week.

You can't delegate your destiny. ~Tony A. Gaskins Jr.

You have to get in there and do the work. When I was coaching my client, he said, "I'm sure you have assistants." Yes, I have assistants but they do meaningless work. They do work that I can do, but work that I don't need to do. They aren't answering emails for bookings without me seeing them. They aren't doing service deals. Any mistakes that are made reflect back on you. I can live with my mistakes; I can't live with someone else's mistakes. I remember delegating my email list to an educated Wake Forest graduate, and there were typos in my email blast. There were words left out and key messaging missing. Humans make mistakes. If I'm going to have to write the email for my staff, then why not just hit send? Why pay someone if all they will be doing is hitting send? I have people approaching me and saying they will handle my mailing list, they'll handle my support email, they'll handle my social media accounts, all so I can do what only I can do. That all sounds fine and dandy, but I don't need all day, every day to do what only I can do. I don't want to write a book or shoot a course every day either, and those are the things that only I can do. Instead I have email answering hours, social media hours, and creative hours. There is time for everything. That gives me variety in my work. Every time I think of turning my email over to an assistant, I get an email that reminds me why I can't. I've turned it over to an assistant before, but the assistant has to call me and ask me how to answer the email. That's a call that I want made because there are no cookie-cutter answers for human beings. If my assistant has to call me to learn how to answer every email that comes in, why am I paying an assistant again? I'd rather be hands-on.

I've delegated before. I delegated the venue search portion of my business, and I'll tell you what happened. I valued finding a venue at $500 per venue. So I had a young lady who I would pay $500 to search and handle the booking of the venue. All I had to do was sign the contract and make the payment. Then eventually I went a different route and hired an assistant at $17/hour. I gave her the same job. She was able to secure about three venues a week. I allowed her to work six hours a week. So now I was getting $1,500 worth of work for $102. I learned a big lesson. The person I was paying $500 per venue started milking my time and started taking two weeks to find a venue. She was doing it because she was busy doing other stuff and probably didn't want to make it look too easy. She was essentially making $500/hour. I then realized that while I had them doing that work, I didn't have any work to do. I had already created what I wanted to create at the time, and I wasn't going to create a new product every week, so I had time on my hands. I wanted to be active. So I went back to booking the events, and all I had to do was a Google search for event halls in whatever city. Then Google would return several options. I'd look at the pictures on the images tab and choose the picture I liked the best and click to that web page. I'd fill out the form and get a reply the same day or the next day. It literally took me 30 minutes to an hour to find a venue. What I learned is that it was easy work, event planners are making a killing, and it was fun. I also learned the ins and outs of that part of my business, so I could make my money back by doing consulting to teach others or put it in a course and sell it because I knew how to do it.

Being hands-on has saved me a lot of money and taught me a lot in the process. One day I'll turn over the wheel, maybe, but I'll know everything there is to know so my staff won't be able to get greedy, lazy, or complacent. I'll share a few of the ways I ran my business with you just in case you have to model yours this way from the ground up.

I run my own social media. The reason I run my social media is because that's my lifeline. I don't want anyone else sending out typos on my behalf. I don't want anyone working for me to get lazy on social media and cut corners. I want my brand to be heartfelt, not cookie cutter. I want my posts to reflect my life and my schedule, not just standard times every day on an automated system. One young lady told me she charges $3,000 a month to manage Facebook pages. So I'd pay $3,000 a month to have my page set up with automatic posts that go out daily? Then what happens if she's living the vacation life and has my posts scheduled and a suicide bomb happens at 10:30 a.m., but I have a post set to go out at 11 a.m. that post totally ignores the tragedy and is talking about something that has nothing to do with what the country is processing in that moment? You can't influence and impact people if you're not feeling what they are feeling and responding to it. Also, because of the way I want to run my brand, that means I'd have to craft every message so that it's in my voice. I have a unique style of writing quotes that can't be easily duplicated. So if I'm going to write the quote, then why not take 10 more seconds to send it and save myself $400 to $3,000 a month?

Another problem with letting someone run your social media is that they will eventually get lazy and they will repurpose other people's content. I've lost a lot of respect for major figures when their Twitter account posted my quotes without giving me credit. I don't think that public figure is a thief or plagiarizing, but the intern they've delegated the task to is cutting corners and doing it for them. For the longest time, I thought this heavy-quoting celebrity was stealing my quotes because his tweets would be one word different from mine. He didn't follow me, so I didn't want to flatter myself. I didn't want to assume that he was taking time out of his day to come to my timeline and repurpose my tweets. Then one day a tweet went out from his account that was my exact quote. I was like, wow, all this time what I feared was happening was actually happening. I sent a tweet to the celebrity and said, "Hey, that's my original quote so don't try to pull that laws of power mess on me." Then I got a tweet back from him that said, "When you mess up, fess up @tonygaskins." My followers were shocked because they all followed him too. Then he tweeted out the quote again and @'d me. I had won the battle. I never got a mention from him again, and I've never checked his page again either. Then one day an associate was at an event where he was speaking. She told me that while he was onstage talking, there were quotes being sent from his page that had nothing to do with the event. Then I realized that he wasn't hands-on and whoever the lazy person was who was running his account was stealing my quotes to build his page's following. This guy was like the number one quote guy on Twitter and everyone followed him, so it was flattering that the person thought my quotes were good enough for that level. That taught me a very important lesson about branding. I then saw the same thing happen on major entrepreneurs' pages, on major pastors' pages, and on major quote pages. I vowed then that I would always be hands-on with my social media. If you use it right, it doesn't take long, and it's not really a lot of work. You just have to give your day a plan.

When it came to my bookings and deals, I was hands-on with those too. I'd seen so many celebrities get taken advantage of because they wouldn't be on the phone when a deal was being made, or they would let someone submit a contract for them. So their handler would tell the company to send the money to their account instead of the client's account. The handler would pay the client. The client thought the deal was for one amount, but it was really for a much higher amount. Then there would be times where a handler would make a side deal without the client's knowledge. So the handler would tell the client, "Hey, we are going to host an event for your brand." The client would be all happy. The handler would tell the client that she was able to get these brands to put their names on the event to make it look more professional. The handler didn't tell the client that the brands actually paid her to be a part of the event. The client thought the brands were doing her a favor, when actually she was doing the brands a favor. I learned from that so I ran my bookings differently. If you want to book me, there is one email to do so and that's booktony@tonygaskins.com. All bookings come directly to my phone, not a manager, agent, or speakers' bureau. So I see every booking. If I want someone to get on the phone with a company instead of myself, it's my wife because my money is her money and vice versa. If I need someone else to get on the phone with a company, then I'm on the line too, even if I'm quiet. But usually what I would do is respond to the email as an assistant. Ninety-nine percent of people will handle business right through the email because everything is in writing and everything is clear. When the 1 percent says, "Hey, can you call me?" I then respond and let them know that I'm just a virtual assistant and I'd have to set up a call with Mr. Gaskins himself. Sometimes the person doesn't want to bother me, so they'll say, "Okay, email is fine." Sometimes they still want to talk, and then I'll get on the phone. When I get on the phone, the person is excited to be speaking directly with me and not a handler. Now that they see that I'm humble, they want to do more fair business. I'll talk to them and let them know what I can do it for and let them know my assistant will get in touch with them. Then I'll email them back as an assistant. I've done that since day one, and I still do it today if I can. But I do have assistants, so the person doesn't really know if they are talking to me or not. No decisions are made without my consent. I've had event promoters tell me that this person or that person will be setting up a booth at my event and I have to ask them, "For what?" Then I have to talk to the person to see what they are selling and how much they were charged. If it's my event, I don't want a handler charging people to sell at my event if I'm not getting a cut of the proceeds.

Sometimes people I follow on Twitter will write in and ask to book me or ask for my rates, and I'll respond as an assistant. If they won't like what they heard, then they will message me personally and tell me again what they want. That taught me a lot about business. It showed me that people are accustomed to dealing with handlers and being given the runaround. It also showed me that they perceived my brand big enough to have an assistant who can make a decision on my behalf without asking me first. That was shocking. I would have to message some people back and say, "Hey, whatever you were told from that email stands. The decisions come from my board and myself." Then they would be like, oh!

I've run into problems with this because being so accessible online can cheapen your brand in some people's eyes, but I need to show them a new way of business. I don't like the fact that you would pay me more if I had an agent than you'd pay me if you were dealing with me directly. Sometimes when I sense that, I stick it to them. I let them know you're going to respect me negotiating my own terms just as you would if an agent had been negotiating for me. If you can't respect that, then we just won't work together. You have to go through some things to learn how it works. Then, once you pay for the knowledge, you can take things into your own hands. I let lawyers and agents handle a couple of deals. What I learned is that they basically just ask for double or triple whatever you're offered and send that in. The companies you're dealing with can only say yes or no. If there's a time period in the contract, let's say they want to lock you in for 12 months to shop a TV show, well the agent will give them six to nine months instead. What I learned is that you should never accept the first offer. Look at the deal and know that it's a sucky deal, then craft the dream deal in your favor and send it in. The company can say yes or no and then you have a decision to make. You can take it and take a loss or you can walk. Sometimes I just take the loss if I see other benefits from the deal.

I've noticed that I can be hands-on in my business because it's all I do. I started businesses to run them, not let someone else run them. I'm a personal brand. If I were Ford Motor Company, then that would be totally different because I'm selling products, not myself. If you're selling yourself and you're representing yourself, then you have to do the work. If you're mass-producing products, then you can delegate certain tasks.

I ran my own social media, I did my own media pitches, and those things built my brand, so now opportunities are coming to me based on what I built. While I was building, no one wanted to manage or represent me, but now that I'm "made," people are ready to represent me. I always ask myself when I look at a rep—*do they make stars or do they manage stars?* I don't need anyone to manage me. If they can't take me higher, then I don't need them. I can manage what I have coming in myself. If you got in the kitchen, created the recipe, and did all the cooking yourself, then you deserve to eat by yourself when it's ready. You don't have to give any away until you've eaten so much that you're full, and now you just don't mind sharing. A lot of entrepreneurs start out with a manager, agent, partner, assistant, or someone else, so they never get to see what it feels like when you have to do all the work yourself. I know what that feels like, so now that I've built it, it's amazing to be able to eat alone for a little bit. I built the table. I cooked the food and set the table. Now I can enjoy my meals. Now that I'm here, everyone wants to come eat too, but a lot of those people saw me when I was cooking and couldn't stand the heat. Now that the food is done, they want a seat at the table, and it doesn't work like that. I have deals coming in every day, but instead of turning those deals over to someone who can't do anymore than I can do, I handle them myself, and I can feed my family without losing 5 to 25 percent. There will come a day when that has to change, maybe, but today isn't that day. The crazy thing about it is that I'm way beyond that day, so most people think. Most people think that to have a seven-figure brand I must have an agent, manager, publicist, and assistant. I know those people and can reach those people, but none are on salary and none handle all of my deals. I haven't signed any exclusive contracts. A part of my hands-on strategy is to never let anyone get too full. If a person gets too full, then they get lazy, so I rotate consultants. It's ignorant to think you can do it all alone and do it at a high level; you need help, you need advice, you need knowledge that you don't have. But you don't have to let any one person feel like they own you or that you're nothing without them. I rotate consultants and put checks in different people's pockets at different times. I don't want to become dependent on anyone.

Our business world has changed drastically because of the Internet. Now I can learn as much as an agent right on Google. There are retired agents who write articles with every tip they would give a client. Because of email there is also a lot more time in the day. I can handle all my bookings because a response takes two minutes. I don't need someone on salary to answer emails because I can answer all the important emails in one hour a day. Why do I need to pay someone for eight hours a day to sit in an office and do one hour's worth of work? Or pay them hourly and then have to fire them because they are milking the clock and taking food out of my kids' mouths. The world has changed. You can be hands-on in your business and never leave the comfort of your home, phone, or laptop. Be in tune with your work and your business practices. Get your hands dirty and know how to do everything in your company. Even when you hire someone, be hands-on. Let them know that you know the ins and outs and what it takes to do their job. They have to know that they can't get anything over on you.

Don't get caught up in the delegation mindset. If you have to delegate everything, then you need to question if you're doing what you love to do. I love my work and if I let someone else do it, I'd miss it. My work is my purpose, and it makes me feel good. If things pile up because I'm doing something else or with my family, oh well. The world will have to wait because I'm only one person, and I am my brand; I am my company. I'm not selling cars, clothes, or toys, so if you're building a personal brand, be personal. The people who are delegating every job are usually info marketers who didn't create the content they're selling, so they don't want to be too hands-on. They just want the money from the business, so they can sip margaritas on an island somewhere. There's nothing wrong with sipping margaritas on an island, but do it on your vacation and use the rest of the time to leave your fingerprint on the world. This way isn't for everybody, but I know it's for some people. If you don't want to be taken advantage of, if you don't want your brand to be misrepresented, if you don't want someone else to be in control of your destiny, then do your work.

Before I close up shop, I need to share with you the one time I started a company that I couldn't be hands-on with. It was a restaurant. I started a soul food restaurant called Tony G's Corner Kitchen. I know a lot of people advise against a restaurant, but this wasn't an expensive deal. The rent was only $750/month because it was a small building with a walk-up window. It sat on the corner in an African American neighborhood. The guy there before me had been there for more than a decade, and he made so much money he was able to move around the corner to a place four times the size with seating inside and a walk-up window. He had the best of both worlds. Everyone who came by the place told us that it was a goldmine and that anyone who had the building did well. I saw that firsthand in the beginning because the restaurant was making about $1,200/day, so in that month it probably grossed about $30,000, and the expenses were about $15,000. Had it kept going at that rate, I could have had an extra $15,000/month sitting in the bank. I was doing the marketing on my social media, so a lot of my followers stopped by, even people from other states when they were passing through Florida. I never stopped by the restaurant. It was open a year, and I made it by about 10 times. I wasn't hands-on with the product. I didn't know the chef or how she prepared the food. I didn't set the standards for food preparation, quality of food, or customer service. I didn't do all the marketing either. I just posted on Facebook, Twitter, and Instagram about the restaurant. I couldn't do the marketing in the neighborhood or the local cities. I wasn't involved in the money. I didn't have access to the accounts to see where the money was going. I wasn't on top of the taxes either. I was just the investor. I let my family run the business. It failed in a year. Nothing I've ever done failed in a year. I couldn't conceive failure. I've had some letdowns and some setbacks, but I couldn't conceive failure. Yes, one could say that the restaurant business is very hard, but I believe that if anyone can do it, then it can be done. There have been small businesses just like that restaurant thriving for years. The guy around the corner wasn't any smarter or more schooled than my family. He had been in the business for 20 years or so. There were ways to make it for sure. From the outside looking in, I could see that a few things were off, but because I wasn't there for the day-to-day, I couldn't address them. One problem was that I didn't fund it like you'd fund a normal restaurant. I didn't put in a years' worth of salary for the staff to get paid and then have everything the restaurant made go into the bank account. I let them eat from the earnings right away. When things got tight because the product was suffering and inconsistent and the marketing was nonexistent, they couldn't get paid because there were no funds. Maybe I handled that wrong, but in my businesses you eat what you kill. If you don't work, you don't eat. If it had been my livelihood, I would have gone and knocked on every door in the neighborhood and offered them 20 percent off their next meal. I would have invited the police station and the fire station to come eat for 20 percent off. I would have gone to the hospital and the group homes and nursing homes and handed out flyers with coupons. I would have made sure my product was at its best every day.

I didn't know where the money was being spent or how it was being spent. I didn't know what extra marketing they were doing. I would be told, "We don't need to market because everyone already knows about it." If you know marketing, then you know that's not true. We all know what McDonald's is, but we still see a commercial every day. When I didn't have any money, I marketed on foot. I went to the malls and handed out business cards with my book cover on it and where you could go buy my book. I went online and added 100 to 400 friends a day to tell them about my book. I did the work, and that's why I didn't fail. I sacrificed. I understood that there would be low months and in those months I had to go without. But when you're living on someone else's funding, you don't see it the same. If you get low, you just want to call your source and ask for more money. I went through that as well with my investor. I would misspend the investment and then have no money. I would have to go back and ask for more money. I would get it sometimes, and then the well ran dry and I had to suffer through it. He wasn't hands-on just like I wasn't hands-on with my investment. There are things that he or I would have advised if we had been hands-on with the investment. When the well ran dry I had to go months without my bills paid, and I had to learn how to budget as an entrepreneur. My family would have to learn the same thing. I had to learn how to get business and how to market in creative ways without a marketing budget. My family would have to learn the same thing. They weren't able to get past the learning curve. People started folding their arms and giving up. It wasn't their baby. It wasn't their idea. It wasn't their problem. We let it go under.

I learned a valuable lesson from that failed venture. I learned that if I'm going to start something, it has to be my baby; and I have to be hands-on if I want it to be ran the way I run a company. I realized that if I delegated everything, it would not be handled the way I would handle it. If it fails, I'll always say I could have done better. The restaurant may have failed even if I had been hands-on and it had been run the way I run my companies, but I'll never know that. The optimist in me won't let me believe it would fail because I've seen others succeed. I was marketing to thousands of people in that area, and it failed. There were other businesses that had no following, and they succeeded. They did something different. They budgeted better. They earned less. They sacrificed through the lean months, and they stored up in the plentiful months. They maintained the standard of their product, and they kept it consistent for the most part. They came to work and worked every day. At my restaurant there would be work for a week or two, then a three- to five-day vacation. There were times where there were one-week to two-week vacations because everyone was tired. Their feet hurt and they were doing 13-hour days, so it was too hard on their bodies. I couldn't argue with that. It wasn't fair for me to sign someone up for that much work. I realized that I couldn't do the work, and if they didn't want to do the work, then we just had to shut the restaurant down. I hate failure. I hate to start something and not be able to see it through. That's why I'm hands-on. I'll probably start another restaurant one day, but it'll be my baby. It'll have my vision, my work ethic will be the standard, and I'll put in what I want to get out of it. It was a learning experience for us all. I can't blame my family—it was their first time running a for-profit business. I don't think they let it fail on purpose. I don't think they did anything shady or sneaky. We just didn't know how to make the restaurant work, and I couldn't be in there with them to see to it that it succeeded or to see whether I could have even made a difference. That's life. You live and you learn, but what I learned is that from here on out I'll be hands-on in every business that I start.

Chapter 12 The Celebrity Factor

Who wants to be a celebrity? It's kind of becoming the thing, or maybe it's always been a thing. I do not see myself as a celebrity, but I am stopped in every city I go to. I think I'm just an Internet celebrity, but today that matters. I'm in a small city called Pompano Beach writing my book, and I was getting into my car at Publix as these three young women were getting out of their car. I asked them if they wanted my cart, and one of them said, "Hey, you're the guy who does those videos on Facebook!" It made me laugh. I've been getting recognized for years now in some of the strangest places. Last week I was in Tampa, Florida, and I went through a Burger King drive-thru and the young lady serving me said, "What are you doing way down here in Tampa? I see you on my TV!" It's strange to me how we see the world as so big with so many people, but in every city I go to someone in a random place recognizes me from online. Although it's been happening for years, I'm not bombarded by people like an A-list celebrity is, so I still haven't gotten used to it. I still have to remind people of my name because a lot of them just know my face, so there is still work to do. You don't think you're a celebrity because you're in your own skin. You see your flaws and your regularness every day, so you don't sweat yourself. You're no big deal to yourself. My wife chops me down to size often because she doesn't treat me any differently than when she first met me, so I'm always just Babe, her husband.

Today anyone can become a celebrity, and it can really change your brand. I see some people as celebrities even if they aren't known by name to everyone in the world. To be honest, some people we consider A-list celebrities are not recognized by name by everyone they bump into. No matter how big we think a person is, they aren't known by every human on the planet. The goal isn't to be known by everyone, but to be known by the people who need you the most. There are ways to become a celebrity without doing anything crazy or ignorant. You can live a meaningful life and do meaningful work and become a celebrity. In fact, everyone is a celebrity to someone, but how many people do you want to influence? We listen to celebrities more than we listen to regular people, and that's why companies use celebrity endorsements. Every major company does a commercial with celebrities because their influence is greater. When we see someone as bigger than us, better than us, more important than us, we listen to him or her. It never was my goal to be seen as better than anyone. I knew that my brand would become bigger than those of many others, but I've never wanted to be seen as better than anyone. I define celebrity differently. Some people may call it an authority figure. There are some keys to gaining that celebrity factor.

Know what you do and do it well. If you have a gift, you have to use it. If you're gifted at something, then you'll naturally separate yourself from the pack. People will see your gift and look at you differently than they look at others. Your gift will speak for itself. You won't have to do much talking or tell the people who matter that you're a celebrity; they'll see it in you. If you hide your gift, then you'll blend in with everyone else, and nothing special will come to you in life or happen for you. You can't be afraid to operate in your gifts and let your gifts take you to higher heights.

Know what you know and stick to it. If you know you're good, it's okay. Don't let anyone talk you down from your greatness. You don't have to flaunt it, but when you have to walk in greatness, you can't shrink from it. You can't be afraid to be great. Many people will try to tell you otherwise just to see if you really know what you know. You can't waiver in your stance. Stand by your truth and live it out.

Be consistent in your gift. You have to use it daily. You can't show up every other week to do what you do. You have to show up daily. Anyone can do something once, but it's the ones who do it over and over again who get the credit and the respect. Consistency is the key, especially if you want to be a leader. People will look to you over and over again to see if you are who you say you are. If they don't see consistency, they won't believe you.

Honestly, I don't like the idea of celebrity, but it's a part of our world. I really don't like when a person knows they are a celebrity and acts like they are a celebrity. I guess that's still some of the regularness in me. I know regularness isn't a word, by the way. I didn't ask to become a celebrity or to be seen as a celebrity by anyone, but people automatically put that title on you when you get to a certain level. I'm only a celebrity to certain people. There are millions and millions of people who have no idea who I am. I remember when some people would come to me online and say, "I'm sorry I didn't know you until today" as if they were supposed to already know me. I would reply, "I'm just like you, and I didn't know you until today either." I guess they said that because they could see that I have verified accounts—on social media, that says I'm a celebrity—and that some people have treated me as a celebrity. When you get that celebrity status to a group of people, even people who aren't in that group will see you differently when they find out you're a celebrity to someone. If you use social media correctly, then it can make a celebrity out of an average Joe without a celeb publicity agent. Twitter verified my page in 2010, and that made a big difference for me. People saw me differently. Facebook verified my page, and that made a big difference. Instagram verified my page, and that made a big difference. People would come to me and ask how I got verified and how they could be verified too. I didn't know what to tell them. I didn't know how or why they do it, but I realized quickly that it made a difference.

Sometimes you can be seen as a celebrity just by association. One of the first clients I got from social media was an R&B singer. I was tweeting wisdom daily and getting a lot of retweets and buzz on Twitter. One day a woman wrote me who was an entertainment lawyer. She said, "Hey, I saw you online and I love what you write. I noticed that you're a life coach, and I have a client who could use your help." I said, "Okay, cool, I'd love to help out." The young lady wasn't a celebrity yet, but I saw her as a celebrity because she knew some celebrities, had worked with some celebrities, and was signed to a label that represented major celebrities. Fast-forward some years and she had gotten on reality TV. Then after being a cast member and building her following online, she was big enough to get her own show. Then when she got her own show, they wanted to bring some balance and have her do some life-coaching sessions, so they called me. I went on her show and talked to her a few times, and from that celebrity association her followers started to see me as a celebrity life coach. I didn't do anything special. I didn't hire a branding firm or a publicist. I just operated in my gift, and it attracted opportunities. The association with celebrities or people with large amounts of followers goes a long way. Perception is reality for most people, so if they see you associated with a person they feel is a celebrity, then you're stamped. Once one celebrity sees you with another celebrity, then you're stamped in their mind too. Most celebs want to know who else you've worked with. In my line of work as a life coach that's confidential, so it becomes a guessing game. I was posting quotes every day so people knew they could come to me for quotes. Then if they saw that much wisdom on Twitter, it made them wonder what a conversation with me would be like. I had been retweeted by major celebrities like P. Diddy, Alicia Keys, and so on, so to many people that made me look like a celebrity. That stamp opened doors and brought about more opportunities. When I tweeted, I didn't sound unsure. I sounded very matter of fact in everything I said. I said it as if I knew I was 100% correct and that you could quote me on it. I literally wanted you to quote me on it. After a while that confidence and surety made me seem like an authority on the subject matter I was addressing. I spoke mostly about relationships in the beginning, so people started to call me a relationship expert. I never once referred to myself as a relationship expert, but the people did. I started being booked for events to speak on relationships, and they would put "relationship expert" on the marketing materials. Then on interviews they would ask me, "How did you become an expert on relationships?" I would lead by saying, "I don't consider myself an expert." I did consider myself an expert; I just never said I was. When you are truly something, you don't have to call yourself that. You just operate in your gift, and people will label you themselves. Then I went from being referred to as a relationship expert to a relationship guru. That scared me. I was shocked that here I was under 30 years old and being called an expert and a guru by seasoned professionals, but I realized it was their perception based on my delivery and my consistency.

Numbers mean a lot; the more you do something, the higher your numbers will go. If you are consistent in your work and you're good at what you do, then your numbers will increase. At a certain number people will start to separate you in their mind. For me it started to happen around 25,000 Twitter followers.

This is because most people only have a hundred to a thousand Twitter followers, so when my numbers reached a certain point, I was validated in some people's minds. It's just how it works. Once you are consistent enough to earn the title like expert, guru, celebrity, or authority, things will start to change for you. Now you can charge more, and you have to charge more because people perceive you differently. I'm the same guy who was coaching at $25/hour, but now that I've built my numbers and my brand and people are labeling me differently, I can charge $350/hour and no one questions it. When I had 34 followers on Twitter, I was a life coach then too. If I had told someone that I charge $350/hour at that point, they probably would have laughed until they passed out. My numbers went up and my labels changed and people started to expect it. When I would say $75/hour, people would say, really, that's it? The flip side of this is that people also expect me to have a high-powered agent and attorney as well, so it's a double-edged sword because when you are labeled a celebrity, it's almost forcing you to not be as accessible and down-to-earth. It's pushing you to another level, and you have to decide if that's where you want to be.

Outside of being a celebrity life coach, I also became a celebrity speaker. I didn't know I was nor did I pitch myself as such, but I started seeing that as my title on event flyers. That really caught me off guard, but I had to take it in stride. Before that title was attached to me as a speaker, people would frown if I told them I wanted $1,500 to speak. After the label changed, people were shocked that I would charge only $5,000 or $10,000. My labels changed before I realized it, and I was charging beginner's rates when people were expecting celebrity rates. It was an adjustment I had to make because I wasn't ready for that. That's one reason having an agent or someone working for you is good, because they aren't afraid to jack up your sticker price, and sometimes they are able to get it. I was so used to pitching myself that I was trying to get used to the celebrity label. I hurt myself a lot of times because I'd want a deal, partnership, or barter with certain companies, and I'd write to them, trying to embrace my new label with my same humble approach, and it didn't work. Imagine getting an email that says, "Hi, I'm Tony Gaskins, celebrity life coach, author, and speaker, and I'm writing you because . . ." A company is automatically caught off guard because they assume that if you were this big celebrity, you wouldn't be making a pitch on your own behalf; you'd have an agent or publicist doing it. That's where the trouble comes in, so although the celebrity label was benefiting my business, I wanted other benefits that I couldn't really get on my own. Celebrities get a lot of free stuff and a lot of deals, but publicists usually pitch companies for those things. Working alone limited some things, so what I had to do with this newfound celebrity is balance it. I had to accept and charge celebrity rates for anything that came in to me; but for the stuff I wanted to go get for myself, I had to pitch as just regular ole Tony, and then let the company look into me and hope they would consider me a celebrity. When I pitched with the humble approach and didn't refer to myself as a celebrity, the company would usually look into my background and write back to me very excited. It was an interesting balance that had to be found. You have to choose what matters most to you—managing the blessings coming to you or going out in search for more than what's coming to you.

If you want to become a celebrity or an authority, by all means go for it. Don't shy away from it. I've seen some speakers referring to themselves as "a regular Joe" or "the guy next door," and guess what: they get treated just like that no matter how big they get. I consider myself to be a humble person, but I didn't label myself "humble Tony." I embraced the label the people gave me. One time a company wrote in for me to speak in South Africa, and they offered me $2,000. I almost spit out my drink. As a speaker you can get way more than that to stay in the States, so I was shocked that they wanted me to fly a round trip of 40 hours and speak for $2,000. Then I found out the reason why they offered me $2,000. They offered me that because they had just worked with another American speaker who referred to himself as "a regular Joe" or something like that, so that's what they offered him and he accepted it. I had to let them know that I was proud of them for getting a speaker to come that far for $2,000, but I wasn't going to be able to do it. That was a time I was happy to email back as my booking manager and hide behind that celebrity tag. I learned then that it's great to be humble and regular, but when your numbers elevate you, accept it.

You can become an authority, but you have to work for it. You have to be consistent, and you have to do something that separates you. One of the best things you can do to become an authority is to create something. Create a product, a book, a course, or something. Do something that not everyone else has done or can do. When you do that and you do it with confidence and you're sure of yourself and you're consistent, then you're sure to be seen as an authority. Remember, there are authorities who are not authorities. There are celebrities who are not celebrities. There are different ways to separate yourself, and there's room for many. I'm sure people who have been doing this for 30 years hate when someone from my generation mentions my name in the same sentence as theirs, but that's just how it works. Just the other day I saw a flyer online promoting a guy's new book, and I'll quote you exactly what the flyer said. It read: "The book includes inspiring quotes from respected pioneers such as Jim Rohn, Tyler Perry, Bill Gates, Tony Gaskins, Mike Murdock, Muhammad Ali, Mark Zuckerberg, Steve Jobs, John Maxwell, Dave Ramsey and much more." I was floored. What it said to me is that you're a celebrity to somebody. Some of those guys listed have never heard of me, but I've heard of all of them. All of them are celebrities to me. I don't hold them all on the same level, some are higher than others, but I know they all have a big names and followings that consider them a celebrities. For me to be listed in that list with those guys, I was blown away.

I sent it to my father, and he said it brought tears to his eyes and that he was going to frame it. That gave me a laugh. I don't know if he was serious or trying to flatter me. It made me want to buy the guy's book to see how he quoted me.

I see stuff like that on Twitter all the time, but usually it's just a tweet, not an actual promotional flyer. I cringe sometimes when I read the tweets because they mention me with people who I know are offended that my name is next to theirs. Then it has happened the other way around too. Sometimes someone will mention my name beside a couple people who have just started inspiring people last year, and I get offended. Karma, I guess. But, I say to myself again, anyone can be an authority if you're consistent and you're sure of yourself, so I can't be mad that the people who just started are already being mentioned beside others who have been at it for years. It's the way it works these days. Social media can make anyone.

There are people who are seen as authorities and celebrities who will tell you that they don't have talent; they just outwork everyone else. That's the name of the game. People want to know that you can be counted on. People want to know that when they need a quote, you'll have a quote ready for them, even if you borrowed it from someone else's page. They don't care who said it first as long as it's readily available when they need to see it. I would have a hissy fit online sometimes about people stealing my quotes, and there would always be a genius who'd say, "Who cares who gets the credit for it? God is the only one who deserves the credit." That response would burn me up. It would burn any writer up. But, once again, it proved to me that the people reading the quote a lot of times couldn't care less that the author isn't credited; they just want the material. That is why you see quote pages on every social media outlet with millions of followers. The quote pages make a living from stealing quotes, but guess what? The person behind the quote page can come out and become an instant celebrity because they've been consistently feeding the people motivation. I've watched it happen more than once where a quote page would build to 500,000 followers from copying, revising, or altering other people's content. Then the creator of the page would come from behind the page and instantly be connected with Oprah and given a book deal by a major publisher. No one cared where the content came from or whether the gift was authentic. All they cared about were the numbers. The numbers meant dollars to the brands. The quotes meant inspiration to the followers, so if you have the gift or you have the passion, then why not be consistent and rise to the ranks as an authority or celebrity and change your life. You deserve it just like anyone else does.

I didn't ask to be an authority or a celebrity, as I've said already, but it has changed my life. It has opened doors sooner than I expected, and it has earned me a great living. My vow is to do it differently though. My vow is to not let it go to my head. That doesn't mean I'll work for free or take less than I'm worth, but it does mean that I won't look down on people. I plan to take every picture and sign every book when I'm passing through an airport or in a store and someone stops me. I want to do it differently. I know that means something to some people. I know realistically speaking that it won't always be possible for me to sign everything and take every picture, but at least a few. I saw a quote once that said, "Do for a few what you wish you could do for many." That has stuck with me and I've adopted that motto even on social media. If I have 10 questions and I can't answer them all, I'll at least answer three to let people know that I saw them and I wanted to chat, but time ran out and I had to get back to work. Go be a celebrity. Go be an authority figure. Just do it for the right reasons and take care of the responsibilities. As the good book says—*where much is given, much is required.* Don't ask for the title or don't work for the title if you don't want everything that comes with it.

Chapter 13 Study the Ant

There are a lot of lazy people in the world today. So many people say they want something, but they don't really want to work for it. They say they want financial freedom, but to them that means an investor giving them enough money to live off of while they play in the sandbox and call it building a business. A lot of people want a handout or a hand up. Not many people want to sweat for it. I've noticed some things while building my brand, and one was that many people think success is made in the microwave. Success is made in the oven. It takes times to become successful, and you have to work for it like there is no tomorrow. I meet a lot of people who get started and right away they want to partner with me. They have 21 followers online, and it makes perfect sense to them why I would align my brand with theirs for a tour. Honestly, I can't be mad at them because I've asked some crazy questions too. A lot of times we ask crazy questions when we're doing something we aren't called to do, and we are looking for the quickest route to the top. I remember when I wanted to make it in something, and I didn't care what it was. I wrote a screenplay and had never read a screenplay or a filmmaking book a day in my life. I wrote the screenplay, and then I went on MySpace trying to connect with people. I saw a guy's play on BET. I thought the play was terrible, but he was on TV so he must have done something right. I looked him up on MySpace and gave him my sob story about how I wanted to be a film-maker. He offered to mentor me. We spoke, and I heard he had another play coming out. I asked him with a straight face to let me cast his next play. His plays went on big tours around the country. I'd never casted anything in my life and never sat through a whole play either. When I asked him to cast his play, he laughed me out of the room. I was out of my mind, but I was hungry and desperate. Had I done my work and studied filmmaking and playwriting, produced a couple local plays myself, and casted them myself, then I could have made a better argument for myself. Instead, I jumped right out of the gate with a list of wants, and I couldn't meet any of his needs.

That's how things go these days. We live in a time where the work is minimal. People are making it with little effort, so it starts to make us all think we can click our heels and become rich and famous. I've had people reach out to me and say, "Hey, I want to be a reality star. Can you help me do that?" People have asked me if I know the producer of these reality shows because they want to get on the show and scream and yell to become famous because they saw other people do it. They don't realize that the people who first started screaming and yelling on TV really thought they were a part of a real show with a real meaning. They later realized they were being used, but by then the money was too good to walk away. Because of that, becoming a reality star started becoming a goal for millions of people. I thought that way at one point too. In my heart I wanted a platform so I could inspire, but I didn't realize that all

I had to do was inspire and eventually I would have a platform big enough to actually make a difference. I thought I had to sell myself short in order to make it. I just wanted a way out of the struggle, so I can't knock people who are looking for a way out. I joined the reality TV casting websites and was looking for shows I could possibly be a part of. I never saw a fit. I was looking for a way to make it. I started creating and pitching my own shows. One time I spent $25,000 trying to shoot a reality TV show pilot to pitch to a network. At least I was willing to do the work, but I was crazy. The world made me think that I had to be on reality TV in order to have a voice and a platform. It was sad at times. After my vain attempts failed, I decided to go back to the basics. I went back to my favorite manual, the Bible, and it told me to study the ant. In studying the ant, I found my answer. I just had to put in some old-fashioned work.

I started working like an ant. I was gathering and storing because I knew that when things got hard, I would have stored up enough that I could be eating good. When I started out, the picking was good. There weren't many young authors like me. There weren't many life coaches. There were always a lot of speakers, but not many like me. I had to go to work and build my portfolio, build my contact list, and lay my foundation. I was storing up experience because I knew that one day the winter would come and things would be harder. The industry started getting cluttered with a lot of fakes, scam artists, and the like, and people started getting confused. It became hard to tell the real from the fake. It was then that people would start to look into your past and check out your body of work to see how long you'd been doing it and if you were serious. There were guys who looked like me but were much older than me who came out with books two years after my first book. At first people thought I was copying the big guys because they saw their books before they heard of me, but then they looked into my body of work and saw that I got started before anyone else they were following at the time. That ant work helped me.

While you're working, you have to work with a purpose. You have to have a relentless pursuit. I was lost at one point in my life, and I was in the street life. I wasn't a kingpin, but I saw kingpins work. I saw guys working around the clock. Although I wasn't on that level, I worked around the clock too. I realized that all of us lost souls could do a lot of good work if we could just change our lives. When I changed my life, I took that same grind into my new line of work. I asked my wife to support my grind and to understand that for a season I had to study and work like the ant. She said she understood, and she gave me the space to work. I worked 40 hours for the man, and then I came home and worked another 30 to 40 hours. I worked seven days a week. I slept early mornings because I would work until 3 or 4 a.m. many nights. While others were sleeping, I was working. While others were partying, I was working. Right now, while others who have book deals are bragging about the book deal but not writing, I'm on Chapter 13 after two days of work. I realize that there is no time to waste. You have to work like you mean it. You're running a marathon, but you have to run it as hard and as fast as you can. I was working like there wasn't a tomorrow most days.

One time my dad said to me, "Son, you have too much going on, and you're working on too many projects at once." I said, "No, Dad; I'm laying a foundation so that when I hit it big, everything will be in place." I knew that a peak would come and I needed to be ready for my break. I'm still not there yet, although you may think I'm talking about now. I still have a way to go. I know what the peak looks like because I can see it from a distance, but I'm not there yet. There is more work to be done. I'm still in the climb. We are all in the climb. You have to work like you're in the climb. You have to be ready for your moment, because moments don't come twice. Each moment only comes once, and you have to be ready for it when it's time. You have to prepare for it, because you truthfully don't know when it will happen. My time is fast approaching, and I know it's on

God's time. I thought I was waiting on Him, but I realize now He's been waiting on me. I know what I have to square away, and I'm almost finished with that work. Once I'm finished with that work, then I know my moment will be coming in any day. I'm preparing for it now.

Ask yourself, how hard am I working? Are you working like there's no tomorrow? Are you partying too much? Are you drinking and smoking too much? Are you talking too much? Are you watching too much TV? What are you doing to move closer toward your goals? What can you cut out that will create more time for your grind? You can't just write your plans and goals and then share them with your friends and family. You have to work for them as soon as the words leave your mouth. You have to get on your grind.

When I started out, I knew I had to build a foundation. For some time, I was caught up in the way of the world. I was looking for the shortcuts, but then one day it hit me. I had to create. I started to change my life, and everything became about the work. I stopped watching TV. I stopped listening to music. I know you probably can't fathom letting your favorite show and your music go, but if you want to make it, you just may have to for a season. You need to cram in some knowledge. You need to get some growth and make up for lost time. When I was at home, instead of watching TV, I would talk to my wife and son and then I would work. When my wife and son were asleep, I would be sitting up working. I would be researching. I would be crafting emails. I would be writing books, work-books, pamphlets, and courses. I was gaining knowledge. I was doing grassroots marketing. If I had to add a hundred friends a day on Facebook or Myspace, that's what I did. If I had to write out tweets, that is what I did. When it was time to go to work, I stopped listening to music. I remember I threw two of my favorite CDs out of the window when I decided to change my life. I know that sounds like I'm making it up, but I literally threw them out of the window like I was throwing a Frisbee.

I realized that the music I was listening to at the time wasn't moving my life forward. The artists had the good life, but I was still broke and struggling. On Sundays, I didn't watch football. During the week, I didn't watch basketball. It was family time and grind time. I told people, "I don't have free time; I have family time and grind time." You have to fit in one or the other. I didn't get to talk to my parents or my sister much at all. I had work to do. There was a season of work that had to be done. Instead of listening to music, I replaced it with audiobooks and podcasts. After I'd listened to enough of them and allowed myself to go back to music, I chose songs that moved my life forward, not backward. I left the junk rap alone and went to the gospel music I grew up on. I need a real song on my heart, a song with a message.

During this time of work, it's not all about physical labor. Work is also working on you. You have to cut off the things and the people who are not moving your life forward. People would get upset with me and tell me I thought I was better than them because I didn't want to watch the TV shows and the sports games. I told them, "Those people you're watching on TV have already made it. That's their work, and they are getting paid nicely for it. On their way to that point they didn't stop to watch you, so why are you watching them?" That upset a lot of people. I would say stuff like that online, and people would be upset. For me social media was work, not pleasure. I was building my brand and my following. I was weeding out the people who were not like-minded. I tweeted my heart and if my tweets upset you, then I knew you weren't trying to grow. I knew we didn't want the same things out of life. I knew my books and my courses wouldn't be for you because you weren't about growing. Now I listen to music, and I watch sports events. I enjoy them a lot. It's a part of my family time. I can relax a little bit now because I've reached a lot of my goals. My goals are still ahead of me, but I don't have to work at the same pace. Now instead of building it's more about sustaining what I've built, and that involves work as well but not in the same way. The foundation has been laid; now I just have to keep doing what I've been doing.

You have to be okay with work. You have to be able to set a goal and make it happen. I wanted to write books, so when it was time I got right to it. I would create a schedule and start writing. I didn't want a book to take me six months to write it. I didn't want to take a year to write a book. I adjusted my plan, and I wrote differently. Considering my generation and my demographic, I didn't want to write really long books either. I wanted quick reads that were filled with power punches instead of light and fluffy jabs. My books had to get to the point and be real and raw. That's how I like to write. To do that I had to be serious about it and make it happen. I would talk to some people, and they would tell me it takes them six months to write a 100-page book. I could respect that, but I had to push myself in a different way because I knew what it took for me to actually get it done. This book will be longer than any book I've ever written. It's been much harder to write because there are a lot more chapters and a lot more content. I realize that even if I take six months to write it, my content will be the same. My wisdom will not change, because the way I've built my brand is etched in stone; I can't change the past. If I'm going to write about my philosophies on brand building and entrepreneurship, I just have to do it. My schedule looks like this:

7 a.m.	Wake up
7:30 a.m.	Eat breakfast
8:00 a.m.	Start writing
10:00 a.m.	15-minute break/snack
10:15 a.m.	Start writing
12:15 p.m.	Lunch break
12:45 p.m.	Start writing
2:45 p.m.	15-minute break/snack
3:00 p.m.	Start writing
5:00 p.m.	15-minute break/snack

5:15 p.m.	Start writing
7:15 p.m.	Dinner break
7:45 p.m.	Start writing
10:00 p.m.	Stop writing/call my wife
10:30 p.m.	Shower
11:00 p.m.	Go to bed and get ready to repeat

By keeping that schedule I was able to write my books in two days. I pushed through, and I just wrote. That schedule ensured that I could publish a book every year if I wanted to. I write from my heart so I didn't want to put a lot of guesswork into it. I took the same approach to creating products or courses. When I felt like someone needed a course, I would sit down and just start writing in my phone what I felt needed to be taught. It would look something like this:

Week 1: How to love yourself
Week 2: Healing from the past
Week 3: Preparing for real love
Week 4: Recognizing the warning signs
Week 5: How to make it work
Week 6: What to do if you have to leave
Week 7: Q&A

I didn't want to make it rocket science. The idea isn't to be perfect, just be worth it. I like to think logical, not magical. There are some magical thinkers out there. It's great if your magical thinking comes quickly, but if your magical thinking leads to you getting stuck and never producing anything, then you have to change that. As soon as I'd finish with the course outline, I'd shoot an email to my designer. My email would read like this:

Hey Bro,

How are you man? I hope all is well! Can you make a new page for me for $100? I'd just want a logo that says "Real Love University," and then put this copy on the page:

Copy: Are you tired of falling in and out of love? Do you want to learn how to truly love yourself and attract the love of your life? And so on and so on.

Then put: In this course you'll learn:

Week 1: etc., etc., etc.

Then under that put a "Pay Now" button, here's the link: (link)

Let me know if you have any questions bro! Thanks a million! I'll pay you as soon as you're done, so let me know.

After sending that email, the new course would be up in less than 24 hours. Then I'd get a flyer made for it and start promoting it. I found the key is simplicity. You can change lives and make a great living by keeping it simple. You may not make millions right away, but you'll do good work and make a good living.

I make sure that the people I'm working with have the ant mentality too. I work fast and hard, so I need the people I work with to do the same. When you study the ant, you'll see that their system makes sense to them. They can build it and make it work for them. It may not look pretty to you, but it works. To you it looks just like a pile of dirt, but to them, it's home. They get what they need, and it works. I've cut a lot of the fluff out of the way by just delivering good content. I've never had a student complain about the content in one of my online courses. I'm building www.TonyGaskinsAcademy.com right now, and it's just going to be online courses without the fluff. I'm not going to oversell and underdeliver. I'm going to tell you what I'm going to teach you, and I'll teach you exactly that. I hired a company to build the site. I hired a guy to shoot and edit the courses, and I'm going to just go and record them. I'm going to work hard and fast and not prolong the process. I'm not going to create so much fluff so that it exhausts me and makes me never want to do another course again. I'm not someone to do only one course and make it my life's work. I'm going to create several courses because we all know several things. We may not be experts in everything but we know enough to help someone else get started who might not know the first thing about it. I'm not the biggest speaker in the world, but I know enough to teach a beginner; so I'm going to teach him or her. I'm not the biggest or best life coach in the world, but I know enough to help someone start their business; so I'm going to teach him or her. That's the point: Do the work and make it simple. Don't overcomplicate the process. Don't get stuck because you're outthinking yourself. Just do the work. Make a plan, set a goal, and make it happen. The more you do it, the better you'll get. My courses may have more features and be more robust in the next five years, but everything is a process. If you try to build Rome in a day, you will fail. First, you have to build Podunk and work out the kinks. Then you can build Smallville. Then you can build Biggerville. Then you can build Betterville. Then you can build Rome.

Make a plan for yourself and get to work. Don't feel strange for cutting out the things and the people who don't move your life forward. If social media isn't a part of your work, then you may have to take a break from social media. If you're not being paid to watch and critique TV shows, then you may have to take a break from some TV shows. If you're not planning to work in professional sports or already working in them, then you may have to miss a few games and matches. You have to work for you first. You have to sacrifice for you first. Don't be afraid to get your hands dirty and do the work. Stop talking about your dreams and start building your dreams. The time is now!

Chapter 14 Expanding the Brand

There always comes a time when we have to expand. We as humans are gifted beyond our wildest imagination, and there is so much we can do. I'm typing on this laptop, and I'm amazed at how this thing works. Are you sure God didn't create this? Well, He did because he created the people who created it. We are powerful. We are mighty and majestic. Whatever great word you want to throw out there, that's what we are. Look around you at all of the technology that you use on a daily basis. Even beyond what you have access to, look at the technology that makes the world turn. There are some amazing things in our world that we take for granted every day. As I started to think about that, I started to realize that I could be and do so much more. I started to ask myself—*why should I settle for less? Why should I settle for one lane and one stream of income?* No matter what you do for a living, there are always one or two more things you could be doing to earn money and leave a mark on the world. We just don't always think about it that way. We get so consumed in the one thing we're doing that we don't make time for anything else. We tell ourselves that there isn't enough time in the day. We tell ourselves that we shouldn't have our hands in too many cookie jars. Well, if you eat one cookie for too long, you may grow allergic to it and not be able to eat it anymore. You might as well try a few others, so you can have some variety in your life. Don't get so used to just one thing. Don't get stuck doing one thing for the rest of your life. Find ways to create an impact on the world and get out of your box. You're too talented to only do one or two things. You're selling yourself short. My mobile detail guy, Johnathan, always reminds me that we're only using 10 percent of our brains. I don't know where he read that, but I think I've heard it somewhere too. It's scary to think that it could be right. I'd like to at least get to 15 percent, sheesh. I've come to realize that we have so much more in us if we just believe and work for it. I believe that I can find a way to expand any brand in a profitable way if I look at it long enough. I believe that no matter how much a person or company is doing, I can find at least one more way they could be doing more and earning more. I'm doing the same thing with myself. I count my streams of income in a very weird and unfair way, but it helps me process things more abundantly. For example, this book: I could count it as one stream of income, but I count it as six or more. The reason is because I count Amazon, Barnes and Noble, Kindle, Nook, iBooks, and Kobo as separate streams of income. The reason I count each of them as a stream of income is because they are all different companies cutting me a check. Yes, another company owns a couple of those e-readers, but on my royalty statement it's a separate sale with a separate name. They also serve different types of people. Physical books are marketed to and bought by certain types of people. One e-reader may be affordable to one group and another e-reader affordable to a different group. Some e-readers are only on certain types of phones. Each outlet serves a different group of people. No one person has all of the outlets, so I count them as different streams of income. It may not make sense to you, but it helps me see abundantly and realize all of the earning opportunities.

Let me explain further how I expanded my brand, so maybe you can look at your own brand in order to see if there are any ways you can tap into a couple of these markets yourself. Or it may help you discover a totally new area that I haven't tapped into.

FIRST, I BECAME AN AUTHOR.

I wrote my first book in 2007. That was actually my second stream of income because I was working a full-time job. I was expanding my brand into my gifts. Until you leave your job, then your job is a part of your brand. The book is technically one stream of income, but I counted it as more because I counted a stream for every company that cut me a check. Back then it was Amazon, Barnes and Noble, Books-A-Million, and Borders. Those were the main ones I received sales from.

THEN, I BECAME A SPEAKER.

After writing a book I thought the next thing I needed to do was spread the word about it, and what better way to do that than to speak? Speaking is one stream of income in my mind although you might speak to several different organizations. When I branched into different topics of speaking, then I started to split up my streams of income because business conferences, relationship conferences, and sports conferences are totally different arenas, and rarely do speakers enter all three. I eventually entered all three.

THEN, I BECAME A SCREENWRITER.

I'm just sharing this because I did it. I didn't make any money from it, but I was offered $1,500 to write someone else's screenplay.

I turned it down. I figured that since I was an author, I could also write a screenplay and become a filmmaker because I saw other people doing it. I wrote the screenplay and actually signed a few Hollywood actresses that I'd seen on some of my favorite TV shows growing up with letters of intent. I was excited, but I didn't pursue it too much. Had I accepted the $1,500 to write for that local filmmaker, it would have been another stream of income.

THEN, I BECAME A GHOSTWRITER.

Because I was writing my own books and doing it fairly easy, I thought I'd venture out and write books for others. I still do that today. The first book I wrote was for an NFL player, and I did it for free. Then I wrote a book for a woman with an amazing story and charged her $2,300 total. Then I upped my price to $10,000, and I started writing for celebrities and other pro athletes. I actually just finished one last month for a celebrity client. The ghostwriting has stuck with me over the years. I'm moving on up to $20,000 because it gets harder every time I do it. I know some people who charge $50,000 and get a percentage of the royalties. I read that the woman who wrote Hillary Clinton's book made $500,000. Ghostwriting could be lucrative if you have the gift and the patience to do it.

THEN, I BECAME AN AUTHOR CONSULTANT.

Not everyone can afford ghostwriting, but they still want to get their books out. I started consulting authors on how to write and publish their books. I charged $500 starting out and then moved up to $1,500 and then to $2,500. Consulting is a great business as well.

THEN, I BECAME A RELATIONSHIP COACH.

My first book was about relationships, and women had more questions after reading it. One day I was on a free teleseminar, and the guy said, "If you've written a self-help book, then you could coach people on that same subject." I was like, wow, that's a great idea. Before that, I was draining myself answering all these questions in the Facebook inbox. Then I switched it up and started converting the leads into clients. I told them I'd love to help them but due to my schedule they'd have to sign up for coaching as one of my premium clients in order for me to fit them in. I started out charging $25/hour. Some of the women hiring me were older than my mother, so I couldn't charge real money at 24 and 25 years old—at least I didn't think I could. I had two days off a week from my full-time job so on Tuesdays and Wednesdays I'd book my coaching sessions. I didn't tell anyone I was working a full-time job. I'd just tell them that my only two days with openings were Tuesday and Wednesday. It made me sound packed, and it helped me convert. It was great that I was off on weekdays too because if I had been off on Saturdays and Sundays, that would have looked a little odd.

THEN, I BECAME A LIFE COACH.

Life coaching is different than relationship coaching because some people just want to get their life in order. They want to go over their goals and make a plan. Some people who come to me for life coaching don't want to talk about relationships, so I count it as separate stream of income and line of work.

THEN, I BECAME A BUSINESS COACH.

Business coaching is totally separate from life coaching and relationship coaching because business coaching is helping people form their for-profit or nonprofit companies. I help them come up with their mission statement, find their lane, identify their target audience, and develop their products. In business coaching, we don't discuss relationships or life in general. There are those people who will buy a block of sessions and talk about a different topic each session; I just consider them a client in three different areas. I started out coaching at $25/hour. I don't get to coach as much now, and the most I've been able to bring myself to charge is $350/hour. I know there are coaches who charge $1,500 to $10,000 an hour, but that's a lot and I'm not there yet.

THEN, I FORMED ONLINE COURSES.

- **For the Love of Me:** This was my first course. I'd built my Twitter following talking mostly about relationships, so people were hungry for relationship wisdom. There was a reality show on TV at the time called *For the Love of Ray J*, so I spinned off of it and titled my course "For the Love of Me." I made it a 12-week course and charged $75 for it. The people who signed up paid $25/month. I had about 125 people sign up, so that totaled $9,375. At that time, I was still on my full-time job earning $1,200 to $1,800/month, so this course was great money for me. I taught it by phone on Tuesday nights from 9 pm to 10 pm. I was on to something. I got the idea from the same guy who taught me about the timely pitch, life coaching, and now group coaching. He said, "If you run out of time and you can't do as much one-on-one coaching, then you can do group coaching." I just took that to mean teaching a course by phone. He didn't say that specifically, but I always took a nugget of info and developed it in my mind in a way that would fit me. I had to come up with the payment structure, the method of delivery for the course, the subject matter, and the length. I learned a lot from that first run. It was a great run.
- **The Love School:** The next time I taught a love course I changed the name because the other one was outdated. I cut down the lessons to eight weeks, and I made the price a one-time fee because a few people defaulted on their monthly payments in my first course. I actually can't remember how much I charged for the course, but it did well enough for me to keep going.

- **Entrepreneur University:** I branched out of the love courses because I realized that I was becoming a pretty good entrepreneur and that I had some insight that I could teach others. I made this course a six-week course, and I charged $350 for it. I only taught it live once, and I had 10 people sign up for it. It was much less popular than the love stuff, but it earned $3,500 for six hours of work. That was much better than my job was paying me for six hours, so I was happy with that. I actually can't remember if I was still on my job or not when I taught this course.

- **Birth Your Book Program:** I wanted to create a course to teach people how to write and publish their own book. The ghost-writing and author consulting had slowed down, and I wanted to make a product that was easily affordable but packed with info. I really gave this course away because it cost only $19.99. And to think, that same course is on my site for $199 today. I gave it away at first just because I thought no one would want it, but hundreds bought it to my surprise. I stopped counting at about 110 people or so.

- **The Life Coaching Certification Program:** This course was my biggest baby. I took it very seriously. All of these courses I've created are a form of life coaching. I consider my books and my speeches a form of life coaching as well. In this course, I wanted to give away the game. I wanted to teach people how to build a successful coaching/consulting business from A to Z. I looked around at other courses, and I beat their prices by $1,000 and charged $1,500 for my course. The first time I taught it I had about 20 people sign up, so that was $30,000 I earned. I was blown away. This course made me the proudest because I'm teaching a six-figure blueprint for life coaches for only $1,500, and I earned more than my measly job paid me in a year. For this course I went the extra mile and wrote a textbook and a workbook with exams. It took me about three days at a beach house to get those things prepared, and then I hit the ground running. I figured I could teach the course three or four times a year and earn six figures from that course alone. It was a great idea and a great investment with double pay because not only am I being compensated for my hard-earned knowledge, but also I'm blessing others who want to do what I've done. I love this course the most, and I still teach it.

- **Real Love University:** I took a break from the love courses for a while because I just got tired of talking about love. I realize now that people never get tired of talking about love. I had to come back to my first love, so in 2014 or so I created the Real Love University and made it a six-weeks course. I charged $197 for the course at first, but then I dropped the price to $97. Hundreds of people have taken it, and if I marketed it for real, there would probably be about 500 to 1,000 people who would sign up. I get about 100 people each course without marketing it; it just sits on my site and gets organic traffic. I don't care to get too many people in the course because I give out a workbook, and I don't want to be mailing out a thousand workbooks. I also do a Q&A for 30 minutes each class, and I hate hanging up the phone with people still on the line with questions. I love this course way more than the love courses I taught in the past.

- **Tony Gaskins Academy:** This website is being built right now. I should be done by the time you're reading this book. This is my baby. I'll house all of my courses on this one site. I have many more courses I'm going to create, and they will all go there. This site will become like an online university. When we reach the point when people are opting out of college because of the debt and the lack of jobs that a degree can get you, this site will be where they turn. I'll be teaching every aspect of a life of peace, happiness, and prosperity.

THEN, I CREATED AUDIO PROJECTS.

- **For The Love of Me:** I took the recordings from my course and put them on iTunes for sale at $9.99 per lesson.
- **Spoken Word:** Remember I told you I was a poet in my former days? Well, I tapped back into the gift, and I wrote some love pieces and some motivational pieces and put them on iTunes, Google Play, and all the other digital outlets.

THEN, I CREATED PHONE APPLICATIONS.

- **iLifeCoach:** This was my first app. This app had about 400 of my quotes from Twitter and also about 60 common questions that I would get asked as a life coach. I answered the questions in blog format. The app only cost me $1,800 to make, and I charged $0.99 for it. It made the money back rather quickly and generated great sales because at that time no one in my industry had an app. I was ahead of the curve. That's how that name was still available in the iPhone app store. We put it on iPhone and the Google phones as well. I've discontinued the app because we are updating it.
- **iLifeCoach by Tony Gaskins:** This was my second app, and it was a free app on an app system that a lot of churches use. I liked it, but it still wasn't what I wanted. I kept it for a while and paid the $155/month for a year or so, then I let it go. I'm building something else right now that will top those other two apps.

THEN I CREATED WORKBOOKS.

- **CEO of Me Workbook:** This workbook is on Amazon, and it's an entrepreneur's workbook. I basically teach my Entrepreneur University course and the Birth Your Book program in this workbook. I could have charged a lot more but I only made it $30.
- **The Real Love Tour Workbook:** This workbook is for my Real Love Tour that I'll mention next. I created this workbook and sold it separately on Amazon as well. It's a guide to self-love, I'd say. I just wanted people to be able to work themselves through some of their relationship issues.

THEN I CREATED MY OWN TOURS.

I produce my own tours each year. I consider this different than just being a speaker because I'm in control and the profit margins are different. I wanted to be in control of my events. I'm sure you can tell by my book that I'm a very hands-on person. I was doing events, and they would have an over-the-top host, a bunch of unnecessary vendors, and some pretty bad speakers. I'm not the best speaker in the world, but I know how to deliver a message in a real way, and my guests always come back a second time. I wanted to do it my way. I didn't want all the glitz and glam because I couldn't afford it. I knew that if I used a nice ballroom and had a good microphone and some comfortable chairs, I could pull it off. I'd recommend this to anyone who has taken the time to build their following online. It's not that hard. I find the venue on Google, set up my ticket page on Eventbrite, get a flyer made by my designer, and then start posting the flyer online. It's that simple. A couple days before the event, I email the guest list and ask for a few volunteers. I get the people I need and meet them at the venue a little early. They help me set up the check-in table and my book table, and I show them how to check people in. I give everyone his or her job and we make it happen. I'm working with complete strangers. For these people with a servant's heart, it's a cool thing because they get VIP treatment because they are coming to see me. They get to see me first, take a picture, and help produce the event. At a lot of stops it would only be the volunteers and me. I like doing it this way instead of having my own team that travels with me. Having my own team means I'm spending a lot more money to produce an event. It also means that some people get complacent, and they find the loopholes in my operation. Once a person settles in and they are able to scope out the operation, then they are comfortable enough to slip a bill in their pocket here and there. They get comfortable and can invite friends to let them in free without telling me. They can get comfortable in all kinds of ways. By my having volunteers, they don't know me yet. They don't know the system or how it works. It's hard to become a criminal the first day on the job because you just don't know if there is a system in place that will get you caught up. You also don't know the person next to you, so you don't know if this person is a raving fan and will be watching you like a hawk and tell if he or she sees you do something wrong. I thought about those things when stringing together a tour on a small budget. People started asking me how I produce tours because their tours kept failing. I just keep it simple.

THEN I STARTED A REAL ESTATE INVESTMENT COMPANY.

I started this company just to build more real assets. I consider my books and products assets, but I also wanted other types of assets. Everything I do has to have a purpose beyond money, so with the real estate I'm doing something different. I want to buy small houses and rent them to single parents or small families who are working hard but just not making a lot of money. I don't want to be a typical landlord. I give my tenants the month of December rent-free. That's pretty much unheard of in the real estate investment industry, but I think more property owners should start doing that. The way it started was one of my tenants was late on her December rent because of Christmas shopping for her three kids. I already had the idea to do it, but I had forgotten about it. When I received a text from her that she was late, I told her that I give my tenants the month of December off and to enjoy Christmas with her kids. She told me she was shocked, and she's never had a landlord do that her entire life. Those words made me feel good. I thought I would be taken for granted and that it would cause a problem with future payments, but to my surprise it made me more appreciated; rent payments come every month and on time. I've paid rent for years myself, and I know how good I would have felt if they had told me I didn't have to pay rent in December.

THEN I STARTED A REFERRAL BUSINESS.

I started making so many connections and I knew so many people that I just became a middleman. I would connect people and get a cut of the profits. I'd have the service provider pay me, or I'd just add my fee on top of the service. It was just another payment for the hard work and hands-on approach that I'd taken to building my brand.

THEN I STARTED A T-SHIRT LINE.

I mention this because I did it, and it can be very lucrative. At the time it just wasn't for me. I wanted to have motivational sayings on shirts, but I spoke mostly on relationships. I sold some shirts when I promoted them, but I didn't feel like promoting T-shirts. I felt like it cheapened my brand too much on a very large scale. Representing myself on deals may also cheapen my brand, but only the people who wrote in to book me knew that. My entire following didn't know I was a one-man show. When I started promoting T-shirts, it just seemed tacky to me, and I didn't like it. I think it's a great idea for many others, but for me it's not where I wanted to be. I'll most likely sell T-shirts on my tours in the future just because it'll be in a closed environment, and it'll be relevant to that tour so it will make much more sense.

THAT'S ALL, FOLKS.

I'm sure there are a few other things I did along the way that I'm overlooking, but if it's not popping up in my mind, then I'm sure it was insignificant. I wanted to walk through those streams of income with you just so you could really get a visual of what I mean. I break down those streams into over 30 or 40 streams of income. Honestly I stopped counting because I already feel abundantly blessed. I share that not to brag or boast but just to give you an idea of all the possible ways you can expand your brand. There are many other ways that I haven't tapped into yet, and they may come in the future. I really just want you to know that you don't have to settle for one stream of income. You can do many things and earn a purpose-based living.

Chapter 15   Building a Team

When you build your team, consider that they will be an extension of you. Your team must hold your same core values. They don't have to be just like you, but they have to believe in your vision. That in itself is very hard to find. I think most of us just settle for what we can find because we don't feel like there is better out there. I've built much of my business without a team, so I can't argue that a team is absolutely necessary to succeed. None of my celebrity coaching clients came as a result of an agent. They found my message online and reached out to me. Only two of my speaking engagements in my entire career have come from a speakers' bureau, and those were from two different bureaus.

Still, I know I'll never be able to govern everything, and I'll need support. I understand that, but I'm in no rush to get there. Currently I'm looking for a manager, and I'll list my stipulations for that manager and explain why I feel that way.

Business Manager Deal Points:

- **A percentage of all deals and bookings handled will go to a manager instead of a salary.** I have that deal point in my plan because a lot of weeks there may be nothing coming in. If I have nothing coming in, then I don't want something going out. The manager would have to budget well or have other clients in order to live. I want it that way because I don't want anyone solely dependent on me other than my wife and kids, and I don't mind if they even get jobs for outside income. In that deal point, I'm also being very generous to the manager because one day there will be millions on top of millions coming in the form of deals, and the manager will be earning a nice check from my companies.

- **A significantly higher commission on all deals and bookings brought to the table will go to the manager.** I have this point in my plan because I want to reward the manager richly for going out and hunting deals. I've built the brand on my own. Now the manager can package and sell my brand to companies for speaking or endorsement opportunities.

- **Media pitches and media materials are included in the job duties.** I put that point in my plan because I want the manager to do some work for the 5 percent of every deal that he or she will be earning. The things coming in already will continue to come in, so the manager can make a living just by answering emails and handling the deals, and no other work would be required. Well, if the manager wants to go out and pitch me, I'd want him or her to make the materials that would be pitched instead of me paying to create those materials.

- **Travel not required, but if needed it will be requested 10 to 14 days in advance. If business manager can't make it, the job status won't be affected.** I put this point in this plan because I want my manager to know that I'm not a child who needs to be followed or governed. I've come this far on my own, and I'm fine continuing to do so, so I'm not looking for "parents" the way I see some people treat their managers. I also want my manager to have the freedom to have other clients, to have a life, and to be there for their family. I miss my family a lot when I'm on the road. I don't want to do that to someone else.

- **Nondisclosure agreement.** I put this point in the plan because I want my manager to know that I don't want any of my numbers disclosed. None of my deals, speaking engagements, or anything can be shared with anyone.

- **Non-compete clause.** By this I don't mean that my manager can't have other clients because I encourage that. This means that none of the deals or speaking engagements I turn down can be given to any of their clients unless my company is paid a finder's fee of 25 percent.

- **Termination by either party should come with a 30-day notice in writing.** I put this point in because I don't want either of us to be blindsided if one of us decides to go in a different direction. I understand that people grow out of positions, and I'm 100 percent fine with that. I put this point in the plan to be courteous.

- **All leads will come through booktony@tonygaskins.com and then be forwarded to the business manager, unless the lead comes directly from the business manager.** I put this point in there because I plan to never have my booking inquiries go elsewhere first. I've known managers to ignore certain emails, accidentally miss emails, or give certain leads to another client without ever notifying the client that it came in. I see public figures put their manager's or agent's email in their social media bios all the time. I've been the one emailing those addresses and not getting a response on serious offers, so I don't want that to happen in my company. I have a family to feed. Most managers don't like this because then they feel like they are being parented or watched too closely. I understand that, but this is how it's going to be in my company until I'm at a level where the process can no longer work that way.

- **Non-reference clause.** This clause means that my manager can't publicly claim me as a client on their website to get other clients inside of a four-year period. The reason I said four years is because my dad told me once that Oprah has a rule that she doesn't stamp anyone inside of four years. I'm not sure if he heard that right, but it sounded good to me. I also put that in the plan because in the past I've brought on a staff member and the next day they would have in their bio, "Publicist or Manager to @TonyGaskins," and they hadn't done anything for me yet. I've also had people use my name and likeness on their sites without my permission to get other clients. I need to see that this person is on my team for the work, not for the glory. I don't want them to try to leverage my name to get paid by others until they've proven themselves for me. Once they've proven themselves and I see that they have integrity and longevity, then I can allow them to use me as a reference to get other clients.

- **Contract can be updated and adjusted with a 14-day notice if both parties agree.** I put this in the plan because I know things change, and adjustments may need to be made. I'm okay with making adjustments as long as it makes sense and we can see eye-to-eye. For example, the four-year rule may be a little stiff, so I may come down on that some if the manager has an amazing reason why they want to put me on their site to gain other business.

Those are my stipulations for a business manager. I may have a manager by the time you're reading this book. I have some candidates, but I haven't made a decision yet. There are other team members I'll have to find, but it's a process. To be honest, you may never find all you need in one person. I have a couple of lawyers I use because they have different strengths. I have a couple of designers I use because they have different strengths. That's why it's hard to build a salaried team as an entrepreneur because you may be committed to paying someone who can't do everything you need.

There are no guarantees when building a team, so you have to be patient, smart, and strategic.

There are qualities I'm looking for in team members that you don't see often. I want someone who is humble. Humility goes a long way. It's okay to be confident. I'm confident, but I'm not arrogant. Confidence comes from strength. Arrogance comes from insecurity. To be confident means you know who you are and what you bring to the table. To be arrogant means you have a false sense of confidence that you've built up to compensate for your insecurities, and that causes you to be mean, rude, and condescending. I want someone who is humble, not arrogant.

I want someone who is extremely hardworking. I want to have to ask my team member to slow down a little, not to pick it up a little. I want someone who beats me waking up in the morning and stays up later than me at night. The person should have ideas flowing and make it a practice to come up with an idea a day.

I want someone who isn't money hungry. Money matters, but I don't want it to be the motive or the focus. If the person can't weather the storm with me as an entrepreneur or take less than what the industry says they should get at times, then I don't want to work with them. I want someone who isn't motivated by money but by the purpose behind the work and where we're going. I will pay nicely but in due time. A person has to earn their keep with me, and I won't turn over everything right away.

I want someone who is selfless. I need team members who put others before themselves when need be and are not self-centered. You can't get much done if you're working with self-centered people who have to have it their way.

Some of those things are common sense, and they come from the heart. That's what we all want and need. It's not rocket science. But if it's common sense, then why is it so hard to find? I even struggle being that person. We want perfection sometimes, but we aren't perfect ourselves. For that very reason I believe in giving chances and helping people grow as I grow. It's even hard to find people who understand that they need to continue growing.

Build your team slowly and wisely. The wrong person can take your business under. If I told you that you could bring in millions of dollars, travel the world, rub shoulders with the bigwigs, and take your gifts to the highest heights and not have to put anyone on salary to ride your coattail, would you take the deal? I'm sure you would. To avoid that, you have to make sure the people on your team are not riding your coattail, but instead they are upgrading your wardrobe, if you get what I mean.

Remember, it all comes down to what you're building and how you're building it. How much work do you want to do? How involved do you want to be in your company? What's your product or service? All of those things matter when building your team. If you're an info marketer marketing other people's products online, then your team choices may not be as detrimental to you. But if you're an influencer or you have a very unique product, then how you choose your team is very important.

I'll tell you one other thing about team building, and this is on the spiritual side of things. The good book says God is a jealous God. To me that means He needs His glory and praise. Well, sometimes I feel like God is doing something with me so that He gets all the glory for my story. When I look at the things that have happened in my life to this point, I can almost cry. Then when I realize that a publicist or an agent did none of it, all I can do is thank God. I say to myself—*I don't have a college degree, I don't have rich parents, I don't have a business mentor, I don't have a team, so how did this happen? How did I speak on three continents and over 10 different countries? How did I become a speaker for the NBA, the NFL, and the NCAA? How did I coach so many celebrities? How did I build a seven-figure brand? How did I create so many books and courses?* When I think about those things, all I can do is thank God. So just maybe, just maybe, you could be being set up for a massive testimony that shows the world that their team must be God. While working alone I have six-figure deals just coming into my booking email from my website. I ask the companies how they found me, and they say their talent scout department found me on social media. I then say—*God, are you messing with me? Are you doing this*

because you want me to spread your name around the globe?
Well, that must be the case because the way this is happening is
blowing my mind! One time I had a major agent with one of the
Big Three agencies in the world. He sent me on meetings with
about 12 production companies, and not one company could
give me a show or even put me on an episode of one of their
existing shows. Then through my LinkedIn, Twitter, and website
I get put on 15 different television episodes across five different
shows, and I didn't have to split the money with anyone. That
blew my mind. I want you to understand that sometimes things
just happen a certain way for reasons beyond our understanding.
If you know what you're looking for in a partner and/or team
members and you can't seem to find it, just keep plugging away.
Don't settle for mediocre people if you aren't a mediocre person.
Don't give in to the hype around having a team if you just can't
seem to find what you're looking for. Keep getting your hands
dirty and stay focused on the work.

No one knows your product and your brand better than you.
So build the team around you and take your time doing it. It will
happen when it's supposed to happen. You can't rush the
process, or you'll ruin the product.

Chapter 16 Learning and Teaching

I've had some success, but it's all relative. My success to some guys is nothing, but to people who come from where I come from and want to do what I'm doing, it's massive success. It also depends on age. I'm not as successful or as known as some people who do what I do, but I'm 32 years old right now. The people who are better known and have more reach have 10 to 30 years of experience over me. Some of them have been doing this longer than I've been living. I'm a firm believer in the mantra that as you learn you should teach. If I learn something today, then in my mind I'm qualified to teach it tomorrow. It's always okay to be the one-eyed king in the land of the blind. If you know something the person next to you doesn't know, then teach them. You can sell some knowledge, and you can give some knowledge. There's a balance that has to be found. I help those who are helping themselves. If there is a really big lesson a person needs to get and I have a course on it, I'll tell them to take my course and then we can talk. If I realize that a person has put in a lot of work already, then I may give them the course for free as a reward for investing in themselves. I've been given help along the way, so I have to give help too.

You can teach for a living, or you can teach just for giving. I do a little of both. A lot of people ask me if I can mentor them, and it's always hard to choose who to mentor. Will you mentor me? Once that meant that a person wanted to learn from you, then go out and implement what they've learned and thank you for all your help along the way. Then I started to notice that the meaning started to change. It started to mean let me use your name to get to where I'm going and then act like I never knew you. There are guys who are reaching millions of people now with their message, and they came to me when they first started because I was doing what they wanted to do. They picked my brain, they met me in person, they copied my every move. They went on to make a name for themselves and never looked back to say thank you. I learned then that some people had a different idea of mentorship.

A lot of people abuse mentorship. I've never had a personal mentor in this business, so I didn't get the chance to abuse it. I had to learn from a distance on teleseminars, and then because I couldn't afford to pay for the whole course, I had to piece together the other half of what I learned on the free call. After being used a couple times for mentorship, I started to be pickier about who I gave my time to. You don't get any time back, so you have to invest it wisely. When people would write me, I would look into what they've done on their own. I wanted to see if they've invested in themselves. Remember, when I got some help from an investor, I had already amassed 25,000 followers on Twitter and been on *Oprah*, *Tyra*, *The 700 Club*, and a host of other smaller media. I'd written two books and become a speaker for major organizations. I didn't just roll out of bed one day with a bright idea and get an investor. In fact, because of my hard work I was able to get a few other people an investment from my investor, and they hadn't done half as much as I'd done. I guess that's just how it works. I wanted to change that and be more careful about it. I know how much you can get done before you need any help, so that's what I was looking for. I stay away from people who only have an idea but haven't taken any action. If you don't believe in it enough to get started, then why should I? I don't mentor women either. I don't have anything against women, but I'm married, and I don't want to build that type of relationship with a woman because I've seen that go wrong with people way more than once. I don't see anyone as competition because we are all unique in our own way, so I don't mind mentoring people who do exactly what I do. I'm not looking to help people who are at the very beginning of their career, because if I pull them to where I am in the climb, it would stunt their growth. There is growth in the climb, and you have to let it build those muscles. I look to help people who are in earshot of where I am on the climb. Maybe they can't reach up and touch me, but if I yell, they can hear me. I'm not looking to throw them a rope and pull them up. I want them to keep climbing just like the people at the very bottom of the mountain who are latching on. They can reach me, and we can hear one another. There is some distance between us, so they won't understand everything I tell them; but as long as they get some of the message, they'll be fine. I'm very sharp and direct with them because due to the distance between us, I don't have time to beat around the bush. I'm focused on my climb, and they are in a hurry to get a little higher as well. We don't have time to fluff around. I tell them what to do on their climb and how to do it. I tell them what to watch out for. I give them every secret I have as direct as I have it. Some of them get desperate and want me to throw them a rope and just pull them up as I climb. I let them know I can't do that because this is a different type of climb, and I can't carry their weight. We don't do this like the rock climbing in the park where one person holds the line at the bottom and releases or holds as you need them to. On this climb you have to climb by grabbing one rock at a time, and it's your hands and feet that will get you to the top. You get stronger as you climb, and you get wiser. This climb takes decades, and the mountain of life is much bigger than any mountain they'll climb for exercise and a challenge.

One thing about my mentorship is that I'll teach every tip and tool I know. I remember sitting down with a celebrity author who self-published a book. I shared every tip and tool I had. The manager and the celebrity told me I'd just done something that no one else offered to do. They told me that people don't do that. I knew that all too well. I've looked up time and time again and made eye contact with people watching me climb. They'll wave to give a slight hello, but they won't yell out a single tip of advice. I'm guessing I look like I've got it figured out or something. Some of those people I caught up to and passed. If they got confused and asked me how I got there so fast, I shared what I'd learned and kept climbing. I guess their pride wouldn't let them ask me for mentorship now that I'd passed them. It gets sad on the climb to the top sometimes.

You have to be willing to give what has been given to you. Sometimes it will be hard to identify exactly what advice you were given. Some of us come from places or from around people who didn't have any advice to give concerning the route we wanted to take. If you find the chance to help someone out, then do so. You'll meet different types of people on the climb. I'll share some of them with you.

You'll meet the talker: The talker has only climbed but so far before returning back to safe ground. The talker will climb a little while talking the head off of someone else who is determined to get to the top. The talker will claim to know more than he or she does. They've done their short climb so many times that it sounds like they have a grasp of the whole mountain. Take some advice from the talker, but know that you'll come to some parts on the climb that the talker has never seen. You have to navigate those parts a little better.

You'll meet the watcher: The watcher stands at the bottom and does not climb at all. They'll encourage you before you start your climb and yell up a couple words of motivation as long as you're within earshot of them, but they won't dare climb with you. You have to appreciate the watcher while you can; they won't be around for long either.

You'll meet the hitchhiker: This person will hop on the back of anyone willing to carry him. He'll ride you until you're too tired to keep going. He'll gladly get off so as not to seem like he's a user; but you'll see him later, as he will be right next to you on the back of someone else he convinced to carry him.

You'll meet the stone-thrower: This person will throw stones to distract you and try to knock you off your path. They'll do it in jest, but really mean it with bad intentions. You have to let the stones make you stronger. They're like training for when the real rocks start to fall. You have to learn how to dodge the stones and keep on climbing.

You'll meet the competitor/hater: This person is going to a different part of the mountain, at a different pace, and for a different reason, but he will see you as competition. He will not help you, so don't even ask. If you try to ask a question, he'll tell you to talk to his manager, but he will tell the manager not to give you a straight answer. Once you realize it's him, just keep climbing.

You'll meet the student: This person will see how you're climbing and want to learn everything you know. Be kind to this person and help them the best you can. Don't treat them the way the competitor/hater treated you. The student may actually pass you one day and be able to reach back and help you.

You'll meet the giver: The giver has climbed the mountain, and they're happy with their progress. You may catch up to them, but they'll keep going at their pace. If you need any advice, they'll give it to you. If you need a little extra water, they'll give it to you. Appreciate the giver. He may never ask you for anything, but if you get the chance to be a blessing, then please do so.

You'll meet the teacher: The teacher is satisfied with his life, but he's still pressing forward. He wants you to know that he sees you climbing hard but realizes that you don't know it all. He'll give you some great wisdom and maybe even a connection or two, but he won't do all the work for you.

Then there are your people: These people may be your family, your friends, your classmates, neighbors, or people you knew in the past. Some of them will keep their distance because they are happy for you and don't want to interrupt your climb. Some of them will keep their distance because they realize they've never done anything to help you, so they don't have the right to ask you for anything. Then there will be some who push you and encourage you because if you make it to the top, you'll make them look good too. They don't want anything. Then there will be those who want you to carry them, to give them your water, to take off your climbing boots and let them wear them, to carry their backpack, to buy them some extra supplies out of your money that you've earned because they didn't want to work for their own. They will claim your success because you're related and expect that anything you get should be theirs too. Because they are closest to you, they will weigh you down the most, distract you the most, and at times make you feel like you should just quit climbing. No matter where they stand in the way, keep going. Do what you can to help, but know that you can't help someone who doesn't want to help himself or herself.

I want to warn you: You'll meet some people who are considered **Others**. They won't fit into any one of those categories I just mentioned. Some of them will be good people, and some of them will be bad people. As you learn about who all exists on the climb, make sure you teach someone else. Mentorship is very important, and what you put into the world will come back around. I'm a firm believer that as long as the world is spinning, what goes around will come back around. You have to be very careful what you send out into the world. It's coming back full force. Make sure it's blessings.

I wish I could help more people, but there is only so much time in the day. Most people have a definition of greatness in their mind, and sometimes people just want to rub shoulders with greatness. You are great in your own way, so there will be people who just want to meet with you and get a little wisdom from you. There are people who I think are doing great things. I've reached out to some of them, and I never get a response after the first response. I think some people are afraid you'll knock them off of their spot if they teach you what they know. They don't realize there is room at the top, and we all have a different spot at the top with our name on it. I can't stand on your spot, and you can't stand on mine. If I don't make it, then my spot just goes unclaimed. Knowing that, I'm not afraid to teach what I know. I want you to reach your spot because I intend to reach mine. This book is a form of mentorship for all the people I'll never to get help one on one. Not every climb is for everyone. A lot of people will disagree with my advice in this book, but they can't refute my climb. I'm where I am for a reason, and I got here off of what I know. It's not the top, and it might not be the best spot, but I'm enjoying the climb. I'll learn more as I go, but along the way I want to teach what I know.

We all need patience. I have a mentee right now who I'm convinced will make it. I think he has the gift. He's unique in his gifting. He has a certain audience just like every speaker has a certain audience. He's desperate right now. He's balancing the dream and the job, and he's been doing so for two years. He's growing a little weary these days. He'll come to me and show me his latest work. I'll give him feedback. A couple of his speeches were so well put together with background music that they brought tears to my eyes. I tell him he has the gift, and he needs to keep pushing. I'm like the teacher on the climb. I won't do the work for him, but I'll give him advice and make a few connections along the way. He'll ask me for a shout-out on my

Facebook page, and I'll tell him no. He'll ask me to partner on a tour, and I'll say no. He'll ask me to just let him open for me at one of my stops, and I'll say no. I don't want to give him anything but time and wisdom. I also need time to see if he's going to stay the course. I want to see if he will find a wife and treat her right. I want to see what type of man he is, not just how good of a speaker he is. I couldn't care less about his speaking if I find out he's not a good man to his woman and kids. I want to invest in the person, not just the gift. Sometimes a gift can also be a curse because it can make us arrogant or complacent. The gift can stunt our growth because we get so much early praise for it that we don't feel the need to keep growing. I have to be careful what I feed when I'm giving to a mentee. I don't ever want to feed ego. I want to feed the heart, the mind, and the spirit.

There will also be people you come across who don't have the gift. The gift's not in them. They just admire your gift because of the doors it has opened, the money it has made, and the platform it has given you. They don't have the gift though. If you meet someone like this, it's not your place to tell him or her they don't have the gift. It's your place to help them discover what their gift really is. That can be hard work, but it's worth it. And always remember some people may just be attracted to the greatness in you. Don't be selfish with your greatness. If a little interaction with you will push someone closer to their own greatness, then do them that favor. I sure wish I could get a little closer to some of the greatness I see in others.

If you're the person who happens to be looking for a mentor, here's what I'll tell you. Don't focus too hard on finding a mentor. Focus on your work. Do everything you can on your own. It's okay to make mistakes. Take your time on the climb. Spend your money on yourself. Work your butt off to get more money to invest in yourself. Learn from a distance. Take their courses, read their books, go to their seminars. Learn enough from them so that when you approach them, they can see how much you've already invested. They may even already know your name because they've seen you in so many of their courses and seminars. Investing in yourself may get you recognized before you even have to ask. Be careful asking for help. Not everyone you ask for help knows how to give. Some people give gifts with a snare in them. Some people give and will hang it over your head every day for the rest of your life. Watch and learn. Don't just look at their gift; look at their life. If you can't find out enough about their life, then you haven't studied them long enough. When you find out how they live their life, you may not want their advice anymore. Learn the measure of a man. By man, I mean person. Learn what matters most, and it's not money, fame, and material success. Judge their heart. How do they treat their spouse? How do they treat their kids? How do they treat the people who can do nothing for them? Pay close attention, and you can learn all you need to know from a person sometimes without even speaking to them.

Do not beg for help. You can ask, but do not beg. You could *use* a personal mentor, but you do not *need* a personal mentor. People will tell you over and over that you need a mentor, but a mentor is not always possible to get. Understanding that, are you going to give up if you don't find someone who can mentor you? Even when you find a mentor, remember that he or she is not God. Please know that they are still making mistakes that they know nothing about. I could be totally wrong about some of my beliefs in this book, but I may not find out about them until five years from now. I'll look back and laugh. Well, if you took everything I said as gospel without testing it for yourself and thinking through it, it could cost you way more than it cost me. Trust your own knowledge too. Don't doubt yourself. You may be more gifted than the person you're seeking out to mentor you. You may end up teaching them a thing or two. The student can teach the teacher, you know. Don't ever worship a human or put a human on a pedestal. Only God deserves to be worshipped, not man. There is nothing that has been done by man that you couldn't do if you really wanted to. Always know your own power, your own worth, and your own potential. Never doubt yourself.

After you've been a student, in whatever capacity that is, then become a teacher. Teach unflinchingly. Teach the truth, your whole truth, and nothing but the truth. Don't let anything die inside of you. Make sure you teach something daily, so that on your last day you will have left everything behind you. Take nothing with you. Every student needs a teacher, even if that teacher is a distant one. If you had no physical teachers, but life was your teacher, then teach what life has taught you because you were fortunate enough to learn from the best teacher. What can you teach that another human never taught you? That's how you should teach. Don't just regurgitate the things you've heard. Dig deeper and find the lessons from life that no one ever spoke out of their mouth to you. There are a lot of quotes that I've heard from others. If I find myself typing one in this book, I delete it, and I dig deeper. I find a deeper truth, a truer truth that comes from my life experiences, and I share that. If I've said something that you've heard before, it just means that we learned from the same teacher—life. Great minds will think alike, so in your learning and in your teaching don't be surprised if you hear the same things and repeat the same things a thousand times over. Be a student, then be a teacher.

Chapter 17   The Indie Life

Most people have to start out independent, but some don't. I have never been signed exclusively to anyone, so my references to being exclusive only come from seeing my clients or colleagues. The contract for this book you're reading is my first time signing with a major publisher. I've been with other publishers, but they were still considered independent or Internet publishers. As TV talent, there are agencies you can sign with that will get you bookings and handle your bookings. I've been signed to one of the Big Three agencies, but it was only because they were trying to get me for a show. As a speaker, there are speakers' bureaus that you can let handle your bookings, and they can also bring bookings to you. I've never been signed exclusively to a bureau either. I've had a couple of non-exclusive contracts, but nothing came of them. There are also publicists who sign talent exclusively and don't allow you to work with any other publicist or agent who will bring deals to you in the same field of play. I've never signed one of those, although I've been offered some.

I've always been independent, and I can't say that I regret that decision. Could I have gotten some bigger opportunities with a major player? Yes! But the indie life isn't as bad as some may think. I've loved not having to split any of my checks. I've loved having complete say-so over all of my work. I've loved not having to wait around on anyone to pull the trigger on a project. I honestly have loved it, and I've gotten so spoiled that I don't know if I ever want to change my decision.

You have a lot to consider when you think about signing with someone in any area of your business. What can they do for you? For me, I want to be able to get this book into bookstores. As an independent author there isn't a way for me to do preorders on Barnes and Noble's website because that option isn't available to independent authors yet. You can do preorders on the Amazon Kindle, but that's not the same. With a major publisher you can do preorders all across the web, and it can help you get into stores and/or make some of the bestseller lists. You have to know what you want out of the deal.

As an independent, you can build your brand on your own terms. You can design your own plan and implement your own strategies. I'll talk about those things in this book as well. You get a chance to build to a point where you can demand more when it's time to sign. If you sign with a major company from day one, you have no leverage whatsoever. Some majors want it like that in all industries. It gives them more leverage, and they can build you and reap the benefits from every stage of your growth. There is a chance that I've had a book earn more independently than this one will earn me with a major publisher. If that is the case, then I'm fortunate to have gotten the opportunity to do that. This book will have perks of its own, and it'll bring a different level of credibility and put me in a different circle of influence. The trade-off may be worth it. I've seen some people sign with a major in different industries and love it, and I've seen some hate it. I think it comes down to you as the talent. If you have the talent, then you can eat either way. If you don't have the talent, you'll flop either way. What you get out of it may depend on you. The worst thing about signing too early from what I've seen is that you don't get to build from your blueprint. You get with the bigwigs and the professionals who feel they know what's better for you than you do. I watched that happen to one of my clients. She was an amazing raw talent. She signed a record deal with a major label, and they put her in the studio with some legends; and they went away from what caught their attention to begin with. She has a beautiful and soulful voice, but they watered her vocals down, and she sounded just like any ole singer. It was a disaster, and after a couple failed singles, they released her. It was their fault, not hers. She did her part, and I think in her heart she knew what was best for her; but she had to follow the direction of the so-called experts.

If you're independent long enough, then you get to do enough work to show the majors what you're good at and what you're not good at. You get to pad your stat sheet and stack your numbers. Then you can go to the table with some data backing what you already know about yourself. Numbers don't lie, so if there is proof in the pudding, then you'll have more leverage at the deal table. I've seen it play out many ways. The bottom line is—you have to be willing to walk. You have to know what you know and know what you will and won't do. Don't compromise your value, your morals, or your beliefs. I have another client who is a singer. She signed with majors across the board, but she's very headstrong. She knows what she wants to do with her career, and she won't let anyone tell her differently. Because of her personality, she's a good fit for brands and television. Everything is working out for her, and she's brought in millions in just a short time. One deal falls through with one major, and another picks her up almost immediately, whereas my other client was dropped and not signed again.

I'll paint a couple pictures for you of two guys in the same industry, so you can get a picture of what I mean about the indie life versus the majors.

Guy A: He's independent. He's talented, and he knows what he wants. He's just as good as anyone with a major behind them, but he doesn't have the connections to the majors. He's rough around the edges, and he rubs the majors the wrong way. He starts building anyway. He builds organically, and the people love him. He becomes an overnight celebrity, and you can't tell the difference between him and those with the majors backing them. He gets endorsement deals, he gets TV appearances, he travels the world working, and he pockets all of his money. He has the gift. The majors can't tell that he's not with another major; they just know he's not with them. He earns hundreds of thousands a year and he only has to pay Uncle Sam. He meets with some majors, but he's asking for too much because he knows what he's worth. The majors keep moving, and they go sign Guy B. Guy A keeps going, and the people keep him afloat. The people build his brand so large that he's being seen more and earning more than the guys signed to the majors.

Guy B: He stumbled into the industry while looking for something fun to do. He has the look. He has the voice. He has the smarts. The people don't gravitate toward him as much because they can tell something is off. He's the replica of Guy A, but not as naturally gifted. He can mimic Guy A close enough to look like the real deal to the majors. The majors come to him and instead of asking the majors what can they do for him like Guy A, Guy B asks the majors what can he do for them. They tell him what he can do, and they sign him before he's even built a true following. They use their connections, and they put him in magazines; they give him one season of a reality show; they get him a book deal with a Top 5 publisher. They pitch him as the real deal to the public, and because of his affiliations, the public tries to buy into it. His following grows because of his placements. He makes hundreds of thousands as well, but he has to give up about 50 percent of it after everyone gets their cut. He's made his runs through the media, and now the majors are done with him; and the people still haven't bought into him. He is hanging on and still able to pull in some money, but he's on his way back to the indie life to start from the bottom and try to build his way to the top.

If you look at both examples, which are real-life examples, you have to determine which person you are. If you're truly talented and you know your worth, then take your time. If the majors want you in the beginning, then they'll want you in three to five years after you have the world behind you. If you know that you're not that talented, but it's a cool gig you fell into, then let the majors carry you. They'll make you seem larger than life, and you just might get good along the ride and have some longevity. You'll make way more money than you would as an independent because of the connections you'll have. Even when the majors are done with you, you could bounce around and keep collecting checks for years to come. If you're Guy A, then you have all the power. You can make a huge impact and earn a killing because you're not giving up any of your money. Imagine being Guy B and having to pay an agent, a manager, a lawyer, and a publisher, then Uncle Sam. By the time you've finished paying, you feel like you've given more than you've pocketed. Depending on what you wanted out of the deal though, it could still feel like a lot of money.

If you couldn't tell, I was Guy A. I'm still him. I'm a black man, I'm young, and I'm country. Being a life coach and in the lane of experts and gurus, it's a tough sell if you're under the age of 40. If I had been an athlete, rapper, comedian, or something like that, it would be a totally different story. Whenever I met with majors, they would say, "But you're so young, who will believe that you know what you're talking about?" The general public, though, they don't really care as long as they can tell you're real. My following saw me teach live on YouTube and Facebook and in person, so they know you can't fake that. They follow all the other speakers and life coaches too, so they know I'm not copying anyone. I have my own style. The people take care of me. The people buy my products, come to my seminars, hire me for coaching, and book me to speak. By them doing that, it attracted some major brands to come and partner with me. Those deals are in the works now. I had to take a different route and prove as an independent that I'm worth it. Even dealing with a publisher, it's the numbers that sealed the deal. There are a lot of young men who claim to know what I know, but what's behind them to prove it? Even if a publisher or a brand hasn't heard me speak or teach, they can see the numbers and the interactions online. They deal with people, so they know that people aren't stupid. People don't spend their hard-earned money on fake people. The numbers speak for themselves, so as an independent you have to get the people. I remember a comedian told me that. It might sound weird, but I used to have three-way calls with these two guys. I won't say their names just in case they don't want anyone to know. One of them is a major radio host right now, and the other is a pretty famous comedian. They saw the hype on Twitter back in the day, and they just didn't believe I was authentic. They thought I was a hustler and a con artist. Of course, they had women telling them that, and all the guys thought that. Coming from where we are from, we just didn't trust other black people who claim to be all positive and uplifting. The struggle was too real to be that motivational. They didn't buy what I was selling, and I couldn't argue with them. I let them have their opinions because I knew that time would tell. The comedian was like me. He didn't know it, but he was the comedian version of me. He was Guy A. Well, in his world Guy B is with the majors and way bigger than him. He's catching up and will eventually surpass Guy B, but it's taking longer because the people have to elevate him because he didn't have the voice and the language and the book smarts that Guy B had, but he's more naturally gifted. Well, the comedian used to tell me all the time, "You need the people! Just get the people behind you and everything else will take care of itself!" I would say, "I hear you, man." There was another comedian who looked up to him, and I mentored that other comedian because he was younger than me. Both of them blew up before me because they are comedians. The world will allow you to make them laugh before they allow you to make them think and feel bad about the choices they're making. They are intelligent guys, but they delivered their intelligence differently. Because they delivered it behind jokes, a lot of times their messages fell on deaf ears, or the people didn't know whether they were serious or not. I just dropped the truth raw and uncut without pulling any punches. I scared a lot of people off, so I knew it would take longer for me to build. Now those guys are all with majors, and I'm still independent except for this publisher. It's a slow grind for me because of the lane I'm in. As a comedian and radio host, it's about time to hang it up at 50 years old. For a life coach, author, and speaker you're just starting to get accepted at 50. I'm sure those guys will transition into more acting, writing books, and speaking.

I said all that to say, you have to get the people. You also have to understand your lane and your timeline. If your industry peaks early, then you have to sign with a major quick. If your industry peaks later, then you have time to get the people behind you and come to the table with more leverage. As a successful independent you can go to the table and throw out an insane dream number to a major. If they don't want to accept it, then you can keep walking because you know you'll earn that amount from what you've built anyway. Our world is changing very fast. There was a time when you couldn't be an author unless you had a publisher. Now there are some self-published authors who are just as respected as authors with a traditional publisher. I know independent authors who are being paid the same amount of money to speak to corporations as the authors with major publishing deals. You have to know yourself and what you bring to the table. Know your strengths. Know your weaknesses, and be honest about it.

There are different deals depending on which industry you're signing in. With a book publisher I can't sign a non-exclusive deal because I can only promote one book at a time anyway, so it wouldn't make sense to ask for a non-exclusive deal. Also with a publisher, you can sign a one-book deal, and they may want a first right of refusal for your next book in that same genre. That's fair, because if you can't come to terms on the second book, you can walk. With your talent and their muscle, if the first book does well, then you'd better get a little more respect on the second book.

When it comes to publicists, the deal's also tricky because you don't want two people writing the same media outlets on your behalf. It's hard to find a publicist with strong contacts across the board, so what I recommend is to ask the publicist what solid pitch they can guarantee. Have the one publicist pitch their strong leads and the other do their strong leads if they have different connections. That way you can still get the best of both worlds. If you've built a strong following and you'll be paying a retainer, then you have the power. If you're not paying a retainer, then you've lost a little leverage, and you may have to sign an exclusive deal to let one publicist work their contacts. You can just limit the contract to a certain amount of time so that if they aren't bringing anything to the table, you're free to go.

As an independent, what I love is non-exclusive contracts. I want people to only get a cut of what they bring to the table. For the life of me, I can't imagine giving someone a cut of something they didn't generate. It just makes no sense at all to me. I've never done it, and I never will, unless they are bringing a whole lot of other stuff to the table.

Don't be desperate! You can package and pitch yourself to an agent, manager, or whomever, and you could end up being shelved for the best years of your career. You will sign and think you've made it and that the work will be done for you, and they'll be thinking you're going to keep working and building your own buzz and then they can get a cut of what you've drummed up. You'll be waiting on each other, and you'll miss some prime time action. If you build your brand, they will come to you eventually. If they never come, it just means you'll never need them. One day you'll get to a point where a deal comes that's so amazing that you have no idea what to ask for. At that time, you'll realize that you need an agent to let you know what the market says you're worth. You can sign with an agent then because the 10 percent you'll be giving the agent won't matter to you because you'll be getting way more than you knew you could get. That just happened to me, and I asked an agent what the deal was worth. I didn't have a deal with the agent, but I still sent them a cut just for giving me the advice. I actually got paid more than what the agent said it was worth, but if I had not asked, I would have probably accepted about 15 percent of what I ended up getting paid because I had no idea what the deal was really worth. You'll know when the time is right, and that's when you should make a move. I tried to force a major publisher, major agent, and major speakers' bureau to sign me very early, but now I'm thanking God that none of them did. It has worked out far more in my favor this way.

Let some people laugh at you now, and you'll have the last laugh later. If you know what you're building, then that's all that matters. Some people won't understand, and they'll look down on you because you're independent; but when their deals have run their course and yours is just getting started and you're getting way more than they ever got, it'll be worth it. The journey is all about enjoying the process and being patient while you're making the journey. Everything happens when it's supposed to.

Chapter 18   15 Minutes of Fame

I plan on having way more than 15 minutes of relevance, as should you. Too many people are trying to get their 15 minutes of fame without seeking to make a difference. I remember when I started out I wanted to be famous because I was broke. I thought being famous would make me rich. I was pitching myself left and right. I remember when I got on the local news as a featured guest. They would do a segment about a local hero. I saw the producer's email somewhere and thought I'd send in an email. I had a BlackBerry at the time with a weird email address. I emailed the producer with a fake name and said:

> Hey, I'm just writing you to let you know that I really would like to see some positive images of young black men on the news. There is so much negativity on the news and anytime you see a black man he's robbing

someone. You could even interview that young Author from the University of South Florida. I just read his book and it was pretty good. That would be some positive news for a change.

The producer emailed right back and said:

That's great to hear. Would you happen to know his name and how I could get in touch with him?

Then I emailed back and said:
Well, his name is Tony Gaskins and the only contact I have for him is what I found in the back of his book, tagaskin@mail.usf.edu *(or something like that)*
Then the producer wrote back and said:

Thank you very much for the tip and we will get in touch with him.

It wasn't long after that I received an email from the producer. She told me she'd heard great things about my book, and she'd love to interview me for their local hero segment on the news. I was so excited. Still, I worried she would find out that the pitch came from me. I felt so bad about it, but then I told another author, and she told me that she used to do the same thing. She actually had a better story of how she would call the bookstore in different voices and ask if they had 20 copies of her book. She said that got her book in bookstores all over. At least that showed me I wasn't crazy. I was normal, and we all want our shine. Still, my heart wasn't in the right place. Those 15 minutes of fame can make you or break you, depending on how you get them.

I often mention going on *Oprah*, but it didn't really do anything for me. It set me free because I told a story from my past that no one knew about, but as far as publicity, it didn't do anything for my career. She didn't promote my book or my business. I wasn't paid for the appearance, so no money came from it. I went on *Tyra Banks* right after, and she showed my book to the world, and my royalty statement later showed that I sold 70 books in that quarter. I was floored. Seventy books after all that work to get on TV? Is this what people are dying to see happen for their book? There were publicists who wanted to be paid $10,000 a month to get you on major shows like that. Instead of paying a fee, I pitched myself every day. I crafted catch pitches on a daily basis. I got so good at it that I started charging $150 a month to do pitches for other people. I found out the hard way that you can do all that work or spend all that money and still nothing may come from it.

With *The Tyra Banks Show*, I was pitching so much that the producers knew me by my first name. They would call me like we went to high school together: "Hey Tony, we have a show coming up and wanted to see if you wanted to be on it." The show ideas were so off base and crazy I couldn't believe they were calling me for it. I think they thought I just wanted to be famous. I did, but not the type of famous they had in mind. The ideas were so far-fetched sometimes that all I would hear was, "Yeah, so this show will be circus monkeys jumping up and down screaming 'I just want to be famous!'" That picture would be in my head after hearing the show ideas. I had to turn them down over and over again. Then finally they invited me as a guest expert with my book in hand after they saw me tell a portion of my story to Oprah. After I did *Oprah* and *Tyra*, I then pitched myself to TBN. I decided to pitch a different part of my story. To *Oprah* and *Tyra* I pitched the toxic lover side of my story. To TBN I pitched the ex-drug dealer side of my story. By saying I'd been on *Oprah* and *Tyra* already I got a call back immediately. They flew from Virginia to my apartment in Florida to film my story. I believe they called it "The Preacher's Son." I just wanted to tell my story. I wanted to turn my mess into my message. I knew it would be my story that would separate me from everyone else. All we have is our unique story, and that's one surefire way to be different from everyone else.

After I pitched to the major shows, I then pitched myself to the local news again. I was really running these stories into the ground. I had a plan though. I wanted my story to be told so I could show people how I had changed my life. Christ was at the center of the change, but I also wanted to teach the actual steps I took to change. I knew that a lot of people needed to change and a lot of people had loved ones who they wanted to help change. I wanted to be a change agent, a catalyst, a life coach, or whatever you wanted to call me. I had a burning desire to help people and to use the wisdom God had given me through all my mistakes in life. I remember my high school put a page up on the website about me. They thought I was going to have a real 15 minutes of fame. They had no idea I made all those mistakes after high school, so when *Oprah* aired, they saw it was really 15 minutes of shame. They took that page down so fast. I asked a little while later if I could come in to speak to the students about the mistakes I made. They wrote me back and told me the students needed to focus on their test coming up so they'd pass. I was hurt. I saw that some people would turn their back on you when you took your skeletons out of the closet. But how bad do you want to help? If you pretend to be perfect or like a knight in shining armor, then you can't help anyone out of their mess. You have to show you had a mess too. I was all out in the open, and I wasn't ashamed of my story anymore. It all came full circle. Last year, I was asked to be the commencement speaker at my high school's graduation. It's all how you handle your 15 minutes of fame or your 15 minutes of shame. If you do enough good deeds, then eventually people will forget the fool you made of yourself or the mistakes you made in the past. We can all make up for our mistakes most of the time.

If you're chasing your 15 minutes of fame, make sure you choose them wisely. Don't take anything that's just handed to you. There may be an opportunity that allows you to expose your mistakes; if you know your mistakes are forgivable and you want to help others, then share it. If you feel it will do more harm than good, then choose another outlet. They say all publicity is good publicity—but that's not true. We see people make a fool of themselves every day and never come back from it. Be smart about your 15 minutes and even if it hurts you in the moment, if you know your heart is in the right place, then keep doing good and it will turn around in your favor.

I went from telling about my shortcomings in relationships to being on TV coaching celebrities on their relationships. I confessed my mistakes in a book then on national TV. I did it so that I could teach from my mistakes and not come off as a person who was trying to appear to be perfect. Some people judged me and questioned how I could give advice if I used to be a terrible lover. Others realized that I was the best person to give advice because I knew what went wrong and I had found out how to do it right. I shared that advice every day online, and celebrities started to see my name. They would read all of my tweets as if they were a book, and then I'd get a direct message from them asking if we could talk on the phone. I'd get on the phone, and I started coaching celebs and everyday people like myself. My 15 minutes of fame changed. It went from 15 minutes of shame to an actual 15 minutes of fame. I went from the valley to the mountaintop, from the sinner to the servant-leader. It's crazy how things can turn around for you if your heart is in the right place. It's very important that your motives are pure. If you're doing it for the wrong reasons, you will get exposed and you will be let down. Be prepared for a marathon, not a sprint. If you think you're going to get on a reality TV show and then be a household name the next day, you've got another thing coming. I remember meeting a client at the airport once. She'd been on TV every week for a year straight, and no one recognized her at the airport. I told her I thought she'd be having to take pictures and sign autographs and stuff, but she said, "No, my show has a certain demographic, and these people in this airport don't watch my show." For some reason I thought being on TV and having millions of viewers would just automatically make anyone a household name, but that's not the case. You have to keep working. There are many people who have been on TV for seasons and once their show is done, they fade into the background as if no one ever knew them.

I got there, and I'm sure you can get there too; you just have to have realistic expectations of what's to come after your 15 minutes of fame. It's not about the flash in the pan; it's about the slow simmer after that. If you flash and then disappear, that will be it. If you make a flash and then you keep cooking, eventually people will take notice and more opportunities will come. It's all about how you capitalize on your opportunities. Don't ever do one thing and think that one thing will carry you forever. You constantly have to be creating and innovating, whether that's new material or new products. You have to keep working.

It's about turning 15 minutes into an hour. You have to be able to prove and keep on proving that you've got the goods. You can't be a one-hit wonder. You have to make an album of hits to have longevity in the game. People are being so bombarded with 15-minute celebrities that they are becoming numb to it. We all know that after the 15 minutes, the next thing we will be sold is a book, a T-shirt, a concert, a seminar, a course, or something else. Knowing that, people have to support the ones who look like the real deal.

Start preparing for your 15 minutes now. Make your hour plan. Map out how you plan to spread your name and keep spreading your name. It doesn't have to be a complex plan. As long as it's genuine and there's consistency involved, then I believe you can reach any goal you set for yourself. People who are not called to be influencers or world-changers stall out. They run out of gas, and they start to hitch their wagons onto the backs of others. You have to make sure that you can always look within and find your motivation. You have to stay motivated no matter what obstacles are in front of you. There is a path to the top, but everyone has their own map. You have to follow your map and trust your inner guide. You can't be sucked into the traps of the world. You can't give in to the easy way out. You can't sell yourself short and try to take shortcuts. Remember, if you take shortcuts, you will get cut short.

There are people who have gone before you and turned their 15 minutes into lifelong careers. If it can be done once, then it can be done again. You want to have influence, and you want to have an impact. There are different levels to influence. You don't always have to be at the top of the mountain to have influence. You can be in the climb and still be influential. Get ready for your moment and have a plan for what you'll do with it. In our Internet age, we see people go viral every day. You can tell the people who planned for it and the people who got lucky. The people who planned for it turn a viral video into a career. They roll out their plan that they've dreamed about for years. We see those who got lucky until their video is played out and then we don't hear from them anymore.

You have to plan for success. You have to prepare for success. And you have to be ready when you meet success. It will knock, but it won't wait too long for you to answer the door. Get ready for your moment. Seek out, not just your 15 minutes, but instead a way to become world renowned, by working hard and being consistent in your pursuit of greatness.

Chapter 19 Designing Your Own Plan

We all need a plan, right? Well, who do you go to for your plan? Why not trust yourself? There are geniuses in the world for sure. Many people have great plans. Some people are paid to be strategic planners. There are mastermind groups. There are teams. There are mentors, consultants, life coaches, online gurus—you name it and they're out there. We can go to a million and one sources to get a plan made. But I believe that there is no better plan than your own. No one knows you better than you. Yes, you may need some tweaking to your plan. You could also get a little advice, but no matter what you add into your plan, you should understand it. I've heard that if you're the smartest person in your circle, then you're in the wrong circle. Well, guess what? You're always the smartest person in the circle, no matter what circle you're in. You can be in a circle with Mark Zuckerberg, Bill Gates, and Warren Buffett, and although those are very smart guys, you'd still be the smartest person in the circle. No one knows you better than you. Mark knows what's best for Mark, not Bill. Bill knows what's best for Bill, not Mark. Sure they can pitch ideas around and advise one another, but at the end of the day each person will have to make the decision for themselves. You'll always be the smartest in the circle; they just may be smarter in other areas. No one is smarter than you when it comes to you, and you can't ever forget that. I understand what they mean by having smart people in your circle though, but I believe most people have taken it the wrong way. Most people picture that as having geniuses around us while we're just sitting there twiddling our thumbs and letting them call all the shots for our life. That's what a lot of people do with their accountants, lawyers, agents, and so on. That's why you see a lot of people go broke or leave this world early. They stopped calling the shots, and other people drove them insane or to the poor house. I saw this happen over and over, but I made a decision to go about it differently for a few reasons. If you don't design your own plan, then you will always need someone else to implement your strategy. If you always have to depend on someone else, then you can never truly be independent. If you don't understand what's going on, then someone can tell you anything and you'd believe it. There will be some things you might miss and some things might not run as smoothly as others right away, but you'll have time to catch up and to grow. Things will become simpler over time, and you'll be able to advance down the line.

When I started my online courses, I needed a system that made sense to me. In my circle I wasn't privy to the guys who could build the fancy sites. I didn't know anyone who knew how to integrate my email list with my shopping cart, so that anyone who buys my course would automatically be added to a list. I lost all my emails that way. Did I let that stop me? No! I just made the system make sense to me, and I did it the best way

I knew how. I had a graphic made for the course. I wrote the copy for the course, so it would be in my voice. Then I logged into PayPal and created a button. I then took the code or the link and sent it to my designer and asked him to put it on the site under the copy. When someone buys my course, I get an email from PayPal letting me know. I'd go in and email the person to let them know their payment was received, and they'd been added to the course roster. I'd then copy and paste their email to a note in my phone. After the registration closed, I'd go in my phone and copy and paste all the emails into the bcc section of an email, and I'd email everyone the call-in information for the course. Then I'd call in on the night of the class and teach the course. If someone had an issue, they would reply to the email address where they received the call information. When I saw the email, I'd respond as my assistant with their answer. If a class had to be cancelled, then I'd go to the note in my phone with all the emails, copy and paste them into the bcc section of an email, and send the updated call time. It was more work for sure! It took more time for sure, but it made sense to me. I didn't know how to create the fancy systems the other guys had because where I come from people don't code. My designers were all self-taught designers. They didn't take a class or go to school for it. The guys I knew had never seen an email list or worked with one. We were all self-taught. I'm self-taught, so we made the system make sense to us. Then I'd meet a guy who looked like me and said he knew how to do it the easier way, but he'd want 50 percent of my business, so I decided to do it my way, the hard way.

It didn't make a difference to the customer how smooth the system was. I never once got a complaint. Well, one time someone asked for a refund because the email I sent to let them know they were added to the class had a few typos in it. That was my fault for rushing, so I had to eat that one. Other than that, I'm guessing the email felt like a personal touch because it wasn't automated. I'm sure they didn't think I was sending the email myself. I really didn't care as long as I had a system that I could manage and I was making a living doing what I love. Coming from my background it's hard to trust people. I figured that if I met someone who knew how to integrate the system, they probably would know how to hack my system too. Or they'd just steal all my emails and be selling the list to info marketers or sending email blasts of their own on the side. I just didn't want someone all in my business like that. So I did it my way, and it made sense. One thing I've never been fond of is needing someone. If I want to do it, I need to learn how to do it or have a one-off job done. I would get calls from clients saying they couldn't reach their web guy and they can't update their site. I hate that. For that reason, I own my domain, and I keep it on my server. That way if something happens, I can hire another designer to build another site and redirect it. I had to create systems that make sense to me. It's slow. It's backward to some people, but it works. I look at some people's systems and I'm blown away by how beautiful they are. I wish I had a system that seamless and beautiful, but I don't know those people. So do I stop, or do I find a way around it? I find a way around it. There is always a way, and you have to make it. You can't get stuck and sit idle because you don't know the right people to make something happen.

The same thing happened when it was time to do my book preorders. My books would cost me about $1,100 to produce. As an independent author there wasn't a way to do preorders on the major outlets, so what I did is make it look fancy and do preorders for signed copies. I'd get a graphic made, write some copy, create the PayPal button, and then start promoting. I'd sell a couple hundred books upfront. Those 200 books would earn me $5,000, so now I'd made my money back on the book before it was released online and also a little profit. Then the hard part came. I'd have to order those 200-plus books to come to my house, and I'd have to go through every order and get the name so I could sign each book. Then I had to go to Staples and buy 200-plus mailing envelopes and write the address on every envelope because I didn't know how to print address labels. Then I'd have to go to the post office and ship all 200-plus books. There I'd see all the eBay shippers with their fancy white shipping packages and their neatly printed address labels taped on all nicely, and they had prepaid postage on the packages because they had a scale system and postage system at their house. I didn't know anything about any of that stuff and didn't feel like learning, so I did it the way that made sense to me. It was harder, it took longer, but it was worth it. I was living the dream.

Next came the tours. I've told you about the tours, but I'm going to tell you again. I didn't know how to make a sponsorship packet or how to get sponsors. I met a lady who said she knew how to arrange tours, but she wanted to charge $8,000 to teach me. For $8,000 she would have owed me a kidney or something. My partner said he would pay for her services, but I didn't want to waste his money like that, so I passed on the $8,000 lesson. Her information was from the golden age anyway, so I knew that it was much harder today than when she did it. I tried to do it, but no one wanted to sponsor me. Why? I don't know, but maybe you have a clue or two about why. I wasn't going to let that stop me. I'd take my Bank of America business card, and I'd use that to book the venue. I'd find the venue by typing "event halls in Atlanta" on Google and then hitting the images tab. I'd look through the pictures until I saw one I liked. I'd click on it, and it would take me to the events and meetings page of the hotel's website. I'd fill out the form and get a response within 24 hours. I learned after a few events that they give you the room for whatever you tell them your budget is unless it's a really fancy hotel or really small hotel or a racist area. I would say $500 to $1,500, and they wouldn't ask any questions and give me the room. I'd put my card on the credit card authorization form because back then the Bank of America business card would let companies place an authorization on the card without actually withdrawing any money from the account. The account would have a balance of like $0.21 because I was balling on a budget. As soon as the hotel signed the contract, before the ink would dry, I would be online promoting the event in order to get some sales. I would get some sales in and transfer the money from PayPal right to my bank account to cover the cost of the room. Then I'd go to the city and staff the event with a few of my guests. I'd tell the hotel I don't need anything in the room but the free water and mints, some chairs, a microphone, and a small stage. They would be upset that I didn't want any food and beverages. I was creating my own plan and making it work for me. Because I didn't have any decorations, no host, no opening speaker, and nothing fancy, all my guests had was my message. My message had nothing to compete with it and that would make it go over way better than it actually was. Then instead of being stuck up and rushing out of the building, I would stay back and sign every book and take every picture even if it took me two or more hours. That was my strategy, and it worked.

I went against the grain, and I did things my way. I earned a great living, and I was doing what I love. It made sense to me. I didn't have to depend on anyone other than my designer. I work so fast and hard that my designers are always reliable because I create so much stuff that they end up being paid what seems like a salary because I'm spending like $400/week with them. If one designer gets too busy, then I realize he's outgrown the job, and I let him go and bring on someone new and put them on the same plan. Then I alternate as I need to.

I shared that with you, as bad as it hurt to be honest, because I wanted you to see how I did it. I want you to know that if you don't have all the tools and all the connections, you can do it your way, and it still can work. I'll upgrade my strategies eventually, but even then it will still have to make sense to me. I'll have to be able to start and stop it. I don't want to have to depend on any single individual to operate my business. Right now I'm trying to start a podcast, but it's too technical for me, so I'm researching and looking for consultants, but no one wants to come in and teach me how to use the recording software and how to set up my system because they want me to need them. I'd rather do the work, so what I'll probably end up doing is paying to take someone's course. The scary thing about that is these info guys online don't teach courses the way I do. They overcomplicate everything and make their little online course feel like you're going to Harvard School of Business, and it's ridiculous. They want to appear as though they are giving you a lot for the money. What they don't realize is they are actually doing too much and demoralizing you instead of motivating you. I decided to take Albert Einstein's advice and get my products to the point that I could explain them to a 6-year-old, the simpler the better. Einstein said: *Make it simple as possible but not one bit simpler.*

Design your own plan. Tweak it as you grow and learn more. Don't get ahead of yourself. Don't let an info guy take you deep-sea diving if you haven't even learned how to snorkel. Many people will want you to need them, but you have to show them that you don't need them until you need them. Don't rush to get to the expert level. There are levels to business. I see some beautiful systems online, but most of those guys have been doing it for decades and met great people along the way. They didn't start at that level. I'm okay with the process. I'm learning as I'm going and when I get there, it will have been worth it.

I'm taking a step up in creating TonyGaskinsAcademy.com. This site is costing me tens of thousands. We will see if it's worth it. Sometimes people just put a sticker price on something because they can, and they know you don't know any better. It may not be worth what you're paying. I'm paying a lot of money, and the media techs are telling me that my students' names and their email info won't be able to be added to an email list in this first phase. So I'm guessing that's pretty hard to do. Or are they just making it hard in order to get more money out of me? I'm taking a chance, and this could work beautifully or be an expensive lesson that I'll be writing about in another book. This site will be a site where students can buy the course and be able to automatically start watching the videos after they pay for the course. Then there will eventually be an app to match it. It's costly, but it's the next level for me. I'll still teach live courses, but this will be something that anyone can take at any time and not have to worry about me knowing they are taking my course or have to worry about being available for a live session. If the media techs can't deliver what they say they can, then I'll learn that later.

A couple years ago, a guy sold me on search engine optimization (SEO). He told me that he charges companies $30,000/month, but it has made them millions. He told me to give him 90 days, and I'd be making so much money that the $5,000/month I was paying him wouldn't be felt. I knew nothing about SEO and how it works. I googled SEO and found out how it kind of works, but I still didn't fully understand. Here I was with someone in my circle who was smarter than me, smarter in the wrong way. My partner agreed to the SEO, so I went through with it this time. We paid $5,000/month for three months. On the third month, nothing had changed. The guy tells me that my metadata was never added. He said he told my web guy to add it and never thought to check back to see if it was done. So on day 90 he tells me that something that was supposed to be done on day one wasn't done and that we would have to start all over. I really wanted to do life in prison for homicide at that moment. I'm still getting over it to this day. I had to prove I was a real Christian then. Now here comes the kicker: I get an email from a guy in India telling me he can do SEO for my site. I ask him what he charges, and he says $200/month. I fell out. At that point I couldn't even afford $200/month; I could but I didn't want to. I asked him to do it for $40/month, and he agreed. The guy did it and sent me a report every Friday with all the work he'd done. The SEO actually worked, and I only paid $40/month. People started writing in for coaching and said they found me because my site came up when they searched "life coach" in Google. After I got enough business from the SEO, I stopped doing it.

I didn't want that much business. I just wanted to see if it really worked. I lost $15,000 to a guy who gave me a strategy that I knew nothing about. He wouldn't give me a refund either. He told me that my site was built all wrong and that he'd rebuild it for free so the SEO would work properly. I'm sure his plan was to rebuild my site and have complete access to it, and then if I decided to stop paying him $5,000/month, he would have control of my site. I also believe that the Indian man who contacted me was probably a rogue worker he uses to do the SEO. He's charging me $5,000/month and paying the Indian guy pennies on the dollar.

From that scam forward, I decided to never implement anything in my business that I didn't fully understand. Also if it sounds legit but I still don't understand it, I don't pay more than I'm willing to lose. The most I'm willing to lose is $100/month. So that guy got me for $4,900/month, and I may never live it down.

I've said all that to say—it is imperative that you design your own plan. Be in the driver seat of your company. Be the smartest in your circle, but have people who are smart in their areas. If it doesn't make sense to you, don't do it. If you feel you need to do it, then get enough information so that it makes sense to you. Find someone who knows it well enough to explain it to a 6-year-old, and let them explain it to you. If it still doesn't make sense, then it may be time to run. There are a lot of smart crooks in the world. When you're building a brand from the ground up, you have to be very careful with who you trust. You can't just let anyone come in and run your business. Be very skeptical. Take your time and watch their patterns. People who know what they bring to the table won't beg you for a seat. They'll tell you what they can offer and leave it up to you to invite them. If a person is too desperate, then that's a sign they may have a leg up on you and a plan to scam you.

Be in control of your destiny and design your own plan. The success or the failure of your company will rest with you. It'll be easier to live with your mistakes than with someone else's.

Chapter 20 The Corporate Crossover

In due time, all things come to pass. If you are consistent, you will get there no matter how long it takes. Some people will get there before you. Some people will start there, but you will get there if you aren't already. I've always been self-conscious about my country accent. I'm also self-conscious about my race, although not as much anymore. I'm self-conscious about my age. I'm also self-conscious about being an independent brand. For all those reasons, I couldn't see when I would get the opportunity to do a corporate crossover. What I mean by corporate is major brands, companies, and so on. Yes, I was called on by different organizations such as the NBA, NBPA, NFL teams, and NCAA teams, but I didn't look at that the same as corporate. I actually wanted to be on salary with a professional sports team as a life coach. I also wanted to be a spokesperson for a major brand. I guess for me this would be validation. I wanted to know that I was just as good as the guys who have a full staff, super agents, proper speech, degrees, and all those things. I'd read some of their wisdom, heard some of their speeches, and wouldn't really be all too impressed. I'd hear some good stuff, but it didn't intimidate me or make me feel that those guys were any better than me. I just needed for my opportunities to come.

I remember asking pro athletes if their team had a life coach. They would all say no. I would then ask them if they felt they could benefit from a life coach being on the team. They all said yes, but that they didn't think the NBA cared enough to invest in them that way. I later found out that it's a team decision, not a league decision. I had no connections to any teams other than through the players, but I didn't feel comfortable asking a player to connect me to a decision maker in the front office. I couldn't ask for anything like that. I just kept doing what I was doing. I mentored a lot of pro athletes at no charge. Some of them I'd visit in their hometown or in the city where they were playing. I'd stop by their home and just talk. I didn't want anything, just to help. I took the same approach I took online with these guys. My goal was to motivate and inspire. Well, one day out of nowhere, I noticed a general manager for an NBA team started following me. Then a couple days later a player development guy from a different team called me. Then players from other teams started calling me. There was a lot going on at once, and I felt I was close to something. I spoke to the GM in the Twitter inbox. Surprisingly, he was a humble and cool guy. I thought he'd be arrogant and condescending, but he was the opposite. About a week or two later, I got a call from the assistant GM, and we talked for a good bit. I was so excited and so pumped up I probably made him think I was crazy. I always do that. I've been waiting for my moment for so long that when it finally came, I could hardly contain myself. Well, we spoke, and then I had some talks with some other teams about coming in and speaking to the team and working with the players. Some of the players liked what they heard when I spoke to them as rookies, and they had kept in touch; then, when they got back to their teams and were asked who they wanted to bring in to speak, they would mention me. I guess your gift will always make room for you. Well this team, which I can't identify contractually, wanted to work with me exclusively. I've always said I didn't want to do anything exclusively, but this was different. This was a dream of mine. When I was little, I dreamed of playing in the NBA or the NFL. I never made it as a player, but here was my chance to play a different role on an NBA team. I'd never heard of a life coach on salary with an NBA team, or I guess you'd call it a consultant because I wasn't actually a staff member. It was all the same for me. I would have done the job for free. They asked me how much I'd charge, and I gave them a dirt-cheap monthly retainer fee. Of course, they couldn't lose. I signed the contract and that was that. I can't speak about the inner workings of what went on while on the job for my first season because some people know which team it is since they saw me at some games, so I'll keep that confidential. All I can say is that it was a great experience! I'm not sure if they will continue the program or not, but I'll be fine either way. I reached my goal. I met guys that I'll know for life and will be able to help any time they need me. I got to experience what it was like to work for a professional sports team, and I wouldn't trade that for the world. I showed myself that anything is possible. Little ole me—no training, no degree, just a gift and some passion. I did something that no one I know has done. I asked around and no one in the league had heard of it either. There were sports psychologists working for teams, former players working as mentors, but no life coaches. I think it's safe to say I was the first life coach in the NBA. A real life coach, like someone who wears the title and makes a living from being a life coach, not a former player who mentors. I share that to say—you are worthy. You can make it. You can achieve your dreams no matter how big they are. If you know who you are and you operate in your gifts, then anything is possible. I think a lot of times we allow our insecurities to box us in. We never grow beyond our insecurities because we put limits on ourselves. I took the limits off and look what happened.

The next corporate crossover came while working in the NBA. There were actually a couple things that happened. We haven't rolled them out yet, so I don't want to say the names of the companies. It's never done until it's done, but I feel good just to be approached and to sign the contracts. One of the companies is a major dating site. I speak a lot about relationships so that really gave me a foothold in that space. I was introduced to a production company once, and they wanted to work with me. I would be a matchmaker and a love coach on the TV show they were trying to produce. The company reached out to this dating site and wanted the site to be a part of the show. I would be the host of the show. The show never happened for whatever reasons. Well, I thought it was dead in the water, but a few months later I get an email from the dating site, saying they are looking for advisory board members and would like for me to join. It sounded good, but my ideas were too good for the money they were offering. Instead I pitched another idea in the form of a partnership, and they loved the idea. We've done all the work, got the landing page ready, and signed the deal. Now we're just waiting to hit the go button. I'm feeling indifferent about it right now because I'm not 100 percent sure it's the way that God wants me to go, so I'm being patient. If it doesn't go, then I won't be mad at all because I know God always moves in my favor. What is supposed to happen happens. What isn't supposed to happen doesn't happen. I trust God, and I trust the process. I don't question anything that is beyond my control. I'm just flattered because I'm a different type of relationship coach. I'm still not polished around the edges. The site is predominantly white, and I'm black, so of course they are trying to build the African American side of things. I'm honored to be chosen as the one they'd like to work with. It's another form of validation. We can think and feel however we want about ourselves, but we still need others in life. We need someone else to see in us what we see in ourselves. It may not happen right away or when you want it to, but if you have the gift, it will happen.

This publishing deal is also another corporate crossover for me. I've been an independent author for the last nine years. It's been a long and fun journey, but now I'm here. I don't know if this will be better or worse because that is still to be determined. I'm sure I'll be honest with you about the experience in a later book, which may or may not be with a major publisher. I can't predict the future, but I can say I'll be honest. This deal came about interestingly enough. It goes back to consistency and social media. It seems like my whole life revolves around Twitter, doesn't it? I know what you're thinking. *What if Twitter goes down tomorrow?* Well, I'm sure we'd find another way. I was tweeting away, and one day I got a follow from a sports psychologist. He seemed legit and in the know. I connected with him in the direct message, and he was eager to hop on a call. We spoke, and it was a good conversation. He was over my head to be honest. Remember, I don't really buy into things over my head. I went my way and he went his. I later noticed that he unfollowed me on Twitter, which could have been an accident but I'm not sure. Nonetheless, I saw him follow me again later. I followed back, and then I connected with him via email in response to an email blast he sent out. I was on his list for months or maybe a year. I wrote to let him know that I'd become a life coach in the NBA and wanted to pick his brain. We hopped on a call and had a great talk. On this call he told me I reminded him of a guy he knows named Jon Gordon. I'd recently heard of Jon Gordon from the guy who hired me in the NBA. He recommended one of Jon's books to me called *Training Camp*. I bought the audio book because I'm not a big reader. I love to listen though. I listened to the audio book, and it was pretty good. I thought to myself—*I can do this*. A lot of the stuff I heard in the book resonated with my spirit, and I felt like I'd said some of the same stuff. Of course, being a conspiracy theorist, I looked to see when the book was published. I thought to myself—*let me see if this guy Jon maybe stole some of my stuff from Twitter and put it in his book*. I think I found out that the book was published before I blew up on social media, so I realized there was no way this guy could have robbed my thoughts. It was another "great minds think alike" moment. I respected his work and wanted to get more of his books, then I realized that he'd wrote so many. Well, Garrett Kramer, the guy who told me I reminded him of Jon, told me that he'd connect Jon and me. I thought he was lying. The next day I noticed that Jon followed me on Twitter. Yes, even though I have nearly 300,000 followers on Twitter, I still pay very close attention. After all, it did change my life. Honestly, it has changed everyone's life. There were so many careers on the brink of extinction until Twitter revived them. Well, I sent Jon a message in the direct message, and we hopped on the phone. We spoke, and he had a great spirit. I mentioned that I had his book, and I heard of it from my boss in the NBA. I told him that someday I wanted to publish with a major publishing company just to see what it's like. He said, "Oh you want to do that for real?" I said, "Sure, why not?" He said, "Well, say no more, I'll connect you and I think they'll love to have you." I honestly didn't think he was serious. But he was. If you refer back to my analogy about the different types of people you'll meet on the climb, you'll see that Jon is a giver and a teacher. I didn't sense any jealousy from him. Although my online following is larger than his and I run my business in a different lane, he's satisfied with his lane and what he's doing. He gave me some tips, and I gave him a couple of mine. I implemented his, and he has implemented mine. It was an exchange, although his was a greater gift than mine. I just gave him a tip about how to quote himself on Twitter and Facebook. Jon told me who his publisher was. It was strange because I'd just heard this publisher's name like a week earlier. I was talking to another entrepreneur who said he would be publishing a book with John Wiley and Sons. It was crazy to me because I kept hearing names in twos. To me it was God creating cosmic collisions on the road to destiny. I heard Jon Gordon's name from two different sources, and then I hear John Wiley and Sons from two different sources. Jon Gordon's stamp to the publisher was better than any agent's stamp. Jon also has the same boss as me. We both work for the Big Guy upstairs, so it was a Kingdom Connection. He connected me to a publisher and didn't ask for anything in return. I know his blessings are steadily rolling in. I'd never really met anyone like that. I can't really ever remember someone making that grand of a connection for me and not immediately asking for something in return. It made me think this publisher must be a little fish in a big pond. I googled Wiley and found out they're the oldest publisher in the game. I also had an agent who wanted to shop my book to the "Big Five," she called it, so I asked her about John Wiley and she said, "Oh yeah, I know exactly who they are. They're the real deal." I told her that since the opportunity came to me before she and I had spoken, I'd have to see what comes of it first. I let her know that if they wanted me, I was going to take the deal because I didn't feel like going through the book proposal and shopping manuscripts phase again. I'd been down that road before. Sure enough the deal was signed. Now, you'll have to check the publisher's name on this book just to make sure everything went as planned, but I believe it'll be just fine.

Right around the same time as the dating site and the publishing deal, another corporate crossover came. This one is with a major car company. I won't say their name because the online commercial hasn't been released yet. I've shot it and been paid for it, so I'm pretty sure it should be online as you're reading this book. This deal came in right through my website booking address. They told me they found me on their own, online. I was wondering if a big-time agent or someone pointed them in my direction, but nope, it was just good ole social media. They visited my site and saw my short bio film on there and said this commercial would be similar. They said I'd be telling my story and promoting this car at the same time. I was blown away. I thought maybe they were just going to use my face and voice and have me as an actor in a commercial, but they wanted me to be in the commercial as Tony Gaskins Jr. The commercial is for online use in order to reach my demographic. It's not TV, and it's not for everyone, but I'll take it. The brand is so big that I was just honored to get the call. I just didn't expect to get the opportunity this soon. Granted, I'm not the only person they are shooting with, but it still means a lot to me. Right after the commercial they came to me with a couple more opportunities as well, so that was just a little more validation that I needed. Just think, all of this came from building an organic brand online—nothing more, nothing less. It's really just mind-boggling to me. I've written this book with a lot of sureties and matter-of-factness, but I can't sit here and say that I really believed that all of this could happen organically. It has happened, and I can't argue with the results or lie about how it happened either. Anyone can disagree with my methods and beliefs, but they can't argue against the results. It's a new day. There was a time when in order to work with a major brand, you needed an agent to represent you to that brand, but today independent beauty bloggers are becoming millionaires through YouTube. There are average, everyday people who turn on a camera in their room and shoot a video and later become a millionaire from those very videos. You have to embrace the change and get with it. Make it easier on yourself and just be true to you.

We will see what comes of these corporate crossovers. I can't predict the future. I'm not sure if they will bring bigger opportunities or if they will turn out to be just a fun experience. Only time will tell. I'm just here to tell you that no matter where you're starting from, it's possible.

Chapter 21   Influencing Influencers

It's one thing to be an influencer; it's another to be an influencer to influencers. If the goal is to have an impact on the world in a positive way, then becoming an influencer to influencers is a great way to do it. An influencer is someone who has massive reach and can impact the actions of others with their words and actions. No, that's not from Webster's dictionary; that's my definition, so hopefully it'll do. The key to influencing influencers is to be sure of yourself and to be consistent in your work. If you're all over the place, and you're operating in your gift one week and, then taking the next week off, you'll never reach anyone that way. You have to be consistent, and you have to know what you know. We oftentimes hear people preface a statement with, "In my opinion," or "I believe," etc. I do it sometimes too. Well, that can take away from your influence if you do that too much. You have to know what you know and really stand behind it. One thing about my online brand is that I never questioned myself within a quote or statement. I spoke as if everything I said was a law from heaven. I did that because I wanted people who may be unsure to know that I was sure. I really was sure. I didn't think I knew what I was talking about. I knew that I knew what I was talking about. Before I said anything, I analyzed it from every angle I could think of. I thought of the arguments one might have from each angle, and I had a counterargument. Even with all of that I still could have been wrong, but you'd have to present a pretty strong case to convince me that I didn't know what I was talking about. Because of that confidence and surety, it helped me rise through the ranks online. My following grew so much faster because I sounded sure of myself. If a person is going to follow you, they want to know that you know where you're going. If you're guessing all the time, then they'd rather just go their own way. You have to know that you know or just shut up. I may not always be right, and sometimes when someone would make a great counterargument, I'd have to delete my tweet. Sometimes my message was just misconstrued because of my bad grammar, but there were times that I didn't analyze my point from the right angle. I had to eat those mistakes. I would post one sure thought, then an hour later I would post a rebuttal to the debaters. I wouldn't address them directly, but my next quote would be to them. It was funny when one would realize I was talking to them and would tweet me again even though I didn't mention their name. I was wrong at times, but I felt right most of the time. I taught by principles of life, not the exceptions of life. There is always an exception, but we can't base our life on that. Thirty years ago my model would have been an exception to the rule, but today my model of business is quickly becoming the majority. I know what I know, and you can't tell me otherwise, especially if the results back it up nine times out of 10. That's how you become an influencer to influencers.

What you have to realize is that we all have insecurities. I have insecurities, although I may not wear a sign on my forehead listing them. I need guidance too; but if I'm going to listen to anyone, they have to sound sure of themselves. They have to sound so sure that I feel 100 percent that they know what they're talking about. I hate it when someone gives advice, and then at the end of it they say, "But I don't know though." It's like, what did you just give all that advice for then? If you're going to advise someone, then be sure about what you're saying, even when it comes back to bite you in the butt. I went on national TV once and advised a celebrity about what to do in her relationship with the father of her two children. She'd had two of his kids, but she still wasn't his wife. Things weren't getting better; they were getting worse. I gave her some advice and told her it was time to take a stand and walk away. I remember getting a call from one of my cousins who asked me how I did that. He said, "Cuzz, you're telling people what to do with their marriage, their life. I'd be afraid to death to do that. What if you tell them something and it ruins their life?" I said, "Cuzz, it's a chance I have to take. If a person isn't sure about their life, and I've weighed the options, and I've looked at hundreds of similar cases and saw how they all turned out and then gave the advice that I thought was best, then I did what I could. I'd rather the person make a definite decision than to be left hanging in the balance." He said, "Man, you're a brave man because I can't do that."

It's not the easiest thing in the world to give advice, but if you know that you know what you're talking about, and you've been put in that position, then people are counting on you. It may be fashion advice, dieting advice, financial advice, or life advice. It could be anything. You have to know that you know. If you don't know, then be one of those people who say, "But I don't know though." But if you want to help impact the lives of many in a positive way, then speak up. If I tell a woman that she should stop letting a man run in and out of her life and take her for granted, how can that hurt her? That was years ago that I told that lady on TV to leave that guy, and she's doing just fine today. I knew there wasn't a downside to having self-respect. It's not like I said she should go hang off the side of the bridge and call him and tell him that she'd be hanging there until he came and rescued her. That would be bad advice. If you can't be sure about what you're talking about, then don't talk about it. If you have studied so hard and long and seen hundreds or thousands of those cases play out, and you feel you can help a person figure something out, then help them.

I tell athletes to cut their own checks, monitor their bank accounts if someone has access to it, and not give their families so much that they have to fall from grace when they retire. You'd be surprised how many don't do those simple things. I give that basic advice as though I'm sure that if they don't do those things, then really bad things can happen. The smart ones listen to that advice. I know that listening to that advice won't bring any harm, so I can give that advice and rest at night. Just like the tips I give in this book. If you do it my way, it may take longer but I know it won't ruin you. I can share these tips with confidence that they won't hurt you to be hands-on in your business, take your time before signing with a major, learn something about every aspect of your business, and be consistent in your gift. I'm very confident about that advice because there's no downside to it. You may let your manager go tomorrow because this book helped you realize that they are just taking a cut for no good reason. I know that letting a deadweight manager go won't hurt you. I wouldn't tell you to cut a manager who is bringing a different deal to the table every month; that would be stupid advice. You may take some of my sure advice and go shock the world over the next five years. Then you'll write me and say, "Hey Tony, I took your advice and became more consistent in my gift and my career has taken off as a result, and I'm reaching thousands of people now." Guess what that means? I became an influencer to an influencer just because I knew what I knew.

I learned quickly that everyone has life questions. If I have the answer to certain questions, then I answer them for whoever I can. I have one client who has tens of millions of followers online and a lot of influence. This client talks to me often. I help where I can, and I give sure advice. But that client has some wisdom that I don't have because they've made more money than I have and had to learn how to handle greedy family members. I asked my client for advice on that matter. My client gave me very sure advice without any hesitation or questioning in the answer. I felt I could trust that answer, and I took that advice. My client is an influencer, I'm an influencer, and we've influenced one another. That's how it works.

There was a time while I was still working a full-time job that I went in to work the morning shift, so I got there like 6 a.m. I sent out a tweet because I was up early. It was a Saturday morning, so most people were asleep in the United States. On the West Coast it was 3 a.m., and on the East Coast it was 6 a.m. I sent out a quote, and I can't remember what the quote was exactly. The next thing I know, I get a direct message from an A- or B-list celebrity. This celeb asks me to give him a call. So I dart outside of work, and I give him a call. Then he says, "Hey, I just wanted to tell you that you've been so instrumental in my growth. You have no idea how many times your advice on Twitter has gotten me through the day. If you ever need anything, just give me a call. If you're ever in LA, swing by my house so we can talk more." I was blown away. I was like, here is this megastar watching my tweets and growing from them. I then would notice that the person's tweets started to sound just like mine. The person started motivating the hundreds of thousands and later millions of followers in the very same way that I do. I'd been an influence to an influencer.

I didn't really understand how it happened, but I knew it started with that tweet to Alicia Keys. Because of that I started telling the guys who were coming to me for mentorship that they should get the attention of a celebrity. I told them to just send an encouraging tweet to a celebrity once a week or so. Well, a couple of the guys went overboard, and they pinpointed the celebrity they wanted to target and sent a quote to the person every day and sometimes multiple times a day. Well, the same thing that happened for me, happened for them. The celebrity would retweet their quotes and as a result, their followers would increase into the thousands. Now they could just tweet their quotes and reach so many more people. It was crazy to realize that these celebrities are human just like us, and they need guidance and motivation just like the rest of us. If you know what you know, lend that advice to someone in need. It doesn't have to be a celebrity. I've coached people who had virtually no following, then fast-forward a couple years and they were reaching millions. I coached their potential, and their potential translated into production and turned into influence.

I recently watched a guy on YouTube start teaching about wealth. When he started teaching, all he had to show for it was a car. I know if he had then all that he has now, he would have shown it all in the first video because you can tell that's just how he is. Well, he started sharing advice, and in the advice he confronted every doubt about him that you may have. He sounded very sure of himself and very matter-of-fact. He was talking about some pretty heavy stuff that was over my head, stuff I'd never heard of. I didn't really want to get into it because it was too hard for me to understand. He couldn't explain it to a 6-year-old, and neither could I. I could tell that he had the gift. I knew that he would rise to the top. I'm not sure how long he'll last there, but I know he will get there. I looked back on YouTube a few months later, and he'd gone from a guy with a car to a guy with multiple cars and a massive house. Outside of that, he'd become an influencer to influencers. He would be hanging out with them, talking with them, and featuring them. I'm not sure how he found them or how they found him, but it happened. I know it happened because of what I'll call the three C's: his confidence, his content, and his consistency. Those three things combined, and he had a winning recipe. The other thing he has going is his complexity. If an athlete or influencer wants to make money, he will sound like he knows more than other people, and that will keep them interested for a long time.

Just like anyone else, you know something. You don't have to argue what you know. You don't have to debate what you know. Just know what you know and keep sharing it. That's all I did, and that helped me build to the point where people who have larger brands and earn more money started coming to me for advice. For the longest time, I didn't know what to tell people when they would ask me how to get celebrity clients. I'm not sure if there is only one way or a surefire way; I just know that no one will follow someone who is unsure of themselves.

If you can't get your gift or product to an influencer, then take a different route. Find someone on the brink of success and connect with him or her and build from there. Help one another. If you have something to offer, they'll be able to tell. If you just want to ride their coattail, they'll be able to tell that too. Know what you bring to the table and don't back down from that. I went from no one knowing my name and having no celebrity clients to some days looking in my text messages and only seeing the names of top influencers. It's crazy to see how that happened. We live in a world today where you can get in front of influencers rather easily. If you have a product, some influencers will promote it for you for a fee. If you know your product is good, then you could pay them once and have a supporter for life. My wife buys these jeans for my sons that she found on Instagram. The woman who makes them is just a regular mom. She made a pair for the daughter of a mega star once, the mega star posted the jeans on her Instagram page, and the lady's company went through the roof. That same mega star retweeted a blog site that I used to blog for, and the blog went through the roof. From that retweet of the blog post the founder of the blog became a celebrity, got a book deal, met Oprah, and now tours the world. If you're consistent, you'll find yourself in the right place at the right time one day, and your life will never be the same. Start positioning yourself to become an influencer, and if you get the chance, leverage the power of influencers you come in contact with. Nearly everyone whose brand grew organically did so with the help of someone with a large reach. Don't run from it if you get the chance, but don't be desperate for it either. You may have to pay your way if a stamp from an influencer costs, but that's marketing and there's nothing wrong with that if you have the money to spend.

If all else fails, do it the old-fashioned way and just work until you get your break. There may not always be an easy way or a clever idea that comes to mind, so you just have to stay the course and wait your turn. There are actually influencers to influencers who no one knows. There are people who don't have a following, aren't online, but yet they influence some of the biggest influencers in the world. They were operating in their gift and happened to be in the right place at the right time and their life changed forever. Their influence helped shape cultures and generations, and the world at large never knew who they were. If you look at the people who have inspired you or just influenced you, you may not know who their influencer is, but that doesn't lessen their influence. I look up to the work of John Maxwell. I've never followed him as closely as I followed Zig Ziglar, but I see myself one day writing as many books as John Maxwell has. He pumps out stuff daily that is life changing. I've never read one of his books because from what I've seen, our message may be similar. I don't want to just copy everything he says, so I don't read his work on a routine basis. I'll look at something once a month, but I see how much he produces and it inspires me. I don't know who his influencer is. I'm fairly sure it's God, but it may also be a person. Whoever influences him has a lot of influence, and we may never know their name. I know my wife influences me, my father influences me, my sons influence me, my mother and my sister influence me, but none of them have large followings. My wife has touched a lot of lives because of her influence on my life. The millions who have seen my name online may never see my wife's name, but they were influenced by her influence on me. I say that just to say, there are many ways you can be significant and have influence in the world. Don't feel like you have to do it the same way I did it or that you need to do it at all. If it's your calling and if it's meant to be, it will come to you along the journey. If and when it does, embrace it and run with it—you'll be a world changer!!

Chapter 22 Work–Life Balance

Out of everything I've talked about in this book, work–life balance is one of the hardest things to master. I'm still getting better at it daily. This has to matter more than anything else, especially if you have a family.

I view success differently now. I judge a person's success by what their spouse and kids say about them, not their money or their fame. My goal is for my wife to be able to say I was a great husband and for my kids to be able to say I was a great dad. When I say that this means more to me than money, I honestly mean it. I know it may sound mushy and like a cliché thing to say, but I really mean it. We have to find balance. The love of my family and my wife changed my life. When you learn how to love, you learn how to live. Love brings balance and stability of its own. Love will make you healthier and wealthier if you treat it right. Your family should be your first priority.

I do understand that in life there will be a season of work. I spoke about that earlier when my wife allowed me to work from 70 to 80 hours a week. There will be those times, but you can't make that a habit. No matter how much money a man has, I tune him out if I don't ever hear anything about his driving forces. Those driving forces for me have to be his family. You have to find a balance if you truly want to be successful. Today I found some balance. I had a choice to make, and I made a choice that I'm happy with.

I'm writing this book at a beach house. Today is Friday, and I've been here since Monday. My wife's cousin graduated from college this morning, so my wife and our two sons arrived last night. I've been writing from 7 a.m. to about 10 p.m. every night this week. I sleep from about 11 p.m. to 6 or 7 a.m., so I'm well rested. Last night I could have been selfish and kept my routine and put the book before my family. Instead I chose to stay up until 12:30 a.m. because that's when they were arriving. I then was up for about another hour and a half getting them settled and talking to my wife. This morning my wife prepared to go to the graduation. She said she would take the boys so I could write. She was being very considerate and supportive. If I wanted to, I could have accepted her generous offer. Instead I told her to leave the boys here with me so they could get some rest. I got up with the boys about 8 a.m. In the back of my head I wanted to lock them in the room and let them play together. I knew that wasn't smart or necessary. Instead we went out on the beach and walked. I fed them breakfast, and we played in the pool. We played an hour or so, and they loved it. After lunch, I put my youngest son down for a nap. At that point I could have started writing, but instead I went in the room with my oldest son, Tony III, and we hung out. My wife returned after the graduation to pick up our oldest son to go out to eat with the family. I was able to get some writing done then. When my wife and son came back, of course she wanted to talk. I sat and ate the lunch she brought back for me, and we talked for 30 or 45 minutes. Then she wanted to lie down to rest her feet. Our youngest was still napping after all that time. Our oldest son was in his room playing games on his phone. My wife told me I could get back to writing. As soon as I sat down to write, our youngest son woke up. My wife was in bed, so I stopped writing and went to get him up and give him some milk. My wife came out, and she got the boys and headed back over to her family's house so I could have some quiet time to get some more writing done.

I told you that long story just to paint a picture of work–life balance. Had I been a workaholic, that scenario would have played out totally different. Instead, I decided to give my sons and my wife some of my time. After all, I've been gone all week long. I put my book down, and I know my 9-year-old paid close attention to that. I didn't mention it, and I showed him that the book doesn't matter more than he does. I've been working on that because my job is so fun and so consuming that it's easy to want to work around the clock. You have to find balance. If you can't find the time, you have to make the time. Put work on the back burner to love.

It's not always easy; there's always work to be done. There are times when my wife has to remind me to put my phone down. I have to constantly check myself. Finding a healthy balance is constant work.

The thing that really stung me the most was a comment that came from my son. I was driving him to school one morning because I try to do that as often as I can since I have to travel a lot. On the way to school he was talking a lot, and he said he just loves to talk a lot. I didn't factor in that he could have just been extremely happy to have some time with me. Sadly enough, even on some of those drives I can get distracted by news on the radio or something I see on my phone at the red light. Social media is a gift and a curse. Anyway, I told my son that it's not always a good thing to talk so much. We had a little debate, and then he said, "Well, I'm quiet sometimes Dad, but you wouldn't know because you're never home to see it." That hurt bad. I cried in my car on the way back home. What did it profit me to gain fame and notoriety and lose time with my family? That's when I started searching for ways to have an impact and create more time.

I know the "work smarter, not harder" crew is shaking their heads right now and saying, "You see, that's why you need a team and to delegate some tasks." But that wasn't my problem. My emails and social media posts didn't take up my time. My TV appearances and speaking engagements were taking up days of my time. I can't delegate those things. I had to make a choice. As soon as I thought I had it figured out, an NBA team hired me. They let me design the life-coaching program, and I stupidly said it would be good for me to be with the team two to three days a week. What in the world was I thinking? It became a travel nightmare. Some weeks I would be in four or five different cities. I'd be with the team on a trip, come home for a few hours, and then have to fly out to another engagement to speak. There were times tears were in my eyes as I walked out the door. How could such a dream become such a nightmare? For that reason, I'm not sure I'll return to the NBA next season, and if I do, I'll definitely have to change my schedule. I want to impact the world, but I'd much rather be able to impact my own home than anyone else's. I'm being transparent with you right now just so you understand that the things you're dreaming and praying for will come with a cost. There will have to be some sacrifices made, and those sacrifices may hurt.

Even when it's hard, I understand that things happen in seasons. This could have been my season of growth where I had to take every speaking engagement under the sun to build my brand and spread my message. I'm sure there will come a different season where a new young speaker is on the rise, and I'm not getting as many calls; then I can sit home and teach online and make a living like that. We have to appreciate the season we are in and make the most of it. That's why balance is so important. Balance doesn't mean you have to choose one or the other entirely, but it means you have to find a way to have the best of both worlds. It's possible. I experienced it today, and I experience it most days. A lot of days I'm able to take my son to school in the morning, go to breakfast with my wife and baby boy, coach a couple clients in the middle of the day, pick my son up from school, take him to practice, have dinner as a family, teach my course, then relax with my wife. That's a full day, and in those days, I experience everything I love. To me that's balance.

While balancing the seasons, it's also very important that you communicate effectively. You can't just do what you have to do and expect everyone around you to understand what's going on. Sometimes when my son asks me why I have to leave so much, I'll tell him that it's how I feed our family. I ask him, do you love your private school? Do you love our nice house? Do you love your iPhone, iPad, Xbox One, and your nice shoes? He'll say, yes, I love all those things. Well, son, how do you think I pay for them, I ask. Then he understands that I'm not leaving him because I don't love him. I'm leaving him because this is my job, and my job is different from most people's. He starts to learn about hard work and that life doesn't always work exactly how we want it to and there are sacrifices we have to make. I never want him to think that it's about material things, but quality of life does matter to us all. I don't want him to settle and not use his gifts because they may take him around the world. He wants to be a pro athlete one day. He's a genius in the classroom, and he's always the top of his class every year, but he's not thinking about engineering right now. He says he wants to be a pro basketball player and a pro soccer player and that he may alternate between the two. I've never seen anyone do that but, hey, it's okay to let the kid dream. Because that's his dream, I point out to him how much NBA players have to travel and how long they're gone. I point out to him that there are NBA games on his birthday, my birthday, and his little brother's birthday, but those guys have to play because it's their job, their gift, and how they feed their families. With that communication he sees that if we don't work, we don't eat. He also sees that even with dream jobs, there's a major sacrifice. It's tough when you think about being a professional athlete and you think about earning $300,000 to $40,000,000 a year, but then you think about how it would feel to miss your child's birthday every year. Yes, you can celebrate on another day, but no day you pick will ever be their birthday, and no day feels like the actual day. That's a big sacrifice. Work–life balance is constant work.

I've communicated with my oldest son so much that one day he motivated me. I was in my feelings, and I think I almost cried in the car when we were talking about my job. I told him that I was so sorry I had to miss his soccer game and that I was going to change my job around so that I could make more games. Then he said, "Dad, it's okay. You're helping people around the world to be good and change their life. A lot of people need you, and I don't know what they would do without you. I get to see you all the time, so it's okay if you're gone some days to help them. I don't ever want you to stop helping people." I'm almost in tears just writing that. I was so blown away that he said that to me. It comforted me. I heard him, but I'm still determined to create more of a balance.

The hard part you'll find about balance is that even when you adjust, things will continue to shift in a way that demands your time. You may find a way to create more time, but the little work you do will explode and get so big that it still requires more time. In a lot of ways, a 9-to-5 job has more structure than entrepreneurship. As an entrepreneur, you're doing what you love, so you can do it for 24 hours straight. You have to discipline yourself and force yourself to stop working and spend time with family. With a 9-to-5 job most times you hate the job so much that when it's over, you don't want to think about it until you have to show up the next day. That makes work–life balance easier. As you're building your dream, be prepared to fight through a nightmare or two. If you can't step away from your work, then it's not freedom. We can't be slaves to our work.

I'd advise you to start working on a schedule tonight, whether you work for yourself or someone else. Create a literal schedule that will remind you of the importance of creating balance. When I decided to make a change, I put everything in my phone's calendar. If you don't make a plan, you won't find balance. If you don't find balance, it doesn't matter how big of a dream you build, it will eventually become a nightmare. It's not something that you can do overnight, and even when you do it, you will have to keep on doing it. I can stay and write until Monday, but I plan to finish tonight or first thing in the morning. Then I'm going home to spend the rest of Saturday and Sunday with my family. I have to have a balance, or I don't have anything.

Acknowledgments

My queen, Sheri Gaskins: For supporting my dreams from day one. She saw something in me that I didn't see in myself. She put up with my crazy ideas, my long nights of work, and the nonstop grind. I'm so grateful for her love and support!

My sons, Tony Gaskins III and Tayden Gaskins: For motivating Daddy to dream bigger and prepare a better future for them. For allowing Daddy to work hard at random times of the day. For always understanding when Daddy has to hop on another plane. You guys are my pride and joy, and I'm doing this all for you!

My mom, Cathy Gaskins: For always speaking positivity over my life. You were the first one who praised my gift of writing, and you never stopped telling me that I should be making a living from my words. I thank you for that!

My dad, Tony Gaskins Sr.: For sacrificing your dreams to work 9 to 5, so I could have a better life. You paved the way for me, and I know my gifts are in me because of you.

My sister, Latesha Gaskins: For supporting and believing in me. Second to mom, you were my first fan and my biggest fan. You promoted me before I had anything to promote, and I thank you for that.

My nieces and nephew: I love you guys, and you are a part of my motivation to keep going!

Wesley Barnett: For being a great friend and helping me get things in order from day one. You always keep it real with me, and I can always count on your insight. Without your help and support this wouldn't be possible.

Big Russ, Russell Collymore: For being my right hand man since the day I met you. It's been over a decade, and you haven't changed. I've seen everyone change in some way, but you've remained a constant in my life. No matter how much money, fame, or success you've seen come my way, you never asked for a dime or any shine. I'm still looking for your flaws because, man, you're one good dude!

Jon Gordon: For speaking into my life and also connecting me with Wiley. Your stamp and support helped me a lot. This book wouldn't be out if God hadn't crossed our paths. Although I know you gave without strings attached, I'm just waiting to see how I can repay your kindness.

I can't list everyone, but if you've ever supported me or spoke into my life, please know that I appreciate you! Every good-hearted person I've met on the journey means something!

About the Author

Tony A. Gaskins Jr. is a faithful husband and father first. He's the son of two humble parents and the older brother to one sister. Tony started building his business and brand with literally no money in the bank. He was working a job earning $8.50 an hour as a group-home counselor and still in college pursuing a degree in criminology.

Tony never finished college because by his eighth year as a part-time student, his business took his life to another level. After three years of what seemed like no progress, he had a breakthrough. After landing himself on several globally televised talk shows and other media outlets, his following started to grow. In 2010 he became a legitimate professional speaker for organizations like the NBA, NBPA, NFL, NCAA, and more. He was invited to speak at colleges and universities around the United States and later to share his message in 10 other countries.

Tony speaks on several topics including business, love and relationships, entrepreneurship, leadership, and more. He focuses on a balanced-life approach and refuses to box himself in to just one topic. Many college athletic teams call on him to tell his story of losing his full football scholarship and to share his tips for the student athletes on how they can avoid the pitfalls. Churches call him in to share a message of relentless faith and perseverance. Other organizations bring him in to share messages about sacrifice and commitment to a goal.

After speaking on 3 continents and in 10 different countries, Tony continued to share his message, and it landed him the opportunity to become the first professional life coach on salary with an NBA team. Tony then went on to work with several teams and players as a trusted mentor in the areas of life, love, and business. Tony is an unorthodox speaker and life coach; his style is all his own. He's real and raw in his passion-filled delivery. He doesn't use note cards or power points. His message is in the fiber of his DNA, and it comes directly from his heart. He is building something that not many dare to build because most are afraid to trust their own abilities. Tony has to do what he feels God put on his heart and do it in the fashion he feels best, regardless of who doesn't understand his vision.

You can expect to see many more books, tours, online courses, phone applications, and life-changing content from Tony in the years to come. Stay tuned because it's just the beginning.

Connect with Tony!

Website: TonyGaskins.com
Speaking engagements: booktony@tonygaskins.com
One-on-one consulting: advice@tonygaskins.com
Facebook: Facebook.com/tonygaskins
Instagram: Instagram.com/tonygaskins
Twitter: Twitter.com/tonygaskins
Youtube: Youtube.com/tonygaskins
Snapchat: tonygaskins
To join the mailing list: TonyGaskins.com
For online courses: TonyGaskinsAcademy.com